INFANT AND ENVIRONMENT
early cognitive
and motivational development

INFANT AND ENVIRONMENT
early cognitive
and motivational development

LEON J. YARROW

JUDITH L. RUBENSTEIN

FRANK A. PEDERSEN

ALL OF
NATIONAL INSTITUTE OF CHILD HEALTH
AND HUMAN DEVELOPMENT

collaborators

JOSEPH J. JANKOWSKI
JOAN T. DURFEE
MYRNA W. FIVEL

HEMISPHERE PUBLISHING
CORPORATION
Washington, D.C.

A HALSTED PRESS BOOK
JOHN WILEY & SONS
New York   London   Sydney   Toronto

Hemisphere Publishing Corporation
1025 Vermont Ave., N.W., Washington, D.C. 20005

Distributed solely by Halsted Press, a Division of John Wiley & Sons,
Inc., New York.

Library of Congress Cataloging in Publication Data

Yarrow, Leon J
    Infant and environment.

    Includes index.
    1. Infant psychology. 2. Cognition (Child psycho-
logy) 3. Motivation (Psychology) I. Rubenstein,
Judith L., joint author. II. Pedersen, Frank A., joint
author. III. Title. [DNLM: 1. Child development.
2. Cognition—In infancy and childhood. 3. Environment. 4. Infant. 5. Motivation—In infancy and
childhood. WS105 Y291]
BF723.I6Y37   155.4'22   74-26522
ISBN 0-470-97178-9

Printed in the United States of America

CONTENTS

FOREWORD xi

ACKNOWLEDGMENTS xvii

1 INTRODUCTION 1

2 METHODOLOGY AND METHODOLOGICAL ISSUES .. 9

   Subjects 10
   Social Characteristics of the Core Sample 11
   Overview of Data Collection 13
      Initial Screening 14
      Pediatric Examination 14

Home Observations........................... 14
Assessment of Infant 15
Observational Methods: Time Sampling Versus
Narrative Records 15
Observation Categories and Procedures 18
Observation Procedures 20
Observer Reliability 20
Observation Categories 21
Measures of Infant Functioning 24

3 DIFFERENTIATION OF THE ENVIRONMENT: THE
DEVELOPMENT OF VARIABLES AND THEIR
INTERRELATIONSHIPS 27

The Social Environment: Aspects of Maternal
Care 28
Modalities of Stimulation 28
Contingency Measures 31
Maternal Affect: Expression of Positive Affect,
Smiling, and Play 35
Social Mediation of Inanimate Objects 37
Higher Order Characterizations of the Social
Environment: Level and Variety................. 38
The Inanimate Environment 40
Variety 42
Responsiveness 42
Complexity.................................. 43
Sex Differences in Dimensions of the Environment 46

4 DIFFERENTIATION OF INFANT FUNCTIONING 49

Measures of Infant Functioning 52
Clusters Derived from the Bayley Scales 52
Gross and Fine Motor Development 53
Social Responsiveness 55

Cognitive-Motivational Functions 56
Object Permanence 58
Language 58
Exploratory Behavior and Preference for
Novelty 59
Interrelations Among Measures of Infant
Functioning 60
Sex Differences in Infant Functioning 64
Conclusion 66

5 FINDINGS AND CONCEPTUAL ISSUES 69

The Social Environment 71
Modalities of Social Stimulation 71
Near Receptor Modalities: Tactile and Kinesthetic
Stimulation 72
Distance Receptor Modalities: Visual and Auditory
Experiences 77
Contingency Measures: Responsiveness to Positive
Vocalization and Responsiveness to Distress 81
Maternal Affect: Expression of Positive Affect,
Smiling, and Play 87
Social Mediation of Play Materials 90
Higher Order Characterizations of Maternal Behavior:
Level and Variety of Stimulation 92
The Proximal Inanimate Environment: Characteristics
of Objects Available to Infants 95
Responsiveness of Inanimate Objects 96
Complexity of Inanimate Objects 98
Variety of Inanimate Objects 100
Combinations of Environmental Variables 103
Some Methodological Considerations 103
Multiple Regression Analysis and Analysis of Variance 104
Relations Between Environmental Dimensions and
Infant Functions for Male and Female Infants 112

6 PORTRAITS OF SOME LIVE INFANTS AND
   MOTHERS 117

   Angela McCloud 122
   Michael Roberts 128
   Leroy Simmons 134
   Daryl Bradley 139
   Jennifer Ford 144
   Rachel Jeffries 149

7 OVERVIEW 155

   Relationships Between the Environment and the
   Infant 157
   Multivariate Analyses 161
   Environmental Influences on Boys and Girls ... 162
   Toward Better Conceptualization and Methodology ... 163
   Models of Stimulation......................... 166
   Bidirectional Influences 168
   Implications for Intervention 170
   Concluding Comments 173

APPENDIX 1 CORRELATIONS OF ENVIRONMENTAL
AND INFANT VARIABLES FOR BOYS AND
GIRLS 177

APPENDIX 2 MANUAL FOR OBSERVATION OF THE
HOME ENVIRONMENT AND MOTHER-INFANT
INTERACTION 189

APPENDIX 3 MATERNAL RATINGS 213

APPENDIX 4 CHARACTERISTICS OF THE
INANIMATE ENVIRONMENT 215

APPENDIX 5 SUPPLEMENTARY INFANT MEASURES—
PROBLEM SOLVING 225

BIBLIOGRAPHY 229

AUTHOR INDEX 245

SUBJECT INDEX 249

FOREWORD

Speculations about the importance of early experience on the development of human personalities have a long history. They go back at least to Plato, who first mentioned the probable importance of early rearing conditions in *The Republic* (Book VI). There he contended that the early conditions of child care are too important for the welfare of the state to be left to the amateur ministrations of mere parents. In *The Laws* (Books VI and VII), he describes a program of early child rearing that is clearly based on hypotheses of what experiences are important for what traits; but he has the Athenian Stranger terminate his opening speech on the matter with this sentence: "I speak somewhat darkly, but I shall endeavor also to bring my wares into the light of day, for I acknowledge that at present there is still a want of clearness in what I am saying." After 2,500 years, there is still a "want of clearness" in what can be said about the effects of early experience.

For hundreds of years, the intuitions of Plato were largely lost. From shortly after the days of Plato and Aristotle, the concept of preformationism reigned in philosophy and dominated conceptions of development. The human infant was seen, and painted in the iconic Madonnas, as an adult in miniature. Preformationism gave way to predeterminism, first theistic and then genetic, and predeterminism tended to make both the conditions of political and social life and the characteristics of individuals inevitable. It was Jean Jacques Rousseau's argument that society corrupts man's native goodness that inaugurated an age of reform. Moreover, his book, *Emile*, on child-rearing and education, brought back some concern for early experience.

It was Sigmund Freud, however, who, in his *Three Contributions to a Theory of Sex,* presented the theory of psychosexual development. This theory provided the chief guide to empirical investigations of the role of early experience in personality development until after World War II. It continues even now to provide one conceptual basis for the choice of independent, environmental variables, and of dependent, personality variables, and also for hypotheses about environment-infant relationships. The notion of instinctual drives is central to psychodynamic theory. The theory emphasizes that the deprivation or frustration of instinctual drives is an important determinant of behavioral pathologies. These frustrated drives include homeostatic needs, sex, and tactile contact.

Competing conceptual bases for choices of variables and for hypotheses about antecedent-consequent relationships have more recently come from the investigations of the effects of early experience in various species of animals. Some of these studies have been inspired by Donald Hebb and the neurochemical theorizing of Helgar Hydén. Other guiding conceptions have come from the theorizing of Piaget, of Skinner and of such others as the writer of this foreword. Yet others have come by way of surprising results from attempts to test the hypotheses of psychosexual experience. I refer to the evidence for the extinction of instinctive responses with disuse and for reduced sensitivity to painful stimuli repeatedly encountered in the work of Levine, of Denenberg, and from my own laboratory. Certain of these latter conceptions, especially those from Hebb and from Piaget, have stressed the importance of early experiences through the distance receptors for the development of intellectual and motivational characteristics underlying competence. Even yet, however, almost any statement about antecedent-consequent relationships is controversial. The "want of clearness" noted by the Athenian Stranger in Book VII of *The Laws* still prevails. The authors of this highly informative new monograph agree. As they say in the first chapter, "Beyond the simple assertion that early experience is important, we are not able to make precise statements regarding what kinds of experience affect which aspects of the developing infant."

This monograph is first of all a description of an investigation. By virtue of the fact that the authors relate their many findings to most of the existing controversies and evidence, this work also becomes a discussion of the state of the existing art in the domain of early experience as it affects the behavior of human infants.

The investigation is broad and eclectic in choices of both the antecedent, environmental variables assessed and the consequent, behavioral variables measured in infants. Unlike a major share of investigations of infancy wherein the infants are brought to a laboratory for brief exposure to more or less traditional experimental conditions, the authors of this monograph have observed the infant in the natural setting of his home. They have chosen as variables the characteristics of both the social environment and the inanimate objects available to the infant. Especially interesting are the characteristics of the inanimate materials available to the infant: variety, complexity, and responsiveness, an innovative and theoretically useful way of characterizing materials and objects. With regard to infant behaviors, they consider eight clusters from the Bayley Scales and eight additional measures that involve problem solving, vocalization, and exploration. The investigation is thus very broad in the choice of both antecedent conditions and behavioral consequences; it is limited by being concerned with only the first six months of life. Moreover, they view development as a dynamic, ongoing interaction between the infant and the environments he encounters. Thus, the consequents need be permanent only if encounters with the environment continue to foster them.

In their data analyses, the authors of this monograph have used the ubiquitous statistic of correlation, but they have used it in an uncommon way. The correlational statistic has more often been employed to investigate response-response relationships. In traditional psychometrics, it is used to assess the relationship of performance on tests, the predictor, to performance in school or on the job, the criterion variable, to assess the relationships among the various components of such a trait construct as intelligence or introversion, and through factor analysis to determine the structure of such constructs. The authors of this monograph also use correlation in this traditional fashion analyzing the intercorrelations among the environmental measures and the measures of infant behaviors. What is uncommon is their correlating independent environmental variables with dependent behavioral variables. In studies of the interactions of infants with their mothers and the inanimate materials made available to them, such a use of correlation is especially uncommon. Their correlating a broad variety of environmental variables with a broad variety of infant variables yields results relevant to nearly every controversy and issue in the domain of early experience. This is a substantial advantage, but obtaining such a multiplicity of coefficients of correlation also runs a risk of spurious relationships. Thus, while their results can hardly establish any hypotheses beyond doubt, they do contribute to strengthening or weakening many hypotheses about early

environmental influences. Such, however, is the nature of progress in the sciences of open systems like biology and psychology.

In the resulting correlations between environmental and infant
variables, the absence of correlations expected from theory or
from previous empirical findings and the presence of other
unexpected relationships are especially interesting. For instance,
kinesthetic experiences appear to be more often and more highly
correlated with infant behaviors at 6 months of age than are
experiences involving the tactile contact dramatized in Harlow's
interpretations of infant monkeys going, when threatened, to the
padded terry-cloth mother surrogate rather than to the wire,
milk-giving one. Another example: measures of the inanimate
environment, especially the responsiveness and variety of the
objects available to the infants, show more and higher
correlations with the cognitive-motivational actions of the
infants (goal directedness, reaching and grasping, and secondary
circular reactions) than do many of the aspects of social
experience. It is also somewhat surprising, despite the recent
uncovering of early sex differences in information processing,
that these relationships are much more prominent in the
behavior of girls than of boys. The size of the relationships
among girls is especially impressive. They range from +.36 to
+.60. What is amazing is the finding that measures of such
specific experiential environmental variables, based on only the
3-hour time samplings during two home visits, can show
correlations of +.50 and +.60 with measures of such specific and
important behaviors as goal directedness and visually directed
reaching and grasping. The fact that these variables can account
for 25% to 30% of the variance in measures of infant development
at 6 months of age implies more stability in the environmental
conditions of homes than we have ever imagined.

Especially interesting also, in view of my contention that
there is a system of motivation with information processing and
action, is the finding of substantial correlations between variety
in both the social and the inanimate aspects of the home
environments and the amount of exploratory behavior at 6

months. Not only does this evidence serve to strengthen the validity of the view that the human infant is at least potentially a highly active information processer, it also suggests that how active an information processer he becomes by age 6 months is to a considerable degree a matter of the variety of his encounters with human beings and inanimate materials. These findings also serve to emphasize the cognitive aspects of motivation and the motivational aspects of competence. Cognition and motivation are separate only as concepts.

These are but samples of the many results from the investigation reported in this monograph. The fact that the authors relate what they have found to the controversies, to the hypotheses, and to the results reported by others gives it the quality of a theoretical overview of the effects of very early experience on the behavior of human infants. It thereby takes a substantial step in reducing that "want of clearness" noted by the Athenian Stranger some twenty-five hundred years ago in *The Laws* of Plato.

                                                        J. McVicker Hunt

Estes Park, Colorado

ACKNOWLEDGMENTS

We wish especially to express our gratitude to the mothers and caregivers who so graciously allowed us to come into their homes with our observation forms, clipboards and stopwatches and to spend long hours observing them and their infants. We are equally grateful to the babies who unwittingly were the objects of our intense concentration.

For their help in facilitating our work on this project, we are indebted to the pediatricians and nurses in the District of Columbia Department of Public Health, in the Group Health Association of Greater Washington, and in the well-baby clinics from which we recruited our subjects. To Dr. Ann Lodge, we are grateful for many contributions, one tangible one being her careful training of Dr. Joseph Jankowski in evaluating infants with the Bayley Scales. Our thanks go to Dr. David Herman of the

Psychological Corporation for his assistance in the computation of split-half reliabilities on the Bayley Mental Developmental Index and Psychomotor Developmental Index.

We recall fondly many hours of lively discussion about statistical and methodological issues with Dr. Samuel Greenhouse. For day to day consultation on the statistical problems and for helping resolve sudden crises in our relations with the computer, we are indebted to Dr. Robert Klein.

To our colleague, Richard Cain, we are especially grateful for his conscientious and arduous labors with the data, and who as our intermediary with the computer firmly bent it to our will.

To many colleagues and friends who carefully read the manuscript and gave many constructive suggestions we owe thanks: Dr. L. Joseph Stone, Dr. Lois B. Murphy, Dr. Richard Q. Bell, Dr. Harriet L. Rheingold, Dr. Howard Moss, Mrs. Pauline Shereshefsky, Dr. George Morgan, Dr. Juarlyn Gaiter, Dr. Robert P. Klein, Dr. Robert Harmon, and Mrs. Mary Walpole.

For their patience, forbearance, and painstaking work in the typing of the manuscript, we are grateful to Martha Weiss and Patricia Simon.

We are especially indebted to our immediate collaborators without whose help this study could not have been carried out. Myrna Fivel and Joan Durfee helped in the development of the home observation system and did a major share of the observations of mothers and infants. Joan Durfee also took a major responsibility for the work on the case histories in Chapter 6. Dr. Joseph Jankowski helped plan the study, recruited the subjects, assumed responsibility for the pediatric and developmental evaluation of the infants, and made a special contribution to the development of the separate clusters of infant functions.

Leon J. Yarrow
Judith L. Rubenstein
Frank A. Pedersen

INFANT AND ENVIRONMENT
early cognitive
and motivational development

1

INTRODUCTION

Long before Freud gave his distinctive emphasis to the crucial nature of early experience, man pondered whether development is simply an unfolding of characteristics present at birth, whether it is determined solely by events in the external world, or whether it represents a complex interaction of both. Belief in the overriding significance of early experience has come to be an article of modern creed. It has been so insistently and regularly intoned that it has acquired the status of dogma. When one tries to marshal the evidence for this deceptively simple belief, one quickly becomes aware of the diverse and tenuous threads out of which it is constructed.

Beyond an assertion that early experience is important, investigators have been unable to make precise statements regarding what kinds of experiences affect which aspects of the developing infant. Very little is known about how a wide range of variation in the natural environment contributes to variation in normal functioning. This is the core issue of this study. A major objective was to assess the impact of early experiences by describing the environments of young infants in great detail and then to look at the relationships between these differentiated dimensions of the environment and the infant's social, cognitive, motor, and motivational characteristics. We studied the infant in his natural environment, observing the amount of time the mother spent holding him, caressing him, and vigorously moving him about. We recorded how often she talked with him and how much of her speech was in response to his signals, whether she responded to his cries or to his positive vocalizations, and how often she presented him with playthings. We also analyzed his inanimate environment—the characteristics of objects within the infant's reach, how simple or complex they were, and the extent to which they were responsive to his actions, whether they changed shape or made a sound when he played with them.

The search for relationships between specific parameters of the environment and specific aspects of development proved to have vast ramifications. We found we were enmeshed in some of the core issues and major controversies of developmental psychology, issues central to many important practical concerns of our time.

For a long time psychoanalytic theory was the main inspiration of research on early development. It provided not only the theoretical framework for the formulation of research problems, but, more important, it specified the variables to be studied. Much of the research on the early environment carried out in the last quarter of a century was concerned with the effects of severe trauma or extreme deprivation of maternal care. Other studies from the psychoanalytic perspective focused on a fairly limited domain of the infant's experience, comparing breast and bottle feeding, abrupt and gradual weaning, harsh and permissive toilet training. For a time, most of the data came from patients' retrospective accounts of their life histories. Vivid and dramatic conclusions were drawn about the effects of severely traumatic and depriving events in early life. In time, prospective human and animal studies extended and elaborated some of these findings. They also raised many questions about the conclusions that had been drawn from the earlier studies.

Prospective clinical studies from a psychoanalytic orientation (Fries, 1935; Levy, 1943; Ribble, 1943) pointed to "inadequate mothering" as a major factor in the etiology of emotional disturbances. Although this research had many methodological inadequacies (Orlansky, 1949; Pinneau, 1955), it dramatized the importance of continuity and warmth in mothering. These findings were extended by studies of children who were separated from their mothers and placed in institutional settings where they had no consistent mother-figure and were given inadequate sensory stimulation (Goldfarb, 1945; Provence & Lipton, 1962; Spitz, 1945). Many of these children were found to be physically and intellectually retarded, and they were unable to establish meaningful interpersonal relationships (Yarrow, 1961).

These findings led to more controlled, experimental studies on animals. Some of these studies found that massive early deprivation resulted in irreversible effects on later development, and enrichment facilitated cortical development (Rosenzweig, Krech, Bennett & Diamond, 1968). Although there were many impressive demonstrations of the effects of early handling or deprivation on the animals' subsequent behavior, many ambiguities remained. For example, "gentling" was first interpreted as optimal stimulation for the animal. Later, it was found that beyond a certain intensity gentling was associated with heightened emotionality in the rat (Levine, 1956). Other findings indicated that there might be a species specificity and emphasized the need for caution in making generalizations to humans.

In one of the first critical evaluations of research stimulated by psychoanalytic theory, Sears (1943) pointed to some of the methodological inadequacies of the studies and the inconclusiveness of the findings. In a sharp critique of the literature, Orlansky (1949) also concluded that the findings were neither clear nor consistent. Similarly, Caldwell (1964) in a comprehensive review of the research on early infant care pointed to inconsistent and equivocal findings regarding the effects of oral gratification, breast or bottle feeding, sudden or gradual weaning, and severe or permissive toilet training. It is evident that these early studies were too literal in their attempts to test psychoanalytic theory. Often they seemed unaware that much more goes on in mother-infant interaction than feeding or training in sphincter control.

In evaluating the more controlled, methodologically more adequate experimental studies of sensory enrichment and sensory deprivation in animals, Thompson and Grusec (1970) concluded that it was not clear which of the many variables that had been manipulated could account for the changes in behavior. Moreover, the relative reversibility of these changes depended on the age at which the deprivation or enrichment experiences occurred.

In a critical review of the extensive literature on maternal deprivation, Yarrow (1961, 1963) pointed out that many different conditions were subsumed under this term: insufficient sensory stimulation and the lack of a consistent caregiver with whom the child could form an attachment, as well as the many traumas associated with separation from the mother and the instability of subsequent caregiving. He concluded that uncritical acceptance of "maternal deprivation" as a global etiological variable only interfered with our understanding of these conditions. It left one with the comfortable feeling that it explained the etiology of emotional and intellectual disturbance and thus there was no need for further research.

We believe the failure to find direct relations between experience in infancy and later development does not negate the significance of early experience, but rather emphasizes the need for framing more differentiated questions and for defining variables much more precisely. The basic strategy of this study evolved out of this conviction. We attempted to differentiate the environment along many discrete dimensions. We focused on specific behaviors of mothers toward their infants and discrete dimensions of the inanimate environment. Rather than characterize environments in global evaluative terms as traumatic or depriving, we attempted to describe variations in the environment along many continua.

Our choice of environmental variables was influenced by a number of recent theoretical formulations. Among these theoretical systems are adaptation level theory (Helson, 1964), operant learning theory (Skinner, 1953), Piagetian developmental theory (Piaget, 1936), and Hunt's synthesis of several of these theoretical positions around the concept of intrinsic motivation (Hunt, 1965). These theories have had significant impact on our conceptualization of the early environment. They have sliced the environment in different ways, they have emphasized different dimensions of early experience, and they have arrived at a different view of the organism. On the whole, the concepts from these theoretical systems can be more precisely defined than the psychoanalytic ones, and the basic propositions they generate can more readily be tested in experimental or natural situations.

There are some basic similarities in these several theoretical approaches, but each one has certain distinctive emphases. Common to several is an emphasis on *stimulus seeking*. They see the infant's activities as directed toward not simply reducing tension but maintaining an optimal state of arousal. The infant seeks variety and change in stimulation. He has an intrinsic motivation to explore the novel. Paralleling this conceptual shift from homeostasis we have changed our concept of the infant from a passive organism to an active one. The infant not only actively elicits stimulation and response from others, he mediates the effects of stimulation through his sensitivities and vulnerabilities. The optimal range on a stimulus dimension will vary for an individual, and it is also dependent on the stimulus level to which he has adapted.

Allied to the view of the infant as a seeker of response from people and objects in his environment is the concept of contingency, a key concept in operant learning theory. Essentially, it emphasizes the importance of a responsive environment, maintaining that the impact of environmental events depends on their temporal relation to behavior. Operant learning theory, however, does not deal with the internal representation of contingent events. This inner representation of contingent responsiveness, its meaning to the organism, was given special emphasis in Rotter's (1954) expectancy theory. More recently, Lewis and Goldberg (1969) and Watson (1966) speculated about the development in the young infant of an expectation that he can have an effect on the environment. They hypothesized that this expectancy develops through his experiences with responsive people and objects around him.

These several theories led to profound changes in our orientation to early experiences. There has been a shift from a pathology-oriented model, based on experiences of trauma and extreme deprivation, to one that recognizes a great range in normal variation. Researchers have come to a much more complex view of early experiences; they do not think of their effects in all-or-none terms. It is no longer a question of whether experiences have effects on the developing organism. Rather, there is an awareness of a continuum of effects that varies with many parameters of the environment as well as with the intensity, the quality, and the patterning of environmental stimuli.

While there seems to be some general agreement on the inadequacies of old models and on the importance of differentiating the infant's experiences along many dimensions, there is still no consensus regarding the degree of differentiation, the level of variables, or the types of variables most useful for the analysis of early experience. For a number of years there have been sharply polarized views. Some have stressed the intangible qualities of mothering, such as warmth, responsiveness, basic acceptance of the infant. Others have emphasized objectively defined variables of sensory stimulation. We came to feel that this controversy was not a useful one. We concluded that many important qualitative dimensions of maternal care could be defined and indexed by quantitative measures of sensory stimulation.

With increased awareness of individual differences in sensitivity to visual, auditory, and kinesthetic stimulation, there has been growing recognition of the need to distinguish the modalities through which mothers interact with their infants, through which they provide stimulation and express affection. The emphasis on sensory stimulation also drew our attention to stimulation from inanimate sources, heretofore overlooked in the study of the natural environment. Information theory especially pointed to such important dimensions of the inanimate environment as complexity, responsiveness, and the variety of objects available to the infant.

Our interest in these methodological and theoretical issues was heightened when the federal government began to take responsibility for the development of compensatory educational programs in an attempt to undo the effects of the severe deprivations suffered by many underprivileged children. More and more, theoretical concerns regarding early experience have moved from the abstract realm to the very real world as attempts are being made to optimize the rearing conditions of infants. Particular attention has been given in recent years to the environments of children of lower socioeconomic status. A number of reports have characterized these environments in terms reminiscent of the early descriptions of depriving institutional environments. These reports, for the most part are based on global impressions, not on careful analyses of mother-child interaction patterns and the child's experiences with inanimate objects. Intervention programs, therefore, have often been developed without detailed knowledge of the important dimensions of the environments of poor families. Moreover, they have been initiated without precise information regarding relationships between certain aspects of these environments and the developmental characteristics of children growing up in these settings.

Because they have been the major target of intervention programs, in this study we chose a sample of black families largely from the inner city. We made detailed observations of the infants and their caregivers in the natural setting, focusing on patterns of interaction and on the character of inanimate stimulation available to these infants. Our strategy was to concentrate on the infant's immediate experience, the proximal environment. We hoped that detailed analyses might confirm or shake some of the simple stereotypes that have pervaded the popular and some professional literature about lower class environments. Basically, we were attempting to establish links between theoretical concepts and environmental variables, with the hope that such conceptual links might eventually provide an orderly framework for planning intervention programs to optimize the environments of young infants. By identifying some important dimensions of early experience and by deepening our understanding of the processes through which the early environment impinges on the child, we hoped our work might be of some value for intervention programs. Even though we were deeply interested in the implications of our findings for the care of young children, the major aims of this research remained focused on basic developmental questions, issues that transcend racial or socioeconomic characteristics.

To recapitulate, a major objective of this study is to contribute to an understanding of early environmental influences. To achieve this objective, there were three major steps: (*a*) to differentiate the natural environment in conceptually meaningful terms through detailed analyses of caregivers' behaviors and the properties of proximal stimuli in the infant's environment; (*b*) to measure varied aspects of infant development, including social, cognitive, motor, and motivational functions; and (*c*) to analyze the relationships between these differentiated dimensions of the environment and infant characteristics.

The following chapters discuss in detail the methodological issues and theoretical conceptions that influenced our choice of the dimensions of the environment and the infant characteristics we measured. In addition, some of the methodological considerations that went into the selection of an observational approach to the natural environment are discussed. The final chapters present the findings and their implications for theories about the influence of the early environment on development.

2

METHODOLOGY AND
METHODOLOGICAL ISSUES

The selection of a sample, the choice of variables, and the development of techniques for obtaining data are critical steps in any investigation. Often in the bare statements of methodology given in research reports, the difficult problems encountered in method development are glossed over, helping to foster the illusion that this is a simple, cut and dried, and essentially insignificant process. Rather than perpetuate this illusion by presenting a simple outline of methods used, we present in this and the following two chapters the theoretical and practical issues we confronted in selecting the variables and in developing the methods for obtaining the data to index these variables. We also discuss the considerations that went into the choice of the sample and the selection of an observational approach for studying the infant's natural enviroment. The conceptual bases underlying the choice of the environmental variables and the characteristics of the infant which we measured are discussed in Chapters 3 and 4. By delineating the many considerations that entered into decisions on the measures, we hope to point up some methodological issues in studying early environmental influences.

SUBJECTS

The core sample consisted of 41 black infants (21 boys and 20 girls) and their primary caregivers, selected from a larger group of 70. Sixteen were first-born, 25 were later-born. All measures were obtained when the infants were between 5 and 6 months of age. The sample was recruited through two sources: public well-baby clinics in the District of Columbia and a private prepaid health plan.

We chose 5–6 months as the age to study environmental effects for several reasons. By this age, the infant has interacted with his environment for a sufficiently long period of time for it to have had some measurable impact. Moreover, the infant is sufficiently differentiated to observe selective influences. We recognize that even a very young infant has some influence on the stimulation he receives, but before the acquisition of basic locomotor skills, a greater amount of the stimulation is under control of the mother. When the infant is ambulatory it becomes increasingly difficult to define his environment.

In some infants studied, there were special problems in obtaining an adequate sample of their mothering experiences. Often the person primarily responsible for the infant's care was not the mother. Mothers who were working or still in school had substitute caretaking arrangements. From the mother's report of the baby's day-to-day schedule, we determined who cared for the infant the largest amount of time during the week. This person was designated the "primary caregiver." We shall use the terms "mother" and "primary caregiver" interchangeably in this report.

One of the first striking findings of this investigation was that in many cases there were several changes during the first months in arrangements for care of the infant. Sometimes the mother shifted back and forth between employment outside of the home and full time care of her infant. Sometimes there were changes in the substitute caregiver, depending upon the availability of a relative, ease of transportation to a caregiver's house, or changes in the mother's work or school schedule. In some families there were shared caregiving arrangements in which several people cared for the infant; often these arrangements were quite variable and unpredictable from week to week, and sometimes they were quite stable. Although we always observed the primary caregiver in interaction with the infant, we came to feel in many cases that our observations were not sufficiently representative of the infant's early experiences. After careful review of the caregiving histories of the 70 infants who were observed, we excluded 29 cases from the main analysis group.[1]

The core analysis group consisted of 41 cases with a caregiver who had been responsible for the infant for 3 months or longer, and where there had been no marked environmental changes in the month preceding the observation. The mother was the primary caregiver in 33 cases, a relative (usually the maternal grandmother) in 5 cases, and an unrelated babysitter in 3 instances.

SOCIAL CHARACTERISTICS OF THE CORE SAMPLE

We found the standard scales for classifying families according to social class inappropriate for characterizing the subjects in this study. The Hollingshead Index of Social Position (1956) illustrates the limitations of these scales. It is based on the father's educational level and occupational status. The mother's contribution to the family's economic resources is ignored. In cases in our

---

[1] The excluded cases represented a diverse group. In some instances, the mother returned to work a few weeks before the observation; in others there were multiple and changing caregivers. These excluded subjects represent infants whose experiences are sharply different from the usual pattern of stable maternal care. Although they do not lend themselves to the central questions of this study, their experiences raise many interesting questions that we plan to pursue.

sample where the mother was more highly educated or employed at a higher level than the father, the scores did not give a true picture of the family's economic status. Moreover, this scale did not lend itself readily to the classification of families where the father was a student or separated from the family. In essence, we feel scales such as this one do not distinguish many important differences in economic status, in lifestyles, or in family structure.

Many studies have concerned themselves with the relationships between social class status and cognitive and personality development, but such a gross formulation is not useful for understanding the underlying processes of environmental influences (Deutsch, 1973). Social class is not a direct index of the stimulation given the child or of the larger patterns of child rearing; there are wide variations among individual members of a social class. We can make only very gross inferences about children's experiences from their social class status. Social class membership per se does not affect the infant's development; rather it is the proximal variables, the kinds of stimulation and patterns of caregiving, that are important. In this research our basic interest was in these variations in the infant's experiences rather than in summary characterizations of their group membership.

There were great variations in the living conditions, lifestyles, and value orientations of the families in this study. Their residences ranged from detached homes in suburban developments and well-maintained high-rise apartments to deteriorated inner-city housing. Most of the families lived in old urban apartments or in attached homes in older neighborhoods in the inner city. The interiors of the homes showed equal diversity—from spacious and amply furnished to dimly lit, crowded rooms with dilapidated furniture. There were great differences among the households in level of background stimulation. Some were bustling with activity, conversation, and a variety of loud sounds; others were slow-paced and quiet.

These households were similarly diverse in family composition. Eighteen cases conformed to the nuclear family model of mother, father, and siblings (44%); 2 were lone mother-infant pairs (5%);

and the other 21 represented some variation of extended families (51%), including various combinations of grandparents, aunts, uncles, and cousins. There were 16 father-absent families. Some mothers were not married, some were divorced; others were separated because the fathers were in military service or employed in another city.

There was a fairly wide spread in age, education, and occupation of the parents. The mother's ages ranged from 16 to 41 years with the mean age 24.2. The fathers were from 18 to 40 years of age; their average was 26.5 years. The range in education was from 7 to 17 years for the mothers and 6 to 17 years for the fathers, with means of 11.6 and 11.5 years, respectively.

The occupational level of the fathers covered the entire spectrum from unskilled manual labor through professional and managerial positions. Ten fathers had relatively unskilled positions, such as parking lot attendant, bus boy, custodian; an additional 10 were in semi-skilled positions, such as truck driver, enlisted military personnel, stock clerk. Thirteen were employed in a variety of clerical, sales, technical, and skilled occupations; these included a lab assistant, several noncommissioned officers in the armed services, a junior mechanical engineer, a draftsman, and a salesman. Four fathers were employed at a professional or managerial level, and four were students or trainees.

The mothers showed some diversity in occupational status. Twenty-five were not employed outside the home. Four were in school; four had professional roles such as teaching or nursing; two were clerks; and six were employed as maids, babysitters, and in similar domestic occupations.

The case descriptions in Chapter 6 describe some of the social and psychological variations among these families.

OVERVIEW OF DATA COLLECTION

Data were collected between September 1967 and July 1968. The study was conducted in four phases. The purpose and time schedule of each phase is described briefly as follows.

Initial Screening

Before an infant was selected for the study, his mother's prenatal record and his birth history chart were reviewed by a research pediatrician. Infants were not included if their mothers had perinatal problems, such as toxemia, systemic infections, or other severe medical problems. Infants who had birth difficulties or perinatal problems, such as low birth weight, respiratory distress, or hypotonia also were excluded.

Following the initial screening of the infants, the pediatrician spoke with the mothers during the routine well-baby examination at 2 to 3 months. The study was described and their participation was requested. Eighty-four percent of the mothers agreed to participate. Interviews with participating mothers were conducted by the pediatrician to obtain background information on the families, such as the composition of the family and household membership, the ages of the parents and siblings, as well as information on caregivers other than the mother. Each family was paid approximately $40 for its cooperation in the study.

Pediatric Examination

When an infant was 4 months old, a complete physical examination, including a comprehensive neurological examination, was conducted by the staff pediatrician to assure that the infant was free from gross physical or neurological impairments. At this time, there was another interview with the mother regarding changes in maternal employment, the household composition, and caretaking arrangements for the infant.

Home Observations

Shortly after an infant was 5 months old, an introductory home visit was made by the observer. The purpose was to introduce the observer to the primary caregiver, to explain the home observation procedures, and to answer any questions about the study. It was intended to help the mother feel more at ease at the time of the observations in the home.

Two home observations were made during the second and third week after the infant was 5 months old. The observations were within 1 week of each other. Each observation consisted of 3 hours of time sampling while the baby was awake. Naps extended the time the observer was in the home: the total time ranged from 8 to 10 hours.

Assessment of Infant

When the infant was 5½ months old, the Bayley Scales of Infant Development (Bayley, 1969) and some supplementary items were administered by the pediatrician in the clinic. At this time the mothers were again interviewed regarding changes in caregivers, in maternal employment, and in household membership.

When the infant was 6 months of age, a test of exploratory behavior was administered in the home by a psychologist.

OBSERVATIONAL METHODS: TIME SAMPLING VERSUS NARRATIVE RECORDS

For a long time, developmental research relied on the interview with the mother as the primary source of information. Much of our data on early experiences have been based on the retrospective recall of the mother. Although many investigators have been uneasy about the validity of data from this type of interview, only in recent years has this approach been scrutinized. Methodological studies point out many distortions and deficiencies in the interview (Yarrow, Campbell, & Burton, 1968). They find discrepancies between the mother's report of an event at one time and her descriptions of the same event at a later time. There are also discrepancies between the mother's report of her interaction with her child and an observer's description of her behavior, a divergence which probably results from the mother's difficulty in viewing her child's or her own behavior with detachment.

The observer is able to view the mother-child relationship from a more impartial perspective. Although an observer's presence in the home may influence the mother's behavior, this effect can be minimized. Certainly mothers differ in their ease of adaptation to another's presence, but if the observer is able to establish a trusting relationship, most mothers will be able to go about their usual activities, responding naturally to the baby.

Two main approaches have been used for recording mother-child interactions. Most common are narrative, or running account records, which are sometimes written, often dictated. The protocols are usually coded some time after the observation (Ainsworth, 1967; Escalona & Heider, 1959; Yarrow, 1963). The second approach involves time-sampling or event-sampling methods, using precoded categories. These may involve continuous recording (Clarke-Stewart, 1973; Gewirtz & Gewirtz, 1965; Moss, 1967; Tulkin & Kagan, 1972) or taking time out for recording (Bishop, 1951; Rheingold, 1960; Rubenstein, 1967).

Both time sampling and narrative records have advantages and limitations. The choice depends upon one's methodological prejudices and on the kinds of data one is interested in obtaining. Narrative records yield richer data, they capture the natural flow of interactions, they permit the observer to be open to unusual or unexpected happenings, and they allow the observer more freedom to select and interpret the events he is recording.

Because of their unstructured nature, however, narrative records have their own shortcomings. Differences in sensitivity and perceptiveness among observers may yield vastly different data. Evaluative biases may unwittingly influence the observations and, without specific guidelines for what is to be recorded, the data obtained on different subjects may not be comparable. For each case we may be left with idiosyncratic data difficult to quantify. Moreover, coding such records is usually time consuming.

Time sampling with precoded categories, on the other hand, avoids some of the methodological shortcomings of narrative recording. The observer records systematically at defined intervals the categories of behavior to be used in the data analysis. Errors due to differential sensitivity and evaluative biases may be minimized by having a common set of categories and by training observers until a high degree of agreement is reached. The time-sampling approach lends itself to observing discrete behavior which may be defined with some precision. Data retrieval is generally more efficient since it consists essentially of the tabulation of frequency scores for various categories.

There are also problems inherent in this approach. After selecting categories, there is no leeway for revisions or elaborations. If there are a large number of categories, time must be taken for recording after each observational time unit. As a result there will be gaps in the data, a loss in the sequential flow of events. This is a serious loss if one is interested in contingencies and chains of interactions.

After weighing the advantages and disadvantages of these two observational approaches, we chose time sampling and attempted to compensate for some of its deficiencies. Since we thought it would be undesirable to attempt to reconstruct sequences after we had recorded the data, we used "interact" categories (Lambert, 1960), categories that encompassed sequential events. For example, we coded all infant vocalizations and all maternal speech; and, in addition, we had a category for maternal speech which followed an infant vocalization. This category defined a particular contingency, the mother's vocal reinforcement of the infant's vocalizations. We also coded several maternal responses to the infant's cries, such as feeding, talking to him, giving a pacifier, and rocking or patting him.

In data reduction we simplified the technical steps involved. Many approaches require intermediate clerical steps, such as tabulating entries in columns. Because these steps are tedious and often boring, the possibility of error is greatly increased. We developed a recording sheet (see Appendix 2) and method of entering events from which a computer keypunch operator could work directly after a small amount of editing. With the raw data entered into a computer directly from the observation sheet, tabulations were made with programmed counting instructions, and standard statistical analyses were carried out using these summary scores.

In addition to analyzing the data at the level of discrete behaviors, we also described the environment at a more abstract level. These measures were derived from two sources: summary ratings made after each observation was completed, and derivative variables based on combining scores of single behavior categories. The higher order composite variables, made possible by computer tabulation techniques that handled several categories simultaneously, are described in detail in Chapter 3.

OBSERVATION CATEGORIES AND PROCEDURES

In choosing variables for a differentiated analysis of the environment, we attempted to order the infant's experiences with people and exposure to inanimate stimuli in terms of a conceptual framework. It was not a tight conceptual framework, tied to any one theoretical system. Selection of the parameters of the environment was guided by concepts from several theoretical orientations: information theory (Miller, Galanter, & Pribram, 1960), adaptation level theory, (Helson, 1964), operant learning theory, Piagetian developmental theory, Hunt's (1961) theorizing about intrinsic motivation, and R. W. White's (1959) conceptual thinking about effectance motivation. Using these conceptual perspectives we tried to translate concepts into categories of observable events, behaviors, and definable properties of inanimate stimuli. Equipped with these theoretical lenses, we looked at environments and observed infants and mothers, going back and forth from theoretical concepts to concrete events and behaviors. After many observations we finally arrived at a set of observation categories.

The observation categories are described briefly in this chapter. They are presented in detail in the observation manual in Appendix 2. They deal with three major types of stimulation: direct stimulation from people, direct stimulation from inanimate objects, and social mediation of inanimate objects. A fourth set of categories is concerned with a small number of infant behaviors. In addition, we noted which mother-infant interaction occurred in the context of caretaking.

Direct social stimulation included (*a*) the sensory modalities in which stimulation was given—visual, auditory, tactile, and kinesthetic; (*b*) the intensity of stimulation (for example, passive touching, active touching, and moving the baby were distinguished from each other); (*c*) stimulation contingent on certain infant behaviors, as in giving the baby a pacifier in response to his cries.

We were also interested in the social mediation of objects in the child's environment—the ways in which the caregiver directed the infant's attention to play materials or highlighted their properties. For example, we recorded whether she presented toys or other objects within view or reach of the infant. We also recorded whether she emphasized or highlighted the properties of objects, such as shaking a rattle to show that it made a sound when moved.

The character and quality of stimulation from inanimate objects is an important aspect of the child's experience that has often been ignored in studies of the natural setting. In this study we recorded the sources of inanimate stimulation by listing all play materials and household objects within reach of the infant. After completing each observation we classified these objects in terms of their complexity and responsiveness (see discussion of the inanimate environment in Chapter 3 and scales for Complexity and Responsiveness of Objects in Appendix 4).

The environment cannot be assessed only in terms of the caregiver's behaviors independently of the infant's behaviors. For example, Moss (1967) found that the amount of infant crying was related to the amount of time the mother spent holding him, a finding which Moss interprets as indicative of infant effects. Our codes contained a selected number of infant behaviors we thought were relevant for assessing environmental stimulation. These codes included such behaviors as focused exploration of objects, positive vocalizations, and crying.

A number of rating scales were also used to describe qualitative aspects of the mother-infant interaction and some relatively infrequent events that did not lend themselves to time sampling. Of the five rating scales of maternal behavior that had adequate reliability, two were used in this report: Expression of Positive Affect and Contingent Response to the Infant's Distress. Coefficients of rater reliability on these two scales were .72 for Expression of Positive Affect and .91 for Contingent Response to Distress. (See Appendix 3.)

Observation Procedures

Observations on 2 separate days were considered necessary to obtain an adequate sample of the mother-infant interaction. The time-sampling cycle consisted of a 30-second observation period and a 60-second recording period repeated through 120 cycles each day, for a total of 240 time-sample units or 6 hours for each child and caregiver.[2] During the observation, the mother or the baby's caregiver was encouraged to go about her usual activities. The observer explained the time-sampling procedure to the mother, emphasizing that the observation required careful concentration on the infant. Most mothers did not attempt to initiate conversation while the observer was engaged in the obser-vation. When the baby napped, the observer was free to talk with her, contributing, we believe, to the development of a comfortable relationship. Information was also obtained about any recent changes in caregivers. Observations were rescheduled if the baby were ill or if the mother reported any major departures from the usual daily routine.

Observer Reliability

Three young women served as observers. Their backgrounds in developmental psychology ranged from a doctorate to a bachelor's degree. The observers had a period of intensive training on the codes. Observer reliability was established on 10 cases before data collection was initiated, and on 10 more cases while data collection was in progress. Spot checks on reliability continued throughout the study.

[2] In five cases a second observation was not conducted because of illness or scheduling difficulties. For these subjects, frequency scores from the first observation were doubled to approximate 2 days of observation.

To obtain reliability data, two observers simultaneously coded mother-infant interaction in the home. The duration of these observations was 1.5 hours. Reliability was expressed as the correlation between the two observers on the frequency of occurrence for each category. A few categories, particularly those with low frequency of occurrence, were dropped because of their low reliability. Of the categories we retained, the coefficients of reliability ranged from .75 and .99. The reliability coefficients for the observation categories are given in the following section.

Observation Categories

In the following material, a list and brief description of the observational categories is given. The manual with detailed definitions and examples of the categories, as well as a copy of the recording form, is found in Appendix 2. The categories were grouped on the recording sheet for the convenience of the observer, while in this presentation, we are regrouping them for greater psychological coherence. Interobserver reliability appears in parentheses. The categories marked with an asterisk are items omitted from the data analyses because the measure was used for descriptive purposes rather than as an independent variable. Other reasons for omitting categories from analyses were low observer reliability or low frequency of occurrence.

I. Infant Behaviors*
    A. Vocalizations
        1. Positive, e.g., cooing, gurgling (.98)
        2. Distress, e.g., crying (.99)
    B. Visual Attention
        1. Directed to the primary caregiver (.93)
        2. Directed to another person in the home (.98)
    C. Focused Exploration, i.e., looking at and manipulating an inanimate object or person
        1. Toys (.97)
        2. Household furnishings (.99)

*Not used in these analyses as an independent variable.

       3. Caretaking materials (.98)
       4. Person (.82)
       5. Self (.97)
  II. Maternal Behaviors
     A. Physical location of caregiver with respect to baby*
       1. Within reach (.99)
       2. Intermediate (.99)
       3. Remote but within view of the infant (.95)
       4. Remote and out of view of the infant, e.g., in another room than the infant (.99)
     B. Context within which interactions occurred*
       1. Noncaretaking, e.g., social play (.96)
       2. Caretaking, e.g., feeding, diapering, bathing (.99)
       3. Mixed (.66)
     C. Sources of social stimulation directed to infant*
       1. Primary caregiver
       2. Other adult in the home, e.g., father, grandmother
       3. Child
     D. Focus of primary caregiver's attention*
       1. Major focus on baby (.96)
       2. Focus elsewhere (.94)
     E. Maternal visual orientation
       1. Looks at infant (.99)
       2. Mutual visual regard: mother and infant looking at each other (.93)
     F. Maternal vocalizations
       1. Any vocalization directed to the baby (.97)
       2. Vocalizations contingent on the infant's positive vocalizations (.96)
       3. Vocalizations contingent on the infant's distress vocalizations* (.93)
       4. Vocalizations which imitate the infant's vocalizations* (.74)
       5. Vocalizations within the baby's hearing but not directed to the baby* (.99)

*Not used in these analyses as an independent variable.

G. Tactile and kinesthetic stimulation
  1. Touch passively* (-.18)
  2. Touch passively with an object* (.99)
  3. Touch actively: pat or caress baby; burp baby (.93)
  4. Touch actively with an object* (.96)
  5. Hold baby (.99)
  6. Move the baby's whole body (.97)
H. Social mediation of inanimate stimuli
  1. Position objects within view (.78)
  2. Position objects within reach (.93)
  3. Position objects in the infant's hand (.75)
  4. Direct attention to objects, e.g., highlight their properties by moving or squeezing the object (.84)
 I. Separate the infant from an inanimate object; either take something away from the infant or change the infant's location so that he cannot handle an object* (.78)
 J. Encourage emergent gross motor responses, e.g., postural control or locomotion (.92)|
K. Affect and animation
  1. Smile (.91)
  2. Play (.81)
L. Responses to the baby's distress*
  1. Social soothing (.81)
  2. Give a play object (.83)
  3. Feed either milk or solids (.90)
  4. Provide a pacifier (.73)
  5. Check or acknowledge the baby's distress but not engage in any of the above (.44)
III. The Inanimate Environment
  A. Physical setting of infant
    1. Change in container, e.g., infant seat, playpen, mother's arms, bed (.96)
    2. Change in room in which infant is observed (.88)

*Not used in these analyses as an independent variable.

B. Play objects within reach of infant
   1. Number of play objects within reach
      a. Toys (.98)
      b. Household furnishings (.96)
      c. Caretaking materials (.99)
   2. Number of different objects (.99)

MEASURES OF INFANT FUNCTIONING

The infant variables were derived from three procedures: a research form of the Bayley Scales of Infant Development, some additional items to measure Problem Solving, and a structured situational test designed to measure exploratory behavior and preference for novel stimuli. During the latter procedure, a measure was also obtained of the amount of vocalization. We did not use as dependent variables any of the infant behaviors noted during the home observations because they were so much influenced by the mother's behavior and the play materials available to the infant. In the test situations we could standardize the conditions of stimulation, thus equalizing the opportunities for infant responses.

The Bayley Test was administered by a research pediatrician in the well-baby clinic during the third or fourth week of the sixth month. Prior to data collection, he had received a period of intensive training with a person experienced in administration of the Bayley Scales. Reliability in scoring the scales was established with 25 black infants, 5 to 6 months of age. One examiner administered and scored the test while the other person observed and scored the items independently. Coefficients of scorer reliability were .95 on the Mental Developmental Index and .96 on the Psychomotor Developmental Index.

In addition to the Mental Developmental Index and the Psychomotor Developmental Index, eight clusters of items were developed from the Bayley Scales: Gross Motor Development, Fine Motor Development, Social Responsiveness, Language, Goal

Directedness, Secondary Circular Reactions, Reaching and Grasping, and Object Permanence.

The Problem Solving cluster consisted of four items administered after the Bayley Scales. These items were scored not on a pass-fail basis but on a 4-point scale. Details of the scoring procedure are given in Appendix 5. The interobserver reliability on scoring this measure was .86.

The situational tests to measure exploratory behavior and preference for novelty (Rubenstein, 1967) were given in the home when the infant was 6 months of age. The infant was seated on his mother's lap at a kitchen table which was covered by a standard white cloth. The purpose of the test was explained to the mother and she was asked not to interact with the infant. The examiner, who had no previous contact with the mother or child, was seated directly across the table from the infant. At the beginning of the test the examiner rang the bell and then placed it on the table within reach of the baby, for 10 minutes. If the infant knocked the bell off the table, the examiner quickly replaced it. The infant's responses to the toy were recorded for a period of 10 minutes, after which a buffer toy was presented for 5 minutes.

The exploratory behavior procedure was followed by a test of preference for novel stimuli; it involved presentation of the now familiar bell paired with each of 10 novel objects. The novel toys included a necklace of pink and blue rubber beads, three uninflated balloons of different colors and shapes, a whistle, a red comb, a gold change purse, a shiny metal bracelet, a multicolored plastic cloth, and a red ring. Each pair was presented for 1 minute. To control for position preference, the positions of the bell and the novel object were alternated on each presentation.

The infant's responses were recorded by pushbuttons activating electric clocks. We observed two types of exploratory behavior: looking at and actively manipulating the bell. The score on each was the total amount of time the infant engaged in each of these behaviors. Also noted was any vocalization by the infant during the time he was involved with the bell. In the test of preference for novel stimuli, four behaviors were recorded: looking at the novel object, manipulating the novel object, looking at the familiar bell, and manipulating the bell. Two measures of preference for novelty were obtained: the amount of time the infant spent looking at the novel objects and the time he spent manipulating the novel objects. After a period of training, observer reliability was obtained on this procedure with nine infants observed in their homes. Reliability coefficients on the separate categories ranged from .95 to .99.

3

DIFFERENTIATION OF THE ENVIRONMENT: THE DEVELOPMENT OF VARIABLES AND THEIR INTERRELATIONSHIPS

There is an almost limitless number of aspects of the infant's environment to which one might attend. Although many studies are not explicit about the rationale for their choice of variables, we have tried to articulate the bases on which we chose the dimensions of the environment to be observed. The environmental variables are on several different levels reflecting the theoretical orientations from which the central questions and hypotheses of the study were derived. Some variables are at the behavioral level describing specific modalities of sensory stimulation; e.g., touching, holding, looking at, and talking to the infant. Other variables are concerned with process, i.e., responses contingent on the child's behavior. Some higher order variables, such as the mother's demonstrativeness in expressing positive feelings, are based on

27

ratings. Others, as indicated in the previous chapter, such as level and variety of social stimulation, are derived from composite scores of several behavior categories. In addition to these social variables, we recorded the number of different objects within reach of the baby and analyzed the Responsiveness and Complexity of these objects.

Although we finally came to describe many dimensions of the infant's experiences, the analysis of the environment was limited by our own theoretical predilections and by the realistic restraints of what could be observed. We focused on the mother or primary caregiver of the infant and only described stimulation from siblings and other adults under certain conditions (see Observation Manual in Appendix 2). We noted the contexts in which the mother interacted with the infant and some aspects of the background environment such as noise and illumination level; but, throughout, our focus was on the proximal environment, the immediate transactions between infant and mother. The test of the value of this level of description lies in how well these variables help one understand early development. This chapter describes the conceptual bases for our choice of variables.

THE SOCIAL ENVIRONMENT: ASPECTS OF MATERNAL CARE

Modalities of Stimulation

Our interest in the modalities of stimulation comes from several sources. For many years there has been a continuing controversy between proponents of "mother love" and the advocates of sensory stimulation. Central to psychodynamic theories is the belief that a warm, affectionate relationship with the mother is essential for healthy development. Others have argued that the infant will thrive if he is simply given adequate sensory stimulation. In many ways this is a pseudocontroversy. The mother's basic feelings towards the infant are transmitted largely through her behavior—through talking to the infant, and touching and holding him. In this study we have not attempted to reduce mother love to simple measures of sensory stimulation, but rather have analyzed the sensory components of maternal interaction and investigated their contribution to development. Our reasoning was that if we find significant relations between the mother's stimulation in given sensory modalities and the infant's development, it is essentially irrelevant as to whether these relations can be attributed to love or to the character of the mother's sensory stimulation.

There have been a few theoretical papers and experimental studies on the role of certain modalities of sensory stimulation. Some theorists have emphasized the importance of tactile and kinesthetic stimulation for maintaining the young infant's internal equilibrium (Frank, 1957; Prescott, 1971); others have elaborated on the role of distance receptor stimulation in the development of social responsiveness (Walters & Parke, 1965).

The Harlows' research (Harlow, 1959; Harlow & Harlow, 1965) on rhesus monkeys dramatized the importance of tactile stimulation. These findings indicated that "contact comfort" was more important in the development of attachment than was drive reduction associated with feeding. Maternally deprived monkeys would cling to a terry cloth "mother surrogate" despite the fact that hunger reduction occurred independently of the terry cloth mother. When frightened, the baby monkeys would flee to the terry cloth surrogate and cling persistently.

Mason (1968) extended the Harlows' findings on the response of infant monkeys to inanimate surrogate "mothers." He found that one of the common effects of maternal deprivation, stereotyped rocking, does not develop when monkeys are reared with a *moving* terry cloth surrogate. He theorized that the moving surrogate simulated the kinesthetic input that the natural mother provides as she carries the infant about. Studies of human infants who have been given supplemental kinesthetic stimulation are consistent with these findings on animals. Kinesthetic or vestibular-proprioceptive stimulation was found to have a reinforcing effect on the smiling response of infants 4 to 5 months old

(Brossard & Décarie, 1968) and to be more effective than tactile stimulation in soothing neonates (Korner & Thoman, 1972). In an earlier study Thoman and Korner (1971) also found vestibular stimulation to be highly effective in stopping the distress call of infant rats; it was also associated with increased exploratory behavior. Cross-cultural developmental studies have also noted the precocious development of infants who are given a great deal of tactile and kinesthetic stimulation by being carried around strapped to the mother's body.

In this study we distinguished two types of near receptor stimulation: tactile and kinesthetic-vestibular. Tactile stimulation was the frequency with which the caregiver touched, patted or caressed the baby. Kinesthetic-vestibular stimulation involved movement of the baby's whole body. It included rocking, jiggling, and carrying him around the house.[3]

Clinical and experimental literature also emphasizes the importance of distance receptor stimulation (Bowlby, 1969; Rheingold, 1961). Because of the young infant's lack of locomotor capabilities, much of the stimulation he receives is dependent on the distance receptors. Fantz (1964) found that the infant's visual system is functional at birth and that he attends selectively to patterned stimuli. Much of the young infant's waking time is spent in visual exploration of his environment. Several investigators have studied the effects of enriching the visual environment of institutionalized infants by placing attractive, colorful toys within view of the infant (Brossard & Décarie, 1971; White, B. L., 1967). Visual stimulation in a social context, on the other hand, has been studied only with regard to the development of the affectional bond between mother and infant. In the present investigation, we have explored the implications of visual stimulation for a broader range of infant functioning—social, cognitive, and motivational

---

[3]Some investigators have called bodily movement proprioceptive, others vestibular, still others kinesthetic stimulation. We have chosen the term kinesthetic-vestibular, recognizing that body movement involves more than one sensory receptor.

development. The measure of visual stimulation was the amount of eye-to-eye contact between the mother and infant, behavior that Robson (1967) has considered especially important for the development of attachment.

The importance of auditory stimulation for language development has been noted many times, but the evidence comes largely from research on extreme deprivation—infants in institutions (Provence & Lipton, 1962)—and from studies of deaf children (Lenneberg, 1967). Little is known about how the beginning of vocalization is affected by the amount of auditory stimulation. Studies of children in institutions have attributed the retardation in language frequently found in these settings to the paucity of verbal exchanges between the caregiver and infant (Provence & Lipton, 1962). Some association between the amount of mother's speech and infant vocalizations has been found in other studies (Beckwith, 1971; Jones & Moss, 1971). The present study obtained, through time sampling, a frequency count of the amount of talking and vocalizing the caregiver directed toward the baby.

Table 1 presents the intercorrelations among the modality measures. The two near receptor modalities were moderately interrelated; the correlation between tactile and kinesthetic stimulation was .53. The distance modalities, visual and auditory, were similarly related (r = .60). The relationships between near and distance receptor stimulation were somewhat lower, with r's ranging from .27 to .43. These data suggest that it is more meaningful to describe mothers according to their predominant patterns of stimulation rather than simply as depriving or stimulating. Some mothers provide stimulation largely through vision or audition, others through the tactile and kinesthetic modalities. The mother who often jiggles and pats the baby may not necessarily talk to him or engage in much eye-to-eye contact.

Contingency Measures

Contingency, the temporal relationship of a response to the child's behavior, is a central concept in operant learning theory.

TABLE 1

Interrelations Among Environmental Measures: Total Group ($N = 41$)

Environmental Measure	Modalities — Kinesthetic	Modalities — Visual	Modalities — Auditory	Contingencies — Contingent Response to Positive Vocalization	Contingencies — Contingent Response to Distress	Affect — Positive Affect	Affect — Smiling	Affect — Play	Social Mediation — With Minimal Social Reinforcement	Social Mediation — With Smiles and Vocalizations	Composite Variables — Level	Composite Variables — Variety	Inanimate Stimulation — Responsiveness	Inanimate Stimulation — Complexity	Inanimate Stimulation — Variety
Modalities															
Tactile	.53	.43	.27	.35	.41	.52	.22	.18	.33	.38	.61	.57	.27	–	–
Kinesthetic		.29	.39	.32	.37	.38	.29	.49	.28	.35	.71	.60	–	–	–
Visual			.60	.47	.25	.55	.66	.51	–	.42	.67	.56	–	–	–
Auditory				.70	.26	.59	.57	.43	-.24	.68	.74	.58	–	–	–
Contingencies															
Contingent Response to Positive Vocalization					.31	.51	.43	.32	–	.52	.64	.45	–	–	–
Contingent Response to Distress						.23	–	.21	.30	.21	.53	.48	–	–	.31
Affect															
Expression of Positive Affect							.46	.70	–	.51	.62	.64	.23	–	.20
Smiling								–	-.29	.24	.52	.31	–	–	–
Play									.20	.50	.60	.77	.26	–	–
Social Mediation															
With Minimal Social Reinforcement										–	.22	.26	.30	.21	–
With Smiles and Vocalizations											.55	.67	–	–	–
Composite Variables															
Level												.76	–	–	–
Variety													.33	–	.29
Inanimate Stimulation															
Responsiveness														.70	–
Complexity															–
Variety															

Note. Dashes represent correlation < .20.

Gewirtz (1961, 1969) especially emphasized the importance of contingent responsiveness in mother-child interaction. For an environment to be functionally effective for learning and for control of behavior, it must provide stimuli that can be discriminated by the child and reinforcers contingent on his behavior. From this perspective, maternal behavior that follows immediately on the infant's positive vocalizations or smiling is likely to increase the frequency of these positive behaviors. Others (Bell & Ainsworth, 1972; Lewis & Goldberg, 1969) have maintained that maternal responsiveness influences the infant's sense that he can affect the enviroment; thus, responsiveness has a pervasive influence on his motivational system.

Our interest in the responsiveness of the caregiver to the infant's signals also stems from studies of institutional environments (Provence & Lipton, 1962) and depriving home environments (Wortis, Bardach, Cutler, Rue, & Freedman, 1963), which have emphasized the lack of contingent interaction in caretaking. In institutional settings, children are often fed, diapered, and even played with by schedule rather than in response to their individual needs at a given moment. The developing apathy and progressive withdrawal of these children have been attributed to the lack of contingent responsiveness (Yarrow, 1961).

This study does not attempt to measure all varieties of contingent response to the child but is limited to two measures: Contingent Vocal Responses to the Infant's Positive Vocalizations and Contingent Response to Distress. Contingent Vocal Responses to the Infant's Positive Vocalization was a count of the frequency with which the caregiver vocalized immediately following the infant's vocalization. This measure incorporates one of the conditions utilized in a now classic laboratory study of reinforcement of infant vocalization (Rheingold, Gewirtz, & Ross, 1959); their social reinforcement consisted of a smile, saying, "tsk, tsk, tsk," and a light touch on the infant's abdomen. Although we recognize that the types of social reinforcement that mothers use are quite varied, we considered the measure of the caregiver's verbal response to an infant's positive vocalization to be a marker variable, an index of her positive interactions with her infant.

Two measures of the mother's responsiveness to the infant's distress were obtained, a time-sampling measure and a rating scale. A time-sampling measure of the frequency of response to distress is clearly affected by how often the infant cries. The baby of a mother whose behavior is highly contingent, one who intervenes when the infant shows minimal signs of distress, might cry infrequently; therefore, the mother's frequency of contingent behavior would be very low. An infant who cries a great deal and whose mother responds intermittently would have the highest contingency score. We felt that a psychologically more meaningful measure of contingent responsiveness is the mother's latency of response. Therefore we developed a rating of contingent response to distress which emphasized the immediacy of the mother's response to fussing or crying. This was a 5-point scale. The low point signified ignoring the infant's distress signals for prolonged periods. A score of 5 indicated that the mother characteristically responded immediately to minimal signs of distress. (See rating scales in Appendix 3.)

Since we tend to think of responsiveness as a general characteristic of mothers, we had anticipated that the measures of contingent response to positive vocalizations and contingent response to distress would be highly correlated. We found, however, a moderately low relationship ($r = .31$) between these two measures. A mother who responds frequently to positive behavior on the part of the infant does not necessarily respond rapidly to the baby's indications of unhappiness or distress. A mother who is responsive to an infant's crying or fussing may often ignore his smiles and coos. Contingent responsiveness is not a generalized characteristic of a mother, but varies with the kinds of signals the infant gives.

The correlations between the contingency variables and the modalities of stimulation were also moderately low, except for one. The correlation between auditory stimulation and contingent response to positive vocalization was .70, indicating that mothers who talk a great deal to infants also tend to carry on a dialogue in response to the infant's vocalizing.

Maternal Affect: Expression of
Positive Affect, Smiling, and Play

Psychodynamic theories have emphasized the importance for healthy development of the affective components of the mother-infant relationship. Meaningful assessment of the complex feelings of a mother towards her infant requires sensitive clinical inferences based on intensive long-term observations. Since it was impossible in this study to assess in depth the mother-infant relationship, we noted interactions characterized by affective exchanges: how often the mother smiled at the infant and the amount of time she spent in play with him. In addition, we attempted through rating scales to integrate impressions of the mother, gleaned from 2 days of observation. These scales summarized qualitative and stylistic differences between mothers that do not lend themselves to simple frequency counts.

Originally there were three ratings: demonstrativeness of positive affect expressed toward the baby, negative affect expression, and ambivalent affect. On only one of these scales did the observers achieve adequate reliability, the rating of expression of positive affect. Although we know there is not a one-to-one relationship between demonstrativeness and depth of feeling, we thought this measure might still have meaning in regard to the affectional relationship between mother and infant. At the very least, we expected that the young infant might respond more readily to strong expression of positive affect than to bland affect. Ratings were made by the observers at the end of each time-sampling observation of the caregiver's characteristic level of demonstrativeness. The rating was on a 6-point scale, ranging from no positive affect and quiet, subdued, or low-keyed positive affect to highly demonstrative, intense expressions of positive affect. (See rating scales in Appendix 3.)

Expression of Positive Affect was moderately related to many other dimensions of maternal behavior but insignificantly related to the characteristics of inanimate objects. Table 1 shows that the highest correlations were .59 with auditory stimulation; .55 with visual stimulation and .52 with tactile stimulation. With contingent response to positive vocalization its correlation was .51; whereas with contingent response to distress, the correlation was only .23. These interrelationships indicate that although positive affect is expressed through the sensory modalities, the sheer amount of visual, auditory, or kinesthetic stimulation is not a simple direct index of the mother's positive emotions towards the infant. The mother who is demonstrative in expressing positive affect does not necessarily respond with dispatch to the infant's distress.

The frequency with which a mother smiles at an infant is another index of her basic feelings towards him. Like Expression of Positive Affect, it is only an indirect clue to the affectional relationship. It is, however, behavior which can be readily observed and reliably recorded. The other affective variable, Play, is a more active expression of the mother's pleasure in the infant. It included mutually enjoyable interactions between mother and infant, such as patti-cake and peek-a-boo; the mother's making fun-like sounds; bouncing the infant on her knee; and vocal fantasy, such as barking like a dog, or meowing like a cat.

Expression of Positive Affect was rather highly correlated with Play ($r = .70$), while its correlation with Smiling was somewhat lower ($r = .46$). These interrelations seem reasonable because Expression of Positive Affect and Play are qualitatively similar, and high scores on both indicate intense forms of stimulation. The low relation between Smiling and Play ($r = .20$) is due partly to the definition of these categories. We attempted to minimize the overlap in these categories by not scoring Smiling separately when it occurred during play. The pattern of intercorrelations between Smiling and other environmental variables suggest that it is associated primarily with distance receptor stimulation, that is, engaging in mutual visual regard and talking to the infant. The moderate intercorrelations of both distance and near receptor stimulation with Play suggest that mothers differ in the preferred modalities of play; some talk animatedly to an infant, and others give him vigorous kinesthetic stimulation—move his whole body and bounce him on the knee. All three measures of maternal affect show higher associations with the mother's contingent responsiveness to the baby's positive vocalizations than to her responsiveness to his frets and cries.

Social Mediation of Inanimate Objects

The mother or caregiver is not only a direct stimulus to the infant, she also serves the important function of mediating inanimate objects. The human infant's inability to locomote until the second half of the first year of life and his limited fine motor skills in the early months make him dependent on his caregiver for the provision of toys.

The variable Social Mediation of Inanimate Objects included two components: (a) the caregiver's active role in positioning objects to make them accessible to the infant for exploration and (b) her activities in making the stimulus properties of the object more salient to the infant by highlighting their properties, e.g., by shaking a rattle, winding up a music box, and waving or banging objects.

We also attempted to describe whether social and affective behavior accompanied the mediation of objects. We counted those time-sampling units during which both maternal smiles and vocalizations and positioning and highlighting of toys occurred. It was hypothesized that the infant's attention to or manipulation of objects might increase through the process of social reinforcement and through the generalization of affect from the mother to the toys. On the basis of this hypothesis we developed two variables: (a) Social Mediation with Accompanying Smiles and Vocalizations and (b) Social Mediation with Minimal Affect. The low correlation between the two variables, $r = .12$, reflects their distinctiveness.

Social Mediation with Minimal Affect was independent of the other social variables (see Table 1). It had zero order relationships with Visual and Auditory Stimulation, Contingent Response to Positive Vocalizations, and Expression of Positive Affect. Although it had a few marginally significant correlations with other social variables, there is such little overlap that this variable can be considered distinct from other direct forms of social stimulation.

Social Mediation with Smiles and Vocalizations is fairly independent of near receptor stimulation, but had moderate to high relationships with other measures of social interaction: $r = .68$ with Auditory Stimulation, $.52$ with Contingent Responsiveness to Positive Vocalizations, and $.51$ with Expression of Positive Affect. Some degree of intercorrelation would be expected since these measures are not independent by definition. For example, the total frequency of auditory stimulation included instances in which the mother talked while giving toys to the infant.

Higher Order Characterizations of the Social Environment: Level and Variety

Although our aim was to achieve maximal differentiation of the social environment, we were also interested in developing meaningful variables that went beyond simple counts of the amount of interaction with the mother. Therefore, we combined several categories into more abstract maternal variables. Depriving environments have been characterized as low in both the amount and richness of stimulation; not only is there a low frequency of interaction with caregivers, but what interactions do occur tend to have a repetitive, monotonous quality. To capture differences in intensity and variation, two measures were developed: Level and Variety.

Level of Social Stimulation is a composite score consisting of the frequency of interaction weighted by the intensity of stimulation. We considered as more intense those stimuli involving a higher rate of stimulus change and a greater number of sensory modalities. By combining frequency and intensity, we hoped to distinguish two caregivers who interacted with the infant about the same amount of time but who differed in the quality of stimulation each provided.

Five degrees of intensity were distinguished:

1. Physical proximity involving simply looking at the infant without other forms of stimulation.
2. Passive physical contact—holding or passive touching
3. Active forms of stimulation occurring alone, such as
   a. smile alone
   b. mutual regard
   c. active touching
   d. vocalization alone
4. Two active forms of stimulation occuring together, such as
   a. mutual regard + smile
   b. vocalization + smile
   c. vocalization + mutual regard
   d. active touching + vocalization
   e. active touching + smiling
   f. active touching + mutual regard
5. Play—reciprocal interaction with high levels of positive affect. It usually involved active tactile, kinesthetic and vocal stimulation.

To obtain the measure Level of Social Stimulation, the frequency of stimulation at these different degrees of intensity was counted and expressed as a standard score. We then multiplied each score by the weight given in the above scale, e.g., the frequency of play was multiplied by five. These scores were then summed for each observation. The interobserver reliability on this composite measure was .99.

Several theoretical positions, information theory most articulately, have emphasized the importance of variety. The basic contention is that varied stimulation arouses the infant and elicits his attention, whereas repetitive, unchanging stimulation is quickly adapted to, and loses its evocative power. We combined several discrete categories of maternal behavior to obtain a measure of variety to index the richness of the infant's experience. Whereas Level of Social Stimulation was defined by properties of the stimuli impinging on the infant, Variety of Social Stimulation was a measure of maternal behavior eliciting different responses and encouraging more differentiated behavior from the infant. It consisted of three measures of manifestly different activities which go beyond routine care of the infant: (*a*) encouraging emergent motor skills, such as postural control or locomotion; (*b*) directing the child's attention to inanimate objects by presenting or highlighting toys (social mediation of play materials); and (*c*) engaging in interactive play, which characteristically elicits smiles, vocalizations, and positive affect. The fourth component was the number of changes in physical contexts, determined by counting how often there was a change in the baby's "container," e.g., an infant seat, playpen, or the caregiver's lap. The rationale for its inclusion was that different containers facilitate different behaviors and provide opportunities for varied visual experience. Each component score was expressed in standard score form and summed. A high score means that the infant was exposed to many instances of these different activities in many different physical contexts. Observer reliability on this composite measure was .95.

Level and Variety correlate .76 with each other, probably because play is a common component of each measure. Play is the most heavily weighted component of Level. Since Level and Variety include many of the specific social stimulation measures in one form or another, moderately high intercorrelations with the individual measures of social stimulation were expected. Level showed correlations ranging from .52 to .74 with these measures except for its correlation with Social Mediation with Minimal Affect, which was more independent ($r = .22$). Variety similarly had correlations with other measures of stimulation ranging from .31 to .77, and its correlation with Social Mediation with Minimal Affect was .26.

THE INANIMATE ENVIRONMENT

For a long time, studies of the early environment have focused almost exclusively on maternal behavior. We know, however, that the inanimate environment is also a rich source of stimulation.

Only recently has attention been given to the impact of the inanimate environment. Studies of institutional settings have pointed to the monotony and drabness of the physical environment and the paucity of objects for the child to look at or manipulate. Experimental intervention studies with institutionalized infants and infants in depriving home environments have attempted to reverse the effects of deprivation by providing increased auditory, tactile, and visual stimulation with play materials. The provision of brightly colored inanimate objects (White, B. L., 1967) and of mobiles over cribs (Brossard & Décarie, 1971) has been associated with significant changes in the functioning of institutional infants. In more controlled experimental studies, Rheingold and Samuels (1969) demonstrated that home-reared infants became fretful and more demanding of attention when placed for even a brief period in an environment without toys. When toys were available, the infants' fussing and demands for their mothers' attention decreased; instead, they actively explored the play materials.

Although it is clear that stimulation from the inanimate environment has significant effects, the more fundamental question is what attributes of the environment are associated with specific effects. Just as we differentiated the social environment into many components, we have distinguished several different dimensions of the inanimate enviroment—variety, complexity, and responsiveness of objects. We have concentrated on the proximal inanimate enviroment, the toys and household objects that are within reach of the infant.

Experimental studies have shown that dimensions such as the complexity and familiarity of inanimate stimuli in the immediate situation serve to engage the attention of the infant; they have not investigated the larger, more interesting question of whether cognitive and cognitive-motivational development is affected. Moreover, these characteristics of inanimate objects have not been studied heretofore in the natural environment.

The choice of these environmental variables was guided by several theoretical orientations: Piagetian developmental theory, particularly as elaborated by Hunt (1961); contingency learning theory (Watson & Ramey, 1972); and concepts from information theory (Berlyne, 1960). Although the deprivation literature has especially emphasized quantity of sensory or social stimulation, theoretical considerations and experimental studies have both pointed out that, by itself, quantity of stimulation is a crude measure.

Variety

The measure Variety of Inanimate Objects is conceptually analogous to Variety of Social Stimulation. It reflects the richness and nonrepetitive character of the inanimate environment. This measure was obtained by counting the number of *different* play objects within reach of the infant. Each object was counted only once over the 2 days of observation.[4]

Our theoretical expectations were that an enviroment high in inanimate variety would provide greater opportunities for the infant's assimilation and accomodation to various properties of objects, thereby differentiating perceptual, cognitive, and motor skills. Adaptation to high levels of variety is also hypothesized to result in motivation to maintain high levels of variation in stimulation. Several experimental studies show clearly the immediate effects of new and changing stimuli. Novel and varying stimuli arouse the infant and sustain his attention; conversely, there is rapid habituation to familiar and unchanging stimulation (Fantz, 1964; Greenberg, Uzgiris, & Hunt, 1970; Lewis, Goldberg, & Campbell, 1969).

Responsiveness

The second dimension of the inanimate environment, Responsiveness, is a measure of the feedback potential of objects. Although there is probably some feedback inherent in any object, some play materials are richer than others on this dimension. There is a conceptual similarity between this aspect of the inanimate environment and the measures of maternal contingent respon-

---

[4]We did not compute a variety score for the 5 cases in which only one observation was made.

siveness to an infant's signals. In a loose sense, it is related to the contingency concept in operant learning theory; it is more specifically related to Watson's (1966) notion of contingency awareness and to Hunt's (1965) thinking about the conditions that influence intrinsic motivation. One of our basic hypotheses is that an object that changes in response to some action on the part of the infant may reinforce his rudimentary sense of mastery, the conviction that he can have an effective impact on the environment.

All toys within reach of the infant were listed on both observation days. Immediately after the home visit, each toy was rated on 5-point scales for its degree of responsiveness in each of four categories: moving parts, change in shape and contour, reflected image, and noise production (see Appendix 5). The four subscale scores were summed to yield a responsiveness score for each toy. A highly responsive toy is one which changes as a result of the infant's behavior; it may emit a sound, change in shape when squeezed, and reflect the baby's image. The score used in the analyses is the average for all toys noted on the two days of observation. Interrater reliability was .90.

Complexity

A third characteristic of play objects is *complexity*. The complexity of a toy is defined by the amount of "information" it provides the infant through various sensory modalities. In experimental studies, complexity has been studied as a determinant of the infant's attention (Brennan, Ames, & Moore, 1966; McCall & Melson, 1970). Theories regarding complexity emphasize a golden mean. They hypothesize that an optimal degree of complexity, defined by the organism's capacity to assimilate the information provided, is most facilitative of cognitive growth (Berlyne, 1960; Fantz & Nevis, 1967; Hebb, 1949).

The complexity of toys available to the infant was rated on five characteristics:

1. The number of different colors
2. The amount of visual and tactile pattern

3. The number of different shapes and the extent of variation in the contours of the object
4. Size of the object
5. Extent of responsiveness of the object

As with responsiveness, the toys within reach of the infant were rated at the end of the observatiion. Rather than rate each component separately, a summary rating was made on a 5-point scale (see Appendix 4). Interrater reliability was .83.

The low complexity toys consist of one basic shape; they are monochromatic, without pattern, small, and relatively unresponsive to the infant's manipulation. The very complex toys have a high degree of either visual or tactile pattern, are made up of several different shapes, are multicolored, are fairly large, and are responsive to manipulation by the infant.

Looking at the interrelations of the three variables of the inanimate environment, we find Variety essentially unrelated to Complexity or Responsiveness. Since Responsiveness was one of the components of Complexity, these two variables were more highly related ($r = .70$). The most striking findings, however, were the consistently low relationships between the variables of the inamimate environment and the variables of the social environment. Most of the correlations were around zero. These data suggest that homes that provide highly stimulating play materials to infants do not necessarily provide equally high amounts of social stimulation.

Table 2 presents the means, standard deviations, and the range on all environmental variables for the core sample of 41 infants. The rating scales are expressed as the *mean* for the two observations, and values are interpretable in relation to the detailed definitions in Appendixes 4 and 5. The frequency scores are the *sum* of the two observations; values may be readily converted to a percentage of the total observation by dividing by 240. Perhaps the most important information in this table is the range of scores; they indicate the striking variation among caregivers. When seen in relation to the moderate intercorrelations

TABLE 2

Means, Standard Deviations, and Range of Environmental Measures ($N = 41$)

Variable	Type of Score	Mean	Standard Deviation	Range Minimum	Maximum
Modalities					
Tactile	Frequency Count[a]	29.3	14.5	5	68
Kinesthetic	Frequency Count	57.0	20.0	5	131
Visual	Frequency Count	23.9	13.3	0	34
Auditory	Frequency Count	61.5	29.2	2	121
Contingencies					
Contingent Response to Positive Vocalizations	Frequency Count	19.6	7.4	0	94
Contingent Response to Distress	5-Pt. Rating Scale	3.4	1.1	1	5
Affect					
Expression of Positive Affect	5-Pt. Rating Scale	3.3	0.9	0.75	5
Smiling	Frequency Count	10.1	7.4	0	28
Play	Frequency Count	11.3	8.3	0	33
Social Mediation					
With Minimal Social Reinforcement	Frequency Count	8.5	8.2	0	34
With Smiles and Vocalizations	Frequency Count	14.5	10.6	0	53
Composite Measures					
Level	Z Score	10.0	1.0	6.7	11.6
Variety	Z Score	10.0	1.4	6.8	12.9
Inanimate Stimulation					
Responsiveness	Four Rating Scales	3.4	0.75	0	9
Complexity	5-Pt. Rating Scale	1.3	0.33	0	3.5
Variety	Count of Different Objects	9.3	5.6	0	25

[a]Frequency counts are based on 240 observation units.

among the dimensions of social stimulation and the independence of the social and inanimate variables, these findings underscore the necessity for avoiding simple generalizations about environments as depriving or stimulating. It is much more informative to describe the patterns of high, average, and low stimulation for any one infant.

SEX DIFFERENCES IN DIMENSIONS OF THE ENVIRONMENT

Although it has long been part of the general folklore that boy and girl infants are treated differently by their mothers, the research evidence is equivocal. Some investigators have reported differences in maternal interaction with male and female infants (Kagan, 1971; Lewis, 1972; Moss, 1967); others have not found clear differences (Clarke-Stewart, 1973). In studying this issue, we made two types of comparisons of mothers' behavior towards boys and girls. One was concerned with the amount of stimulation. It involved comparisons of the means for the boys and girls on both the social and inanimate environmental variables. In the second analysis we looked at the patterning of stimulation. That is, we analyzed the interrelationships among the variables separately for boys and girls.

On two variables, Level and Variety of Social Stimulation, the mean scores for male infants were significantly higher than females (Table 3). In this sample mothers interacted with male infants more frequently and at higher intensities of stimulation, and there was greater richness and diversity in their interactions. Other environmental measures showed a trend in the same direction because there is some degree of positive intercorrelation among them, but the differences are not statistically significant.

In a study of white middle-class 3-month-old infants, Moss (1967) found no significant sex differences in maternal behavior. There were, however, sex differences in the infants' sleep time and irritability. Controlling for the fact that boys cried more and slept less, he found mothers to be more arousing and stimulating in

TABLE 3

Means and Standard Deviations of Environmental
Measures for Boys and Girls

Variable	Type of Score	Boys		Girls		t
		Mean	SD	Mean	SD	
Modalities						
Tactile	Frequency Count[a]	33.2	13.6	25.2	14.6	—
Kinesthetic	Frequency Count	62.7	13.7	51.1	23.9	—
Visual	Frequency Count	27.6	15.3	20.0	9.6	—
Auditory	Frequency Count	69.4	31.5	53.3	24.7	—
Contingencies						
Contingent Response to						
Positive Vocalizations	Frequency Count	24.7	22.2	14.3	9.4	—
Contingent Response to						
Distress	5-Pt. Rating Scale	3.6	1.0	3.1	1.2	—
Affect						
Expression of Positive						
Affect	6-Pt. Rating Scale	3.4	1.0	3.1	0.8	—
Smiling	Frequency Count	12.2	7.9	8.0	6.2	—
Play	Frequency Count	12.5	8.9	10.1	7.7	—
Social Mediation						
With Minimal Social						
Reinforcement	Frequency Count	8.9	8.9	8.0	7.7	—
With Smiles and						
Vocalizations	Frequency Count	16.2	12.9	12.6	7.5	—
Composite Measures						
Level	Z Score	10.68	1.68	9.28	2.10	2.38*
Variety	Z Score	11.12	2.56	8.83	2.45	2.94**
Inanimate Stimulation						
Responsiveness	Four Rating Scales	6.9	0.86	6.5	1.95	—
Complexity	5-pt. Rating Scale	2.5	0.5	2.7	0.79	—
Variety	Count of Different Objects	10.1	5.5	8.4	5.7	—

[a]Frequency counts are based on 240 observation units.
*$p < .05$, two-tailed test.
**$p < .01$, two-tailed test.

their interactions with boys, while they engaged in more imitation
of their infant girls' vocalizations. Our findings on Level and
Variety of Social Stimulation are partially concordant with his
results. Mothers are significantly higher on these variables for
boys. We did not control for irritability since the frequency of
fussing and crying was comparable for male and female infants in

our sample. We found no differences in amount of maternal vocalization. Our measures, however, were not strictly comparable with Moss's measures. Lewis (1972) found that 3-month-old male infants were held more by their mothers. Our measures of tactile and kinesthetic stimulation showed only a trend in that direction. Lewis reported that females received more verbal stimulation, which our data did not support even though our measure of maternal vocalization was very similar to his. In another observational study, Clarke-Stewart (1973) found no consistent sex differences in mother-infant interaction. Kagan (1971), on the other hand, found complex interactions between sex, socioeconomic status, and maternal behavior. From the available studies, it seems that simple generalizations about differences in maternal behavior toward boy and girl infants cannot be made with any assurance.

We came to similar conclusions concerning the interrelationships among the variables. Comparing the matrices of intercorrelations for male and female infants, we found somewhat greater independence in the dimensions of the environment for boys than for girls. Considering the entire matrix of environmental variables, the median intercorrelation is .40 for the girls and .21 for the boys (see Tables A and B in Appendix 1).

Can we interpret these findings to mean that the environments of infant boys and girls are fundamentally different, that they are more differentiated for males than for females? Such conclusions are not warranted by our data. Although there were many more significant intercorrelations among the environmental variables for the girls, there were relatively few statistically significant differences in the magnitude of the correlations. Of 120 correlations in each matrix, there were only 6 instances where the corresponding values were significantly different from each other.

4

DIFFERENTIATION OF
INFANT FUNCTIONING

Our view of the infant has changed dramatically during the past decade. Not long ago the young infant was seen as an undifferentiated organism who responded globally and diffusely to stimulation. More and more, research is documenting the infant's sensitivity and capacity to respond discriminatively to a wide range of stimuli. It is being recognized that there are many parameters of individual differences in behavior patterns and sensitivities. There are differences in activity level, in vigor of expression of needs, and in intensity of response to stimulation. Infants also show differential sensitivities to auditory, visual, and tactile stimuli. At any one developmental level, there are also wide variations in responsiveness to people, in fine and gross motor abilities, and in the level of different cognitive functions. This variety of individual differences has sharpened our awareness of the many components of infant functioning.

Just as we believe that it is essential to analyze the early environment on many dimensions, so do we feel that a global measure of infant developmental status is inadequate. In studying the influence of the early environment, we hope to go beyond statements about the effects of general stimulation to an understanding of the selective relations between specific components of the environment and specific aspects of infant functioning.

We did not attempt to measure the entire spectrum of infant temperamental and personality characteristics. Rather, on the basis of theoretical considerations, we restricted our attention to the infant's social responsiveness, early evidences of language, motor functions, and to certain cognitive and cognitive-motivational characteristics.

For a long time psychologists have clung tenaciously to a global concept of intelligence. In recent years, however, there has been a growing dissatisfaction with this concept. First, there is the question as to whether intelligence is a domain of functioning independent of and isolated from personality and motivation. Second, global measures of infant intelligence have failed to show substantial predictive value. Finally, theories of intelligence have emphasized its multidimensional character.

It has become apparent that the infant's cognitive functioning is closely intertwined with his motivation to explore and to master his inanimate environment and that his capacity to adapt flexibly, to change his responses, and to try out new behavior patterns is essential for solving cognitive problems (Dember, 1974; Hunt, 1961). Wechsler (1950) commented that despite Terman's findings on the high level of curiosity in gifted children, there have been no attempts to extract curiosity as a factor of intelligence. From another perspective, increasing attention has been given to the infant's capacity to be aroused, to give more than fleeting attention to people and objects in his environment, and to attend selectively to stimuli, characteristics that are on the borders of cognitive and motivational functioning. These qualities of behavior were often noted by skilled clinicians but not measured systematically, as have pure cognitive functions. Increasingly, serious attention is also being given to concepts like effectance motivation and competence, which epitomize the overlap between intellectual, personality, and motivational characteristics. A number of investigators and theorists have described varied aspects of behavior that do not fit into the traditional mold of cognition or motivation (Anderson & Messick, 1974; Bronson, 1971; Murphy, 1962; White, R.W., 1959).

Research over many years with many different measures of the infant's developmental status has failed to find substantial relationships between global indexes of infant development and later measures of intelligence. It is likely that global evaluation of the infant may mask important parameters of individual variation that are predictive of later development. McCall, Hogarty, and Hurlburt (1972) and Lewis (1974) have emphasized that specific skills may have functional utility at a given developmental period, but lack long-term significance, and may not be predictive of later development. Other early abilities may be transformed in the course of development and appear in qualitatively different forms at later ages. These abilities may be useful predictors of later characteristics even if the transformation processes are not fully understood.

Perhaps the most fundamental reason for rejecting a global index of development is that it does not faithfully reflect our theories of intelligence. Almost 50 years ago, Spearman (1927) articulated a conception of adult intelligence that included a notion of differentiated skills and abilities. More recently, Guilford (1966) presented evidence to contradict the view of intelligence as a unitary characteristic. With regard to infant intelligence, Piaget has had a singular influence in directing attention to the processes of cognitive development. The basic focus of interest in his theoretical system is in the development of specific internalized action sequences, the schemas. Schemas such as looking at, grasping, and mouthing an object initially appear in isolation; but they are soon combined into coordinated patterns to form more complex patterns such as means-ends relationships. All these considerations raise questions about the usefulness of a single global measure of functioning.

MEASURES OF INFANT FUNCTIONING

At the time of our investigation, several efforts toward more differentiated measurement in infancy were in progress. Kohen-Raz (1967), empirically isolated, through a Gutman scalogram analysis, five areas of functioning from the Bayley Scales: Eye-hand, Manipulation, Object-Relation, Imitation-Comprehension, and Vocalization-Social Contact-Active Vocabulary.

Infant scales with more clearly defined theoretical bases were also being developed by Corman and Escalona (1969) and Uzgiris and Hunt (1974). Both these ordinal scales were designed to measure early cognitive development in terms of Piaget's sensori-motor stages. These scales were still being refined at the beginning of the present study; moreover, the Kohen-Raz Scales did not appear sufficiently differentiated at this age level, since there were only four scales applicable to the 5- and 6-months infant. Therefore, we decided to develop our own differentiated measures of infant functioning from the varied items on the Bayley Scales of Infant Development.

Clusters Derived from the Bayley Scales

The procedure for grouping the Bayley items involved several steps. First, items were sorted on a conceptual basis, according to the class of response elicited, such as fine motor, gross motor, and vocalization. Other items were classified according to the cognitive functions they tapped, i.e., object permanence and secondary circular reactions. Still others were grouped in terms of more abstract psychological processes, such as goal directedness. Each cluster included the lowest item that at least one child failed, up to the highest item that at least one child passed. The age placement of the items ranged from 1.6 to 12 months.

For each cluster, Spearman-Brown split-half reliabilities were computed; for two clusters with only two items, tetrachoric correlations were obtained. Clusters with split-half reliabilities of .70 or higher were accepted with no further question. Clusters with lower split-half reliabilities were examined, and some items were reassigned to other clusters and some dropped. Four clusters, Auditory Responsiveness, Tactile Exploration, Social Discrimination, and Imitation were not used because they did not reach a satisfactory level of split-half reliability. The eight remaining clusters had reliabilities renging from .74 to .92. Table 4 presents the items and the split-half reliabilities for each cluster. The score on each cluster was the number of items passed.

The eight clusters were Gross Motor Development, Fine Motor Development, Social Responsiveness, Language, Goal Directedness, Secondary Circular Reactions, Reaching and Grasping, and Object Permanence. Six additional infant measures were derived from two sources: (*a*) a series of supplementary items designed to measure problem solving and (*b*) a test from which we obtained a measure of the infant's vocalization rate and several measures of exploratory behavior and preference for novel stimuli. The conceptual and empirical considerations guiding the choice of these variables are described in the pages that follow.

Gross and Fine Motor Development

In early infancy an important index of the maturation of the central nervous system is the infant's gross and fine motor development. Some of the most fundamental changes occur in these characteristics during the early months of life. The acquisition and refinement of locomotor and prehensile skills underlie the development of other abilities. The emergence of locomotor skills enables the infant to expand his environment, to initiate contact with a greater variety of objects and persons. The refinement of prehensile skills permits the infant to explore and manipulate objects, enabling him to discover their properties and use them in the service of other goals—for solving problems and obtaining tactile and auditory feedback.

The Gross Motor cluster was composed of 17 items measuring several aspects of head and trunk control and the early stages of locomotion. It consisted of items such as sitting and rolling from back to stomach and different aspects of standing, stepping, and

TABLE 4

Cluster Derived from the Bayley Scales

Cluster Name	Split-Half Reliability		Item No.	Age Placem.	Description	Percent. Passing
1. Gross Motor	.90	Motor Scale	13	2.3	Sits with Slight Support	91
			18	4.2	Head Balanced	100
			19	4.4	Turns from Back to Side	91
			20	4.8	Effort to Sit	81
			22	5.3	Pulls to Sitting Position	77
			23	5.3	Sits Alone Momentarily	67
			27	6.0	Sits Alone 30 Sec. or More	41
			28	6.4	Rolls from Back to Stomach	40
			29	6.6	Sits Alone Steadily	26
			31	6.9	Sits Alone with Good Coordination	13
			33	7.1	Prewalking Progression	23
			34	7.4	Early Stepping Movements	10
			36	8.1	Pulls to Standing	60
			37	8.3	Raises Self to Sitting Position	1
			38	8.6	Pulls Self to Stand	1
			40	8.8	Stepping Movements	3
			42	9.6	Walks with Help	1
2. Fine Motor	.92	Mental Scale	56	4.7	Retains Two Cubes	71
			59	4.9	Recovers Rattle in Crib or Playpen	68
			69	5.5	Transfers Object Hand to Hand	74
			70	5.7	Picks up Cube Directly and Easily	63
			77	6.3	Retains Two Cubes (3 Offered)	44
		Motor Scale	15	2.7	Hands Predominantly Open	96
			16	3.7	Retains Cube Briefly	96
			21	4.9	Partial Thumb Opposition— Radial Palmer Grasp	83
			24	5.4	Unilateral Reaching	90
			26	5.7	Rotates Wrist	77
			30	6.8	Secures Pellet—Radial Raking	13
			32	6.9	Picks up Cube—Radial— Digital Grasp	44
			35	7.4	Secures Pellet—Inferior Pincer Grasp	6
			39	8.6	Brings Two Objects Together at Midline	21
3. Social Responsiveness	.84	Mental Scale	26	2.1	Social Smile	88
			27	2.1	Vocalizes to Social Stimulus	73
			35	2.6	Anticipatory Adjustment to Lifting	96
			53	4.4	Approaches Mirror Image	91
			61	5.1	Likes Frolic Play	68
			65	5.4	Smiles at Mirror Image	57
			76	6.2	Playful Response to Mirror	50
			81	7.6	Cooperates in Games	7
4. Goal Directedness	.82	Mental Scale	60	5.0	Reaches Persistently	83
			71	5.7	Pulls String Secures Ring (?Purposeful)	76
			80	7.1	Pulls String to Secure Ring (Purposeful)	56
			82	7.6	Attempts to Secure Three Cubes	14
			96	10.5	Unwraps Toys	8
		Motor Scale	25	5.6	Attempts to Secure Pellet	64

TABLE 4

Cluster Derived from the Bayley Scales—Continued

Cluster Name	Split-Half Reliability		Item No.	Age Placem.	Description	Percent. Passing
5. Visually Directed Reaching and Grasping	.92	Mental Scale	37	3.1	Reaches for Ring	90
			46	3.8	Closes on Dangling Ring	88
			49	4.1	Reaches for Cube	88
			51	4.4	Eye Cooperation in Reaching	88
			54	4.6	Picks up Cube	88
			63	5.2	Lifts Cup	90
			64	5.4	Reaches for Second Cube	48
			70	5.7	Picks up Cube Directly and Easily	63
			73	5.8	Lifts Cup by Handle	84
6. Secondary Circular Reactions	.92	Mental Scale	66	5.4	Bangs in Play	86
			72	5.8	Enjoys Sound Production	83
7. Object Permanence	.90	Mental Scale	31	2.4	Reacts to Disappearance of Face	96
			62	5.2	Turns Head After Dropped Object	61
			75	6.0	Looks for Dropped Object	58
			86	8.1	Uncovers Toy	6
			88	9.0	Picks up Cup and Secures Cube	13
			91	9.5	Looks for Contents of Box	4
8. Vocalization and Language	.74	Mental Scale	21	1.6	Vocalizes 3–6 Times	84
			30	2.3	Vocalizes 2 Syllables	88
			55	4.6	Vocalizes Attitudes	87
			79	7.0	Vocalizes 4 Different Syllables	36
			84	7.9	Responds to Name and Nickname	23
			85	7.9	Says Da-Da or Equivalent	6
			89	9.1	Adjusts to Words	1
			101	12.0	Uses Expressive Jargon	8

walking. The Fine Motor cluster consisted of 14 items concerned with prehensile controls, such as picking up and retaining cubes, picking up a small pellet, unilateral reaching, and bringing two objects together.

Social Responsiveness

The infant's increasingly discriminating awareness of people, his differentiation of himself from his mother, and the development of a repertoire of responses to other people are especially significant aspects of his growth during the first year. They mark the beginning of his functioning as an autonomous human being. Moreover, the character of the behavior he initiates towards others, as well as the quality of his responses to them, sets up a system of reciprocal interactions in which he influences people and in turn is influenced by them.

The cluster, Social Responsiveness, contained eight items from the Bayley Scales measuring the infant's responses to various types of social stimulation. It included behavior such as smiling and vocalizing in response to the examiner's smiles and speech, making anticipatory adjustments preparatory to being picked up, and responding with pleasure and actively participating in a social game.

Cognitive-Motivational Functions

In this study, we were especially interested in a group of infant behaviors that we called cognitive-motivational functions. We believe that a close interdependence exists between these two domains of functioning, which have usually been strictly separated. The four cognitive-motivational variables—visually directed reaching and grasping, secondary circular reactions, goal directedness, and problem-solving—reflect the infant's transactions with the environment. They are on a continuum from simple efforts to secure objects to persistent attempts to circumvent a barrier to secure an object not immediately available. These behaviors can be considered expressions of the infant's motivation to assimilate, learn about, and master the environment. We have speculated that they may be precursors of later ego functions, of what R. W. White (1959) called "effectance motivation." It is likely that they contribute in a significant way to the development and elaboration of purely cognitive skills.

Visually Directed Reaching and Grasping

This cluster, with nine items, measures the ability to coordinate vision and prehension, a step necessary to the development of exploratory behavior and the manipulation of objects. It consists mainly of items measuring varying degrees of skill in reaching for and grasping objects. The cluster also had a motivational component. It involved attending to objects and attempting to make contact with them, an effort to bring visual images under the control of motor activities. According to Piaget, the coordination of prehension and vision is crucial to appreciating the objective reality of the world.

With the development of visually guided manual activity, the child is able to make genuine alterations in the environment essential to the secondary circular reaction.

Secondary Circular Reactions

This behavior, which involves the repetition of responses to produce interesting results, is Stage III of Piaget's sequence of sensorimotor stages. It is motivational in that it requires intentionally repeating actions to elicit feedback from objects in the environment. In Piaget's view, secondary circular behavior is a necessary antecedent to problem solving, the deliberate repetition of actions to achieve a goal. The cluster consisted of only two items: bangs object in play, enjoys making sounds. Unlike reaching and grasping, where the infant's behavior is for the purpose of acquiring the object, the child who evidences secondary circular reactions is much more interested in the environmental consequences of his actions.

Goal Directedness

This cluster was composed of six items that measured the infant's directed attempts to secure objects under a variety of conditions, e.g., attempting to secure cubes out of reach, unwrapping a loosely wrapped toy, and working persistently to obtain a ring which is out of reach. These items were more concerned with persistence of effort than with the motor skills required to obtain objects. In a broad sense, they reflected the strength of the infant's motivation to attain difficult goals. They were measures of the child's capacity to direct his attention to objects, and to persist in his efforts to obtain these objects in the face of difficulty. Some investigators conjecture that the low level of functioning of institutionalized infants and infants from very depriving home environments might be attributed to their apathy and depressed motivation to reach out and act on the environment as much as to poorly developed prehensile or cognitive abilities (Provence & Lipton, 1962).

Problem Solving

This cluster was not derived from the Bayley Scales. It was a special group of four items presented after the completion of the Bayley Test (see Appendix 5). These items were scored not on a pass-fail basis, but on a 4-point scale. According to Piaget, problem solving is the "coordination of secondary schemata and their application to new situations." It requires the perception of means-ends relationships, and behaving in a manner appropriate to achieve the goal. This stage, Stage IV, represents an advance over secondary circular reactions in that "the child no longer merely tries to repeat or prolong an effect which he has discovered or observed by chance; he pursues an end not immediately attainable, and tries to reach it by different intermediate means." To solve these problems, e.g., pulling a cloth to secure an object out of reach, reaching over or around a transparent obstacle to obtain a rattle, requires some understanding of objects in relation to each other, and a capacity to persist in working towards a goal that is not easily accessible. The cognitive-motivational character of this variable is apparent in that it requires the integration of cognitive abilities with the motivation to secure objects.

Object Permanence

One of the most significant advances in cognitive growth is the development of object permanence, the recognition that objects exist when they are outside of immediate sensory experience. This capacity, present in early infancy in only rudimentary form, is a first step in the development of symbolic thinking. The cluster, Object Permanence, consisted of such items as looking in the direction of a dropped object, making an effort to uncover a toy which has been covered with a tissue after a brief exposure, and attempting to find a cube hidden under a cup.

Language

The role of language in cognitive development is currently an area of active theorizing, investigation, and intense controversy

(Chomsky, 1959; McNeill, 1970). It is one of the few functions measured in infancy found to be predictive of later intellectual development (Cameron, Livson, & Bayley, 1967; Moore, 1967), although these findings have been restricted to girls. Several studies have noted that the language function particularly is vulnerable to early environmental deprivation (Provence & Lipton, 1962; Yarrow, 1961).Infant vocalizations also appear to be readily influenced by brief experimental manipulations such as contingent social reinforcement (Rheingold, Gewirtz and Ross, 1959; Schwartz, Rosenberg, & Brackbill, 1969; Todd & Palmer, 1968).

Our goals in this study were not to map out the process of language acquisition, but simply to see how early linguistic development might be related to parameters of environmental stimulation. We distinguished two components of language, one dealing with the amount of vocalization, the other with the beginnings of communication. The quantitative measure, Vocalization during Exploration of the Bell, was obtained during the exploratoty behavior test. It was the amount of time the infant vocalized during the ten-minute period when he had an interesting toy. The other language measure, Vocalization and Language, was derived from a cluster of eight items on the Bayley test dealing with the qualitative aspects of language. It included expressive behaviors, such as vocalizing attitudes, saying da-da or equivalent, as well as some receptive aspects reflecting comprehension of words. Although we feel it is important to distinguish qualitative and quantitative aspects of language, we do not know whether these rudimentary forms of speech have any genotypic relationship to the later use of symbols to stand for concrete objects and behaviors or to represent complex relationships.

Exploratory Behavior and Preference for Novelty

For a long time theories of motivation have been locked into a drive-reduccion model, with the belief that the reduction of stimulation is the major source of motivation. More recently, we have come to recognize that stimulation seeking is a fundamental characteristic of sentient organisms, and that obtaining stimulation is intrinsically rewarding (Berlyne, 1960; Fiske & Maddi, 1961). According to these views the organism's search for new, varied experiences is gratifying in itself. There is an intrinsic motivation (Hunt, 1961) to explore objects and people and to seek new experience. In the process of seeking stimulation the infant learns about his environment. He attends to stimuli, and by listening to sounds and looking at and manipulating objects he learns about their properties.

The development of exploratory motivation is not maturationally determined alone, but is influenced by the child's experience. Because of our interest in understanding its environmental correlates, we measured some early manifestations of exploratory behavior and response to novel objects. These procedures have been described in detail in Chapter 2. In brief, the baby was presented with an attractive novel toy, a small metal bell, for 10 minutes and the amount of time the infant looked at and manipulated this interesting object was recorded.

Preference for Novelty was measured in the same testing session by presenting a series of 10 unfamiliar toys for 1 minute each paired with the bell used in the exploratory behavior procedure. Preference for the novel was indexed by the amount of time spent looking at or manipulating the novel objects.

Theoretical speculation about response to novel objects in infancy suggests that it involves several important cognitive capacities. It requires the capacity to discriminate new from familiar objects. Response to a new stimulus is also influenced by the rate of habituation to a familiar stimulus, a process which is thought to be related to speed of information processing (Lewis, Goldberg, & Campbell, 1969).

INTERRELATIONS AMONG MEASURES
OF INFANT FUNCTIONING

The correlations among the separate measures of infant functioning are given in Table 5. We hoped through these analyses to gain some understanding of the degree to which these measures of

TABLE 5

Intercorrelations Among Dependent Variables: Total Group (N = 41)

Infant Variable	General Status		Social	Language		Motor Development		Cognitive-Motivational				Object Permanence	Exploratory Behavior		Preference for Novelty	
	MDI[a]	PDI[b]	Respon-siveness	Vocaliz. During Explor.	Language Quality	Gross	Fine	Goal Directedness	Reach and Grasp	Second Circular Reaction	Problem Solving		Look at Bell	Manipulate Bell	Looking	Manipulating
General Status																
MDI[a]		.73	.71	-.25	.48	.59	.74	.86	.77	.67	.60	.66	—	.24	—	.32
PDI[b]			.29	-.30	—	.92	.86	.76	.71	.63	-.21	.47	.22	.42	.24	.45
Social Responsiveness				—	.61	.22	.30	.56	.34	.52	.26	.47	—	—	—	—
Language																
Vocalization During Exploration					—	-.31	-.24	—	-.28	-.21	-.26	—	—	—	—	-.23
Language Quality						—	—	.39	—	—	—	.29	—	—	—	—
Motor Development																
Gross							.78	.68	.65	.61	.62	.47	—	.41	—	.43
Fine								.76	.87	.62	.62	.51	—	.46	.28	.35
Cognitive-Motivational																
Goal Directedness									.76	.70	.58	.64	—	.29	—	.27
Reaching and Grasping										.72	.53	.51	—	.32	.33	.41
Secondary Circular Reactions											.41	.46	—	—	.23	.29
Problem Solving												.45	—	.28	.22	.47
Object Permanence													—	—	—	.22
Exploratory Behavior																
Look at Bell														.51	.43	—
Manipulate Bell															.55	.29
Preference for Novel Stimuli																
Look at Novel																.50
Manipulating Novel																

Note. Dashes represent correlation < .20.
[a] MDI = Mental Development Index.
[b] PDI = Psychomotor Development Index.

61

infant functioning are independent or overlapping. They also indicate the extent to which more complex functions are dependent on simpler, more basic skills.

The individual clusters in relation to each other and to the general developmental indices, the Mental Developmental Index and the Psychomotor Developmental Index, showed moderate to high correlations. The exceptions were Language and Social Responsiveness, which were clearly distinguished from the other measures. The correlations between Language and the other clusters ranged from -.03 to .39, with a median of .11. Social Responsiveness was more highly related to the other infant variables; the correlations ranged from .22 to .56, with a median of .34. The Social Responsiveness and Language clusters were more highly related to each other than to any of the other infant clusters (r = .61). They were more highly correlated with the Mental Developmental Index (r = .71 and .48, respectively) than to the Psychomoter Developmental Index, (r = .29 and .06, respectively). The other measure of language, Vocalization During Exploration of the Bell, was similarly independent of measures from Bayley Scales.

Of great interest were the relations of the four cognitive-motivational clusters—Goal Directedness, Visually Directed Reaching and Grasping, Secondary Circular Reactions and Problem Solving—to the individual clusters and to the two Bayley developmental indexes. The correlations among these four clusters ranged from .41 to .76, with a median of .58.

The Goal Directedness cluster, which consisted of six items, had the highest relationship with the Mental Developmental Index (r=.86). It was also highly related to the Psychomotor Developmental Index (r = .76). On the whole, it showed higher correlations with the other clusters than did any other variable; the range of the correlations was .39 to .76, with a median r of .64. These findings indicate that very early in infancy, such motivational characteristics as capacity to sustain attention and persist in efforts to secure objects play an important role in the child's total functioning.

Visually Directed Reaching and Grasping, like Goal Directedness, was cluster with high generality, as evidenced by its correlation of .77 with the Mental Developmental Index, and of .71 with the Psychomotor Developmental Index. This cluster was also highly related to the Fine Motor Cluster ($r = .87$), Goal Directedness ($r = .76$), and Secondary Circular Reactions ($r = .72$). These findings give some support to the view that visually directed reaching and grasping and fine motor skills are basic to the development of secondary circular reactions and goal directed behavior.

As might be expected, the Gross and Fine Motor clusters were highly interrelated ($r = .78$). They were also highly related to the Psychomotor Developmental Index, the correlation with Gross Motor being .92 and with Fine Motor, .86. The correlations of these clusters with the mental scale were somewhat lower; there was a higher relationship between the Mental Developmental Index and the Fine Motor cluster ($r = .74$) than the Gross Motor ($r = .59$). These findings emphasize the special importance of motor functions in early infancy. They aslo point up some of the reasons why later intellectual development cannot readily be predicted from early infant measures. It is extremely difficult to isolate and measure pure cognitive functions at this age.

On the whole, the relations between the clusters derived from the Bayley test and the four measures of exploratory behavior— Look at Bell, Manipulate Bell, Look at Novel Object, and Manipulate Novel Object—tended to be much lower than the interrelationships among the clusters. The correlations ranged from $-.23$ to .47. The relationships with the Mental Developmental Index tended to be low and insignificant for both exploratory behavior and preference for novel stimuli. In general, the manipulative items, Manipulation of the Bell and Manipulation of Novel Objects, had higher relationships with the test clusters and the Bayley Psychomotor Developmental Index than the visual measures, Looks at Bell or Looks at Novel Object.

The highest correlation was between Problem Solving and time spent manipulating the novel objects ($r = .47$). The magnitude of the intercorrelations, on the whole, indicate that the exploratory behavior procedure measures distinctive characteristics.

SEX DIFFERENCES IN INFANT FUNCTIONING

There is some evidence that behavioral and temperamental differences between boys and girls appear very early (Korner, 1973). However, when one looks carefully at the literature on the first year of life, the findings are inconsistent. Using studies of habituation as an example, one finds discrepant results, depending on the particular stimuli being studied, the type of response measured, and the age of the infants. Some studies find more rapid habituation for males, some for females, and some find no sex differences (Kagan & Lewis, 1965).

Findings are also inconsistent when we look at the data on measures similar to those used in this study. On the standardization sample, Bayley (1965) found significant sex differences at only a few age levels on the Mental and Psychomotor Developmental Indices. Comparing male and female infants at 15 age levels (1 to 15 months), there were only two significant differences on the Mental Developmental Index and one on the Psychomotor Developmental Index. At 4 months, males were significantly higher than females on the Mental Developmental Index, whereas at 10 months females were significantly higher. On the Psychomotor Developmental Index, males were significantly higher than females at 8 months. Three other studies on infants between 6 and 8 months were unanimous in finding no sex differences on the Mental Developmental Index, but their findings on the Psychomotor Developmental Index were less consistent. Kohen-Raz (1967) found that 6-month kibbutz and institution-reared males were higher than females of similar background on the Psychomotor Developmental Index. With an unusually large sample (N=3,037), Willerman, Broman, and Fiedler (1970) reported diametrically opposite findings; 8-month-old females were significantly higher on the Psychomotor Developmental Index. Goffeney, Henderson, and Butler (1971) found that 8-month-old females scored higher than males on a measure of fine motor development derived from the Bayley Scales.

The present study found that boys and girls were not significantly different in mean scores on the Mental Developmental Index or the

TABLE 6

Means and Standard Deviations for Measures
of Infant Functioning

Infant Variable	Boys (N = 21)		Girls (N = 20)		t
	Mean	SD	Mean	SD	
General Status					
Mental Developmental Index	116.0	19.1	107.9	23.3	—
Psychomotor Developmental Index	111.9	15.9	107.2	20.6	—
Social Responsiveness	5.2	1.7	4.8	1.9	—
Language					
Vocalization During Exploration	27.3	36.9	19.9	21.2	—
Language Quality	3.2	1.6	2.9	1.3	—
Motor Development					
Gross	7.8	2.8	6.6	3.3	—
Fine	8.7	2.9	7.4	3.8	—
Cognitive-Motivational					
Goal Directedness	3.5	1.5	2.5	1.7	2.05*
Reaching and Grasping	7.6	2.1	6.6	2.9	—
Secondary Circular Reactions	1.8	0.5	1.4	0.9	—
Problem Solving	4.4	2.8	3.6	3.1	—
Object Permanence	2.9	1.3	1.9	1.4	2.30*
Exploratory Behavior					
Look at Bell	223.8	79.3	282.9	87.9	2.27*
Manipulate Bell	288.0	120.7	339.2	117.9	—
Preference for Novel Stimulus					
Look at Novel	219.0	83.5	252.2	83.9	—
Manipulate Novel	374.5	143.4	418.1	113.2	—

*$p < .05$, two-tailed tests.

Psychomotor Developmental Index (Table 6). Of the eight clusters derived from the Bayley Scales, there were only two significant differences. Boys scored significantly higher than the girls on Goal Directedness and Object Permanence. Considering the large number of tests of significance in the many studies cited and the inconsistent nature of the scattered significant differences which have emerged, it seems tenable to assume that there are no consistent sex differences on the Bayley Scales.

On measures of exploratory behavior and preference for novel stimuli, Rubenstein (1967) reported no significant sex differences. In the present study, girls were significantly higher than boys on one of the four measures, Look at Bell.

We also looked at the intercorrelations among infant measures to determine whether there might be sex differences in the patterns of relationships. In the total matrix of 120 correlations, there were only three instances in which the relationship of a pair of variables in the male group was significantly different from that in the female group (see Tables C and D, Appendix 1). Since this finding is well within chance expectations, it is reasonable to conclude that the patterns of interrelationships among the infant measures are essentially the same for male and female infants.

On the whole, the few significant differences we have found do not make a strong case for early sex differences. Before one can draw any firm conclusions about sex differences, studies are needed in which many relevant variables are controlled.

CONCLUSION

We have shown that there is a moderate degree of differentiation of the infant on the various clusters developed from the Bayley Scales. Social Responsiveness and Language were quite independent of gross and fine motor development, cognitive-motivational functions, and object permanence. Exploratory behavior and preference for novel stimuli were well differentiated from functions measured by the test clusters. The amount of vocalization the infant showed during exploration was unrelated to other infant behaviors.

Not all aspects of infant functioning, however, were found to be independent of one another. The cognitive-motivational variables— Goal Directedness, Reaching and Grasping, Secondary Circular Reactions, and Problem Solving—were rather highly intercorrelated with each other, with motor development, and with the Mental and Psychomotor indexes. There may have been methodological factors that contributed to this overlap. Since these measures were obtained in a single testing situation there may have been common extraneous factors, such as level of alertness or fatigue, which influenced the results. Moreover, all the cognitive-motivational measures involved some components of hand control.

If tests were available with more diverse response requirements, perhaps greater differentiation in the infant might be found. Nevertheless, these intercorrelations reflect a true underlying interdependence of functions at this early developmental period. Prehensile skills, such as those measured by the cluster, Visually Directed Reaching and Grasping, are basic to the infant's performance on the measures of Secondary Circular Reactions, Goal Directedness, and Problem Solving. We want to emphasize, however, that performance on these tasks requires more than prehensile abilities. In addition to the common skills involved, there is a pervasive motivational component. These findings suggest that the traditional approach to measurement in infancy, an exclusive concern with infant skills, needs to be reexamined. It might be more meaningful both for characterizing infants and for predicting later functioning to devote more attention to assessing early motivational differences.

5

FINDINGS AND CONCEPTUAL ISSUES

Conventional formulations regarding early experiences have usually been in general terms. They have asked simply whether early experiences influence development. In this study our questions were more differentiated. We were interested in the extent to which there are generalized effects of stimulation on development and the extent to which there are specific effects, that is, whether certain dimensions of the early environment influence the development of specific infant functions.

Many studies have shown that severe stimulus deprivation in early life is associated with developmental retardation and personality distortions (Casler, 1961; World Health Organization, 1962; Yarrow, 1961); other studies have shown that these deficiencies can be prevented or ameliorated by enriching the experiences of infants and young children or by specific experimental manipulation of some aspect of the infant's experience. Almost no studies have finely differentiated the early environment and looked at the relations between specific dimensions of experience and infant characteristics.

We analyzed relationships between parameters of the environment and infant functions for the total sample of 41 infants; then these relationships were examined separately for boys and girls. There were many more significant relationships between the environmental variables and infant functioning for females than for males. We believe it is meaningful, however, to combine the male and female groups in analyzing the relationships for two reasons: the direction of relationships is the same for boys and girls for most variables; and the number of significant relationships was increased rather than decreased by pooling the male and female groups. In the exposition of significant findings for the core sample, we have taken the parsimonious perspective that environmental effects are not fundamentally different for boys and girls. This issue is discussed in more detail when the data for boys and girls are presented separately.

Discussion in this chapter is organized around seven major sets of environmental variables described in Chapter 3: the modalities of stimulation, the responsiveness of the mother to the infant, maternal affect, the mother's mediation of play materials, the level and the variety of maternal stimulation, and the characteristics of inanimate objects available to the infant.

First we discuss the social environment. We look at the stimulation provided through each of the sensory modalities, i.e., visual, auditory, tactile, and kinesthetic. Then we examine the mother's responsiveness to the infant, distinguishing responsiveness to his positive vocalizations and responsiveness to crying or fussing. Third, we consider the mother's positive affect towards the infant. Complementing our interest in the mother's direct stimulation, we examine how she encouraged the infant's attention to inanimate objects. Then we look at more general stimulation variables: a measure of the intensity and frequency of stimulation (Level of Social Stimulation) and a measure of diversity (Variety of Social Stimulation).

Following discussion of the social variables, we present the findings on the inanimate environment. Although many enrichment programs have emphasized the value of stimulating play materials in undoing deprivation effects, few studies have analyzed the inanimate environment in the home and assessed its role in development. In this study special attention is given to the relationship between the infant's development and the variety, complexity, and responsiveness of the toys and the common household objects available to him.

These findings are considered in the light of other research and from the perspectives of several theoretical orientations. We presented the theoretical meaning of the variables in discussing the choice of the environmental and the infant variables in Chapters 3 and 4. This chapter discusses the theoretical concepts in an effort to "explain" our findings. Some overlap is inevitable, but in this chapter we have often gone beyond the theories. We have tried to think freely about the findings and to interpret our results in ways that go beyond any formal postulates of these theoretical systems. We have elaborated on and synthesized concepts from several theoretical positions. There are many hypotheses about the role of certain dimensions of the environment and about the mechanisms by which they operate; yet no coherent, unified theory has been formulated about environmental influences on early development. By drawing on concepts from many theories in an eclectic manner, we hope to take some small steps toward an integrative theory of early experience.

THE SOCIAL ENVIRONMENT

Modalities of Social Stimulation

The dramatic findings of animal and human deprivation studies led to the hypothesis that a direct association exists between amount of stimulation and the development of the infant and young child. In recent years there has been some research and theorizing about the role of stimulation in *specific* modalities. As a result, one or another of these modalities has been championed as of singular significance. Experimental studies that have attempted to analyze the effects of one type of stimulation, i.e., auditory, visual, kinesthetic, or tactile, have often concluded that the particular variable with which they were concerned was prepotent. Few attempts have been made to compare the modalities of stimulation and to ascertain if they have different effects on certain functions. Here, we analyzed the relationships between each of these modalities and general developmental functioning, as well as the relationships to specific aspects of cognitive, cognitive-motivational, and social development. In essence, we were interested in testing whether stimulation through certain modalities might selectively facilitate certain aspects of development.

Near Receptor Modalities: Tactile and Kinesthetic Stimulation

Tactile and kinesthetic-vestibular stimulation are frequently not distinguished in discussing an infant's "contact needs" (Frank, 1957; Harlow & Harlow, 1965; Kulka, Fry, & Goldstein, 1960), with the implication that their impact on development is similar. Both involve direct physical contact; but kinesthetic stimulation adds movement of the baby's body, and, by changing proximity to the mother's face and the perspective of surrounding objects, may be associated with greater variation in visual input.

The measure of tactile stimulation in this study included behavior such as patting, stroking, or caressing the baby, often occurring while the baby was held. Kinesthetic stimulation included picking up the infant, carrying him, rocking or jiggling him, and moving his entire body. We found that, compared with tactile stimulation, kinesthetic stimulation had many more relationships that are significant. Table 7 presents the relationships between infant functioning and stimulation in both the near receptor modalities, kinesthetic and tactile, and the distance modalities, visual and auditory.

TABLE 7

Relations Between Modalities of Social Stimulation
and Infant Functioning

Infant Variable	Near Receptor Stimulation		Distance Receptor Stimulation	
	Tactile	Kinesthetic	Visual	Auditory
General Status				
Mental Developmental Index	—	.41**	—	.23
Psychomotor Developmental Index	—	.36*	—	—
Social Responsiveness	.21	.36*	.31*	.37*
Language				
Vocalization During Exploration	—	—	—	.29*
Language Quality	—	.24	—	—
Motor Development				
Gross	—	.25	—	—
Fine	—	.31*	—	—
Cognitive-Motivational				
Goal Directedness	.33*	.57**	—	.21
Reaching and Grasping	.24	.25	—	—
Secondary Circular Reactions	.33*	.28*	—	—
Problem Solving	—	—	—	—
Object Permanence	—	.44**	—	—
Exploratory Behavior				
Look at Bell	—	—	—	.27
Manipulate Bell	—	—	—	—
Preference for Novel Stimuli				
Look at Novel	—	—	—	—
Manipulate Novel	—	—	—	—

Note. Dashes represent correlation $< .20$.

*$p < .05$, one-tailed test.

**$p < .01$.

Tactile Stimulation

The fundamental importance of tactile stimulation has been repeatedly stressed in theoretical papers from a psychoanalytic perspective (Frank, 1957; Spitz, 1957). Harlow's (1959) research on rhesus monkeys deprived of contact with their mothers dramatized the role of this modality. Our results indicate that tactile stimulation has limited bearing on early developmental functions. Only two infant measures showed significant positive correlations with tactile stimulation: Goal Directedness and Secondary Circular Reactions.

These results are similar to experimental findings that tactile stimulation, when compared with other modalities of reinforcement, (Brossard & Décarie, 1968; Haugan & McIntire, 1972), does not appear to be of overriding importance. Moreover, contact alone does not seem to be especially effective as a soothing stimulus in the neonatal period (Korner & Thoman, 1972). On the other hand, Casler (1965) found that supplementary tactile experience, 20 minutes a day for 10 weeks, significantly influenced the development of institutionalized infants. Perhaps supplementary experience in any modality will have some effect on infants reared under conditions of extreme deprivation.

Although we would not conclude that touching and patting the infant are unimportant, our data indicate that in the context of other parameters of stimulation in the home environment, tactile stimulation shows few distinctive effects. It may be that most home-reared infants are given adequate tactile stimulation so that "more" has no discernible effects. Also, there are subtle qualitative differences in handling infants that may not have been captured in our categories of tactile stimulation. An affectionate caress or holding the baby closely is far different from the business-like touch of a diaper change. If we had distinguished such variations, perhaps we would have found differential effects of tactile stimulation.

Kinesthetic Stimulation

Among all the sensory modalities, kinesthetic-vestibular stimulation has singular significance. It has both general and specific effects. It is significantly related to general measures of development, The Bayley Mental Developmental Index and the Psychomotor Developmental Index, and to five specific functions: Social Responsiveness, Fine Motor Development, Goal Directedness, Problem Solving, and Object Permanence.

These strong and pervasive relationships are consistent with the findings of several cross-cultural studies. Many investigators have noted the precocity of African infants during the first year:[5] among the Ghanda (Ainsworth, 1967; Geber, 1958; Kilbride, Robbin, & Kilbride, 1970), the Zhun-twa of Botswana (Konner, 1974), Zambian infants (Goldberg, 1974), the Senegalese (Lusk & Lewis, 1972), and the Kikuyu of Kenya (Leiderman & Leiderman, 1974). All these studies have noted acceleration in motor development. Some have also found superiority on the Bayley Mental Developmental Index (Leiderman & Leiderman, 1974), in object permanence (Goldberg, 1974), in language development (Liddicoat & Koza, 1963), and in social responsiveness (Ainsworth, 1967). In all these cultures the infants are given a great deal of kinesthetic stimulation because they are carried about almost constantly during the early months of life. In the process they are treated to a variety of sights and sounds as the mother moves about the village and works in the fields. When not being carried, the infants are in almost constant proximity to their mothers who respond rapidly to their crying. Much stimulation is also given by other adults and children. Thus, it may be an oversimplification to attribute the precocity of African infants to kinesthetic stimulation alone.

Although the literature on kinesthetic stimulation in our culture is relatively sparse, clinicians have speculated about its role in development (Ambrose, 1969; Bowlby, 1969; Brody, 1956). Institutional environments are notably lacking in this type of stimulation, and several investigators have interpreted the stereotyped rocking frequently observed among institutionalized children as representing attempts to obtain proprioceptive-vestibular stimulation (Provence & Lipton, 1962; Spitz & Wolf, 1946). Experimental studies with institutionalized infants also find that compensatory kinesthetic stimulation effectively increases infants' social responsiveness and alertness. Brossard and Décarie (1968)

---

[5] In a recent review of this literature, Warren (1972) concludes that the precocity of African infants has not been demonstrated convincingly because of the methodological inadequacies in many of these studies.

found that combinations of stimulation that included a kinesthetic component were more effective in reinforcing smiling than combinations of modalities that did not include kinesthetic stimulation. White and Castle (1964) found that institutionalized infants who had received extra rocking and were blindfolded to control for visual stimulation showed longer periods of visual alertness than a control group of infants who were not given any extra handling. These findings underline the need for research on kinesthetic-vestibular stimulation in intervention programs. Moreover, there is need to study the effects of different amounts of kinesthetic stimulation in home-reared infants of different ages. During some developmental periods the infant may be especially sensitive to this type of stimulation.

Several investigators have noted the effectiveness of vestibular stimulation in terminating crying (Ambrose, 1969; Bowlby, 1969; Korner & Thoman, 1970, 1972). Among neonates, Korner and Thoman (1972) found body movement to be more effective than tactile contact in quieting and in promoting visual alertness. In one study, premature infants were given supplementary kinesthetic stimulation (Freedman, cited in Ambrose, 1969) by being rocked for 30 minutes each day. Compared with matched controls, these infants made significant weight gains. These data in humans are strengthened by the results of several animal studies discussed in Chapter 3 (Mason, 1968; Thoman & Korner, 1971).

Why does kinesthetic stimulation seem to have such pervasive effects? Describing their findings on neonates, Korner and Thoman (1972) hypothesized that the vestibular system is likely to be a mediator of early stimulation because it is one of the earliest myelinated (beginning at four months gestational age) and is fully mature at birth. Our speculation is that appropriate kinesthetic stimulation serves to maintain an optimal state of arousal. The kinds of activities involved—rocking, jiggling, and moving the whole body—can be either soothing or arousing, depending on the state of the infant when it is initiated. Being in an optimal state permits the infant to attend and respond to people and objects in his environment. Moreover, arousing kinesthetic stimulation is probably more resistant to habituation than is tactile stimulation. Supporting this view are Casler's (1965) observations that infants habituated very rapidly to tactile stimulation. In addition, as already noted, some types of kinesthetic stimulation, such as being carried, may also be associated with greater visual stimulation and opportunities to see objects from varying perspectives.

Two infant variables, Goal Directedness and Object Permanence, showed a strong association with kinesthetic stimulation. These relationships seem to be especially meaningful theoretically. The finding on Goal Directedness, a measure of the infant's persistence in attempting to secure objects out of reach, supports the interpretation that kinesthetic stimulation enhances the general level of alertness and interest in the environment. With regard to object permanence (which at 6 months is present in only a very rudimentary form), our speculation is that kinesthetic stimulation not only increases the infant's awareness of an external environment but also helps him define the boundaries of his own body. This in turn facilitates his awareness of objects existing independently of him. Essential to the development of object permanence is the ability to discriminate between the self and the outside environment.

Distance Receptor Modalities: Visual and Auditory Experiences

With regard to visual and auditory stimulation, we found no significant correlation with general development, but very specific and conceptually meaningful correlations with the infant's social responsiveness and amount of vocalization. Both visual stimulation (mutual redard between mother and infant) and auditory stimulation (vocalizations directed to the infant) were significantly related to social responsiveness. Auditory stimulation was also related to the amount of vocalization the infant showed while exploring a novel object. Stimulation through the visual and auditory modalities was not related to any other infant functions.

These findings are plausible and meaningful in the contexts of the findings of other studies and a variety of theoretical speculations. Our measure of visual stimulation, mutual regard, is one of the few interactive categories in the study. It is an index of reciprocal behavior initiated by either mother or infant, and sustained or turned off by the response of either person. The special appeal of a mother's face to a child, and specifically her eyes, has been noted by several investigors (Bergman, Haith & Mann, 1971; Kaila, 1932; Spitz & Wolf, 1946; Washburn, 1929). Visual stimulation in the form of eye-to-eye contact or the moving face has been found to elicit social smiling during the third or fourth week of life (Wolff, 1963). Robson and Moss (1970), in turn, have pointed out that the infant's capacity to fixate on the mother's eyes, to smile, and to follow her visually are especially important factors in evoking positive maternal feelings and in making the baby seem like a real person. Most of this theorizing has been with regard to the development of the normal affectional bond between mother and infant. There is clinical evidence that the tie of a blind infant to his mother is significantly delayed, as are other social responses dependent on eye-to-eye contact (Fraiberg & Freedman, 1964; Robson, 1967). Although fleeting spontaneous smiles appear at the usual time in blind infants, mutual visual regard is apparently required to maintain true social smiling (Freedman, 1964). Mutual regard may be an important variable in isolation, but we believe its great significance derives from the fact that it is a marker variable indexing a variety of other social responses. It is often associated with a whole configuration of social stimuli, such as facial animation, approach movements, smiling, and vocalizing.

Because visual interaction is a component of almost all social exchanges, the correlation found between amount of mother-infant mutual regard and the infant's social responsiveness seems especially important. This finding is similar to the results reported by Moss, Robson and Pedersen (1969), who found a significant relationship between the amount of mother-infant visual regard at 1 month and the infant's spontaneous social approach to a stranger at 8 and 9½ months. Although the samples in these studies differ in social background and age, there is a convergence in the findings. They indicate that different components of sociability, approach behavior and responsiveness, are affected by visual interaction with the mother.

The role of auditory stimulation in the development of social responsiveness has received less theoretical attention. In a longitudinal study, Wolff (1963) reported that, as early as the third week, social smiles were evoked more frequently by a high-pitched human voice than by a variety of other auditory stimuli. Shortly afterwards, visual stimulation appears to make a greater contribution to the eliciting of smiles. Brackbill (1958) included vocalizations directed to the infant as one of several social reinforcers in her investigation of instrumental conditioning of smiling in infants between the ages of 3½ and 4½ months. She used physical contact as well as visual and auditory reinforcers. Consequently, the relative importance of the separate modalities could not be assessed. In another investigation of conditioning the smiling response, Brossard and Décarie (1968) attempted to sort out the relative efficacy of different combinations of reinforcers. They found that auditory stimulation was not significantly different from any other type of stimulation, but the sample (four subjects in each condition) was too small for the results to be conclusive.

Our data show that talking to the infant and engaging him in mutual visual regard are equally related to social responsiveness (correlations of .37 and .31, respectively). Since social exchanges between mother and infant involve a constantly changing configuration of facial features as well as stimulation from the human voice, it may be superfluous to look for a distinctive contribution of either. It is likely that both types of stimulation complement each other in the development of social responsiveness. Maternal vocalization has an on-off quality, which may encourage the infant to orient to the mother's face. With his attention thus directed to her, the infant appears interested in and receptive to the mother, which in turn heightens the likelihood of mutual regard and other pleasurable social interactions. Auditory stimulation was also significantly correlated with the amount of infant vocalization during a period of exploration ($r = .29$), a finding we discuss in greater detail in relation to maternal contingencies.

These findings on the role of auditory stimulation and mutual regard add to our understanding of the role of the environment in early social development and emphasize the complexities of the relationships. Walters and Parke (1965) proposed that it is primarily distance receptor stimulation that affects the development of social responsiveness. Our results do not support this contention. We find that both near and distance receptor stimulation have correlations of comparable magnitude with social responsiveness. They both affect the infant's responsiveness to people; neither is unique.

The intercorrelations of the environmental variables indicate that kinesthetic stimulation was quite independent of auditory and visual stimulation. Nevertheless, we are aware that we have not isolated the modalities experimentally. Kinesthetic stimulation was not given mechanically by an inanimate mechanism. While the mother may look at the baby and talk to him without moving him, she is less likely to hold him, move him about, or rock him without looking at him; moreover, talking frequently accompanies these activities. The overlap among these measures, however, was not so great as to obscure their differential effects.

In summary, both near and distance receptor stimulation have a significant impact on development in early infancy, but their impact is selective. Auditory stimulation is related to the development of social responsiveness and the beginnings of language, whereas mutual regard between mother and infant is related only to social responsiveness. Kinesthetic stimulation is also related to social responsiveness; in addition, it has important relationships to early cognitive and motor functions and cognitive-motivational characteristics. All modalities are important avenues of stimulation for the young infant. Some seem to have widespread effects on early development, others are more selective.

These findings cannot be interpreted as simple one-way relationships. Infants who involve their mothers in mutual regard, who vocalize and smile at them, are likely to elicit more auditory and visual stimulation; the infant's responsiveness in turn reinforces the mother's talking and looking. Infants who adapt comfortably to being held and rocked probably elicit more tactile and kinesthetic stimulation, whereas the infant who becomes tense and uncomfortable when he is held or cuddled, in time comes to receive less of these types of stimulation. Interaction between the infant and his mother is reciprocal and mutually reinforcing. The responses he elicits from his caregiver depend on his behavior, and he in turn is molded by what she does. He also mediates stimulation through his sensitivities. Individual sensitivity to tactile, auditory, visual, and kinesthetic stimulation varies widely (Escalona & Heider, 1959; Murphy, 1968; Thomas, Birch, Chess, Hertzig, & Korn, 1963), and the effects of stimulation in these modalities are undoubtedly moderated by these sensitivities.

Contingency Measures: Responsiveness to Positive Vocalization and Responsiveness to Distress

The importance of a responsive environment has been stressed by psychodynamically oriented clinicians and experimentalists alike. Clinicians have been especially concerned with the mother's sensitivity to the child's communications and the harmful effects of her failure to respond appropriately to his cues. From another perspective, operant learning theory has been explicit in specifying the temporal conditions under which responsiveness to the child's signals serve to reinforce desired behaviors.

In this study we distinguished two types of responsiveness to the child. The two measures were the frequency of the caregiver's contingent vocal responses to the infant's positive vocalizations and the latency of the caregiver's response to the infant's distress signals. Table 8 shows the correlation between these two maternal contingencies and infant functioning. Their patterns of relationships are very different.

TABLE 8

Relations Between Contingent Social Stimulation
and Infant Functioning

Infant Variable	Contingent Response to Positive Vocalization	Contingent Response to Distress
General Status		
Mental Developmental Index	—	.32*
Psychomotor Developmental Index	—	.37*
Social Responsiveness	.22	—
Language		
Vocalization During Exploration	.30*	—
Language Quality	—	—
Motor Development		
Gross	—	.28*
Fine	—	.33*
Cognitive-Motivational		
Goal Directedness	—	.38**
Reaching and Grasping	—	.29*
Secondary Circular Reactions	—	.30*
Problem Solving	—	—
Object Permanence	—	—
Exploratory Behavior		
Look at Bell	−.37	—
Manipulate Bell	—	.21
Preference for Novel Stimuli		
Look at Novel	—	—
Manipulate Novel	.31*	.24

Note. Dashes represent correlation < .20.

*$p < .05$, one-tailed test.

**$p < .01$.

Contingent Response to Positive Vocalization

Contingent Vocal Response to the Infant's Positive Vocalizations was related to two measures of infant behavior: Manipulation of Novel Objects ($r = .31$) and Vocalization During Exploration ($r = .30$). Although neither correlation is of impressive magnitude, the latter relationship with amount of infant vocalization does have considerable theoretical interest. Vocalization in infancy is thought to be important for later language development because it is from these early vocalizations that mature speech sounds are differentiated (Staats & Staats, 1963). Moreover, as noted earlier, language is one of the few infant accomplishments that has been found to relate to later measures of intelligence (Cameron, Livson & Bayley, 1967; Moore, 1967). Our findings complement and extend laboratory operant studies of social reinforcement of vocalization rates (Haugan & McIntire, 1972; Rheingold, Gerwirtz and Ross, 1959; Schwartz, Rosenberg and Brackbill, 1969; Todd & Palmer, 1968; Weisberg, 1963), which found that contingent responses to the infant's vocalizations act as reinforcers.

Our results go beyond establishing that vocalization rates are affected by social reinforcement in the immediate situation. We have found that a mother's contingent response to the infant's vocalizations in the home environment affects the amount an infant vocalizes in a totally independent situation. The measure was the amount of time the infant vocalized during a 10-minute period of exploration and manipulation of a toy. It was obtained during the exploratory behavior test approximately 2 weeks after the home observation. The methodological independence of the environmental and infant measures makes these findings especially provocative. Another study of the home environment at 3 months (Jones & Moss, 1971), found a positive relationship between the amount of infant vocalization and the frequency with which the mother's speech was contingent on the infant's vocalization. In the latter investigation, as in the laboratory studies, the infant vocalization and maternal contingent reinforcement both occurred in the same situation. Our data are especially striking since they show an effect that appears to have generalized beyond the immediate reinforcement situation. These findings in the natural environment are concordant with operant learning principles derived from experimental studies in the laboratory.

We have noted that Auditory Stimulation, i.e., *all* speech directed toward the baby, was also significantly related to Amount of Infant Vocalization ($r = .29$, Table 7). We were interested in determining whether it was the contingent or the spontaneous components of the mother's speech that contributed to this relationship. When we distinguished these components, we found no relationship between the mother's spontaneous speech and amount of infant vocalization. The correlation between Auditory Stimulation and infant vocalization was determined by the contingent component. Other evidence of discriminant validity is found in the fact that Contingent Response to Distress, a rating of responsiveness to fussing and crying, was unrelated to amount of infant vocalization.

We stress these results in spite of the modest quantitative relationship because it appears that the mother's contingent speech is a potent reinforcer of infant vocalization. A recent study (Haugan & McIntire, 1972) compared vocal imitation, tactile stimulation, and food as reinforcers for infant vocalization. Rates of vocalization were increased with each type of contingent reinforcement, but *vocal* imitation was consistently the most effective in conditioning infant vocal behavior. We did not attempt to control for other behaviors that may have accompanied vocal reinforcement. The mother's contingent speech may be closely associated with other types of social reinforcers. Mothers who listen to their baby's cooing and respond by talking to them may be more attuned in general to their infant's positive behaviors. They may be more sensitive to them and more expressive of positive feelings.

Experimental studies with 3-month-old infants suggest that eye contact must accompany vocal reinforcement if it is to be effective in influencing vocalization rates (Bloom & Erickson, 1971). Research so far has yielded little on how the many maternal behaviors operate as reinforcers in combination with one another. It is possible that some infants are especially sensitive to certain types of reinforcement; and, alternatively, some mothers may be more comfortable providing one kind of reinforcer than another. Some infants may enjoy being bounced vigorously in response to their coos; others may be uncomfortable with such intense stimulation and may prefer being talked to quietly. Mothers and infants thus learn to adapt to each other's preferences. For social reinforcement to be effective there must be mutual adaptation.

We found no positive relations between maternal contingent speech and the Bayley language cluster. This cluster measured expressive and receptive language and included qualitative aspects of the infant's speech such as vocalizing attitudes and use of expressive jargon. We had expected that this variable would be related to responsive maternal vocalization. In looking carefully at the cluster however, we find a gap in the age placement of individual items. There are no items in the 5–6 month age range. Thus, the cluster may not have been sensitive to subtle developmental changes during this period.

Contingent Response to Distress

While the mother's verbal reinforcement usually occurs when the infant is in active, alert states, her response to his distress occurs during periods of fussiness and irritability. At these times the infant is in a high state of arousal and tension associated with hunger, fatigue, or other conditions of disequilibrium. Responsiveness to the infant in periods of high arousal has been shown to be related to measures of attachment between mother and infant (Bell & Ainsworth, 1972; Schaffer & Emerson, 1964). In this investigation we were concerned with the broader question of the effects of contingent responsiveness to distress on development.

In contrast to the few specific relationships with Contingent Response to Positive Vocalizations, the mother's Contingent Response to Distress shows a facilitating effect on the development of a number of important functions. Rapid response to distress is associated with higher scores on the Mental and Psychomotor Developmental Indexes, the Gross and Fine Motor subscales and three of the four measures of cognitive-motivational functions: Goal Directedness, Reaching and Grasping, and Secondary Circular Reactions.

These results are thought provoking when seen in relation to the findings and theoretical speculations of other investigators. Moss (1967) speculated that responding to the infant's cry increases the mother's reinforcement potency, thus enabling her to have a positive influence on many areas of the infant's development. Lewis and Goldberg (1969) suggested that the infant's awareness of a contingent relationship with his caregiver promotes his cognitive development and his expectation that he can have an effect on his environment. They reported a significant relationship between maternal contingent behavior and the infant's habituation to a redundant visual stimulus, a measure they believe is a primary indicator of cognitive development.

The moderate but significant correlations of Contingent Response to Distress with Goal Directedness and Secondary Circular Reaction suggest that response to the infant's distress may facilitate the infant's motivation to interact with the environment. Goal Directedness, indexing persistent attempts to secure objects not immediately available, and Secondary Circular Reactions, involving repetition of actions to produce feedback, may be early expressions of the infant's attempt to master the environment. Thus, it is likely that response to an infant's cries does more than reinforce crying. It reinforces active coping with the environment, reaching out to obtain feedback from people and objects. Moreover, in time, an infant whose mother is quickly responsive to his cries may come to feel that through his own actions he can have an effect on other people and on his environment.

In a study of the mother's responsiveness to the infant's cry and the development of mother-infant attachment, Bell and Ainsworth (1972) reported that a rapid response to an infant's cry resulted in a decrease in crying during the first year of life. They speculate that the infant's use of the cry as social communication is enhanced by the mother's contingent response. They reject the notion that a rapid response to crying may "spoil" the child and interfere with the development of competence (Etzel & Gewirtz, 1967), but do not give data to confirm this assertion. Our results indicate that a rapid response to crying does not interfere with the development of competence but may actually facilitate it. Motor development and cognitive-motivational functioning are enhanced by rapid intervention during periods of high arousal and tension.

The findings of the present study shed light on the issue of whether a baby is spoiled by "giving in" to his cry. If rapid response to his cry contributes to the infant's motor skills and enhances his persistence and interest in eliciting feedback, he may require closer monitoring. Some mothers may perceive this behavior as a sign of competence, others may see it as inordinately demanding, an indication of being spoiled.

Our measure of responsiveness to distress emphasizes the timing of the mother's intervention. Future studies need to test other important concomitants of the mother's contingent behavior. The meaning of her response will depend on its appropriateness to the signal the infant has given, whether he is hungry or fatigued or is simply bored and desires more varied stimulation. Wolff (1969) pointed out that young infants begin very early to communicate different types of discomfort in their cries, and some mothers are able to make fine distinctions in response to them. Also influencing the infant's perception of the mother's response is the affect accompanying it, whether the mother is calm and accepting or tense and anxious. The few studies that have concerned themselves with these more subtle aspects of maternal responsiveness (Ainsworth, Bell, & Stayton, 1971; Brody, 1956; Escalona, 1968; Yarrow & Goodwin, 1965) have found them to be significantly related to early development.

A conclusion that rapid responsiveness to an infant's distress is beneficial to his development is an oversimplification. It is difficult to prescribe appropriate timing of responsiveness to an infant's cries or unhappy vocalizations. A symbiotic relationship can exist in which the mother is overresponsive to minimal cues, with the consequence that the child's developing initiative and autonomy are impaired. At the other extreme, unresponsiveness to the point of rejection is detrimental to the infant's well being. A sensitive balance needs to be struck between oversolicitude and ignoring. It may be beneficial for the infant to learn to tolerate small delays and to have opportunities to master tension, at least for short periods. Learning to delay gratification becomes increasingly important at later ages.

Maternal Affect: Expression of Positive Affect, Smiling, and Play

The development of a basic trust in people and the expectation that the world is satisfying and predictable are thought to come about through the infant's earliest affective interactions with his mother. Studies of depriving environments have dramatized the harmful effects of the lack of a warm, affectionate relationship in early infancy. The extreme case is the child care institution where the quality of care is characterized by lack of variation in affect; caregivers in poor institutions rarely show strong positive feelings to their wards. Many studies have documented the apathy and inability to establish meaningful relationships of children growing up in these settings (Bowlby, 1951; World Health Organization, 1962; Yarrow, 1961). Yet it is extremely difficult to capture through direct observation the varieties of expression of affect and the subtle nuances that index the many facets of love and acceptance.

Expression of Positive Affect

The measure, Expression of Positive Affect, simply distinguished differences in intensity of affect expression. It is not a measure of the depth of the affectional relationship nor does it define the global characteristics of warmth. It is a rating of the general expressiveness of the mother towards the infant, of the intensity with which she expressed positive feelings.

This variable was significantly correlated with four measures of infant functioning that have a common element of stimulation seeking: Social Responsiveness, Goal Directedness, Secondary Circular Reaction, and Manipulation of Novel Objects (Table 9). These correlations were all of low magnitude, within the range .26 to .30, but they include some of the major areas of infant functioning. These findings indicate that high levels of maternal positive affect serve to maintain the infant in an optimal state of arousal and thus increase his responsiveness to people, sustain his attention to the environment, and support his active attempts to explore and obtain feedback from objects.

Smiling and Play

From the time-sampling observations, there were two additional measures of maternal affect: the frequency with which the mother

TABLE 9

Relations Between Maternal Affect and Infant Functioning

Infant Variable	Expression of Positive Affect	Smiling	Play
General Status			
Mental Developmental Index	.23	.20	.26*
Psychomotor Developmental Index	—	—	—
Social Responsiveness	.26*	.27*	.27*
Language			
Vocalization During Exploration	.24	—	—
Language Quality	—	—	—
Motor Development			
Gross	—	—	—
Fine	—	—	—
Cognitive-Motivational			
Goal Directedness	.30*	—	.30*
Reaching and Grasping	—	—	—
Secondary Circular Reactions	.30*	.32*	—
Problem Solving	—	—	—
Object Permanence	—	—	.40*
Exploratory Behavior			
Look at Bell	—	—	.20
Manipulate Bell	—	—	.35*
Preference for Novel Stimuli			
Look at Novel	—	—	.20
Manipulate Novel	.28*	—	—

Note. Dashes represent correlation $< .20$.
*$p < .05$, one-tailed test.

smiled at the baby and the amount of time she spent playing with him. Of these two affective variables, Play was related significantly to six infant variables; smiling only to two: Social Responsiveness and Secondary Circular Reactions (Table 9). Play was related to the Bayley Mental Developmental Index; to Social Responsiveness; to Goal Directedness; to Object Permanence; and to the exploratory behavior measure, Manipulates Bell. Play included a variety of activities with the infant, such as tickling him, holding him overhead, rolling him on the bed, and engaging him in patti-cake and peek-a-boo. The latter game, peek-a-boo, is one of the classic person-permanence games. Inasmuch as person permanence is thought to be a prerequisite for object permanence, the relationship between Play and Object Permanence ($r = .40$) is especially meaningful theoretically. The baby's experiences with the mother's face going out of sight and reappearing in a context in which there is strong expression of positive feelings helps build his appreciation of the fact that his mother exists when she is not completely in view. Kinesthetic stimulation involved in play activities also helps the infant clarify the concept of himself as distinct from his mother. The relationships of Play with Secondary Circular Reactions (r = .32) and with a measure of exploratory behavior, Manipulates Bell (r = .35), are also of theoretical interest. Murphy (1972) has noted in discussing play with infants:

> As he enjoys the contact with his mother, he gradually cathects the wider environment. The more feedback he gets, the greater is his investment and drive to explore and discover new experiences. Thus he develops "curiosity" which continues to lead him to new discoveries, perceptions, and concepts of the world around him [p. 123].

We are cognizant of the limitations of our measures of affect; nevertheless, the fact that they show significant relationships with theoretically important aspects of the infant's development highlights the importance of the concept. This aspect of the mother-child relationship has not been handled adequately by either its proponents or its antagonists. Some tend to be content with affect as a global, intuitive variable without precise definition. Others reject it because of its lack of definition. It is time we came to grips with the problems of defining these elusive components of the mother-infant relationship.

Social Mediation of Play Materials

In addition to her activities in providing tactile, kinesthetic and auditory stimulation, both spontaneously and in response to the infant's signals, the mother plays an important role in directing the infant's attention to his inanimate environment. There has been some theoretical discussion of the mother as a mediator of stimulation, in providing inanimate stimuli and in making their properties more salient to the infant (Yarrow & Goodwin, 1965); but research has generally ignored this aspect of maternal behavior. In analyzing the mother's role as a mediator of stimulation, we were especially interested in whether there were differential effects when social reinforcement accompanied the presentation of play materials. Two measures of social mediation were used. The first, Social Mediation with Minimal Affect, was the frequency with which the mother provided play materials for the infant or highlighted their properties with bland affect and without talking. The second measure, Social Mediation with Accompanying Smiles and Vocalizations, was the frequency with which she presented play objects or directed the infant's attention to their properties while smiling or talking in the same time unit.

The data indicate that the two types of social mediation operate differently (Table 10). The presentation and highlighting of play objects with minimal social reinforcement seem to affect the

TABLE 10

Relations Between Social Mediation of Play Objects
and Infant Functioning

Infant Variable	Social Mediation with Minimal Social Reinforcement	Social Mediation with Smiles and Vocalizations
General Status		
Mental Developmental Index	—	—
Psychomotor Developmental Index	—	—
Social Responsiveness	—	—
Language		
Vocalization During Exploration	—	.49**
Language Quality	—	—
Motor Development		
Gross	—	—
Fine	—	—
Cognitive-Motivational		
Goal Directedness	.30*	—
Reaching and Grasping	—	—
Secondary Circular Reactions	—	—
Problem Solving	—	—
Object Permanence	—	—
Exploratory Behavior		
Look at Bell	.28*	—
Manipulate Bell	—	—
Preference for Novel Stimuli		
Look at Novel	—	—
Manipulate Novel	—	—

Note. Dashes represent correlation $< .20$.

*$p < .05$, one-tailed test.

**$p < .01$.

infant's orientation to the external environment. He is more likely to inspect an object at length and to strive persistently to secure objects than is the infant who is seldom given play materials.

We expected that the presentation of play materials with accompanying social reinforcement would have stronger effects on the infant's cognitive-motivational development and his exploratory behavior. From the perspective of social learning theory, we would have predicted that the mother's smiles and verbalizations would reinforce the infant's attention to objects. No such effects were found. Instead, this type of social reinforcement was related to the amount of vocalization the infant engaged in while exploring an object. This unexpected finding suggests that the mother's smiles and verbalizations when presenting him with play objects reinforce the infant's expressive behavior had social communication rather than his attentiveness to objects. Apparently the infant's vocalizations in the exploratory behavior test situation are generalized responses based on reinforcements in other situations.

Higher Order Characterizations of Maternal Behavior: Level and Variety of Stimulation

In an attempt to explore some conceptually different dimensions of the infant's experiences than are given by simple frequencies of discrete caretaker behaviors, we derived two composite measures: Level of Social Stimulation and Variety of Social Stimulation.

Although it is known that the amount of time a mother spends with an infant is important, frequency measures do not capture important qualitative differences between mothers in intensity of stimulation. Therefore we developed a measure, Level of Social Stimulation, which included both the frequency and intensity of the mother's interactions with the infant. Among the criteria of high intensity were rapid stimulus change and simultaneous stimulation in several different sensory modalities, e.g., actively touching, moving, and talking to the baby at the same time.

The variable, Variety of Social Stimulation, is defined quite differently from Level. Variety measures the richness and diversity of experiences provided by the infant's caregiver. It is an index of the many different types of social stimulation to which the infant is exposed: playing, providing toys, encouraging motor skills. It also includes changes in the physical context in which the interactions occur. All of these activities go beyond routine caretaking.

These two measures of social stimulation, Level and Variety, were highly interrelated ($r = .76$, Table 1), but Variety yielded more correlations that were significant (Table 11). Both variables were significantly correlated with the Bayley Mental Developmental Index; Social Responsiveness; Object Permanence; and two cognitive-motivational variables, Goal Directedness and Secondary Circular Reactions. In addition, Variety of Social Stimulation was related to four other variables: Vocalization to Bell; Fine Motor Development; Reaching and Grasping; and a measure of exploratory behavior, Manipulation of Bell. Variety together with Kinesthetic Stimulation stand out as the most highly significant dimensions of the social environment because of the breadth of their influence on infant development.

Among the highest correlations between social stimulation and infant functioning are those of Level and Variety with Goal Directedness ($r = .45$ and $.48$, respectively). It appears that this important cognitive-motivational function is influenced by both the intensity and diversity of the mother's interaction with the infant. The mother who interacts vigorously with him and shows a wide repertoire of behaviors—playing, encouraging his motor skills, providing toys and play materials—and engages in these activities in a number of different settings facilitates the development of motivation to act on the external environment.

An equally high relationship between Variety and Object Permanence is consistent with what one might expect on theoretical grounds. Varied maternal behaviors in many different contexts furthers the development of the infant's awareness that

TABLE 11

Relations Between Level and Variety of Social Stimulation
and Infant Functioning

Infant Variable	Level	Variety
General Status		
Mental Developmental Index	.32*	.34*
Psychomotor Developmental Index	−	.23
Social Responsiveness	.35*	.34*
Language		
Vocalization During Exploration	−	.31*
Language Quality	−	−
Motor Development		
Gross	−	−
Fine	−	.26*
Cognitive-Motivational		
Goal Directedness	.45**	.48**
Reaching and Grasping	.25	.28*
Secondary Circular Reactions	.32*	.35*
Problem Solving	.21	.20
Object Permanence	.31*	.47**
Exploratory Behavior		
Look at Bell	−	−
Manipulate Bell	−	.32*
Preference for Novel Stimuli		
Look at Novel	−	−
Manipulate Novel	−	−

Note. Dashes represent correlation $< .20$.
*$p < .05$, one-tailed test.
**$p < .01$.

the mother exists independently of the immediate situation. As noted before, the development of person permanence and object permanence go hand in hand.

The derived measure Variety has important theoretical implications. Information theory stresses that varied and changing stimulation serve to arouse and orient the infant to the environment and maintain his attention to external stimuli. Piaget (1936) and Hunt (1961), in particular, articulated the importance of variety of stimulation, maintaining that the young child is especially responsive to change in stimulation. In line with Piaget's formulation, Hunt proposes that the infant's earliest response repertoire becomes differentiated through change in stimulation. As the infant adapts his responses to the distinctive properties of varied stimuli, there is differentiation and refinement of sensorimotor skills and cognitive structures. As the infant begins to accommodate to a wider and wider range of circumstances, new experiences evoke his interest. In short, he becomes curious about more things and he develops initiative. The essence of the issue as formulated by Piaget (1936) is summarized in Hunt (1961, p. 262): "The more new things an infant has seen and . . . heard, the more new things he is interested in seeing and hearing; and the more variation in reality he has coped with, the greater is his capacity for coping." The relationships between Variety and the cognitive-motivational functions support this proposition.

The findings on the measures Level and Variety of Social Stimulation have methodological as well as theoretical significance. Since the components of these measures are positively correlated, the reliabilities of Level and Variety are *higher* than any of their constituent measures. Thus, although it is often difficult to achieve high reliability for complex ratings, one can develop composite measures with adequate interobserver reliability. Although we have emphasized the importance of differentiating the environment, it is apparent that global variables can be meaningful if the constituent behaviors are defined.

THE PROXIMAL INANIMATE ENVIRONMENT: CHARACTERISTICS OF OBJECTS AVAILABLE TO INFANTS

For some time, there has been a continuing dialogue, with sharply polarized views, on the relative importance of mothering (Bowlby, 1969; Brody, 1956) and inanimate stimulation (Casler, 1968; Levine, 1962). A number of laboratory investigations and some intervention studies bear on the controversy. With one exception, (Brossard & Décarie, 1971), these studies have not compared inanimate with social stimulation, but have restricted themselves to the effects of either supplementing maternal care or to special varieties of inanimate stimulation. Several investigators, (Sayegh & Dennis, 1965; White, B. L., 1967), have concerned themselves with the provision of stimulating objects to children as an antidote to depriving institutional and home environments. These studies have pointed to some important dimensions of the inanimate environment which most studies of home environments have ignored.

In this study we analyzed three aspects of the inanimate environment in the home: the variety of objects available to the infant, the complexity of these objects, and their responsiveness. The relations between these dimensions of the inanimate environment and infant functioning are presented in Table 12. Each of these measures showed significant relationships with some aspect of infant development. These relationships however, were selective. No significant relations were seen between these environmental variables and language or social development, but they did relate to several aspects of cognitive and motivational development.

Responsiveness of Inanimate Objects

Experimental studies have shown that visual and auditory feedback from objects in the environment, particularly when this feedback is contingent on the infant's behavior, will elicit periods of sustained attention (Foster, Vietze, & Friedman, 1973; Rovee & Rovee, 1969; Uzgiris & Hunt, 1970; White, B. L., 1967). The question with which we are concerned is whether feedback-producing objects in the natural environment have effects that generalize beyond the immediate situation in which the infant is handling these objects. Our measure of responsiveness is an index of the feedback potential of play materials that were within reach of the infant.

Responsiveness had significant relationships with many aspects of infant development. In addition to the Bayley Mental Developmental Index and the Psychomotor Developmental Index, significant correlations appeared with indexes of motor development, cognitive-motivational functioning, and preference for novel

TABLE 12

Relations Between Dimensions of Inanimate Stimulation
and Infant Functioning

Infant Variable	Inanimate Stimulation		
	Responsiveness	Complexity	Variety
General Status			
Mental Developmental Index	.27*	—	.36*
Psychomotor Developmental Index	.28*	—	.51**
Social Responsiveness	.21	—	—
Language			
Vocalization During Exploration	—	—	—
Language Quality	—	—	—
Motor Development			
Gross	.27*	.22	.42**
Fine	.33*	—	.37*
Cognitive-Motivational			
Goal Directedness	.30*	—	.41**
Reaching and Grasping	.46**	.32*	.38*
Secondary Circular Reactions	.51**	.46**	.33*
Problem Solving	—	—	.50**
Object Permanence	—	—	.30*
Exploratory Behavior			
Look at Bell	—	—	—
Manipulate Bell	.21	—	.40**
Preference for Novel			
Look at Novel	.28*	.30*	.35*
Manipulate Novel	—	.35*	.48**

Note. Dashes represent correlation $< .20$.
*$p < .05$, one-tailed test.
**$p < .01$.

stimuli. Responsiveness was more highly related to Secondary
Circular Reactions ($r = .51$) and Reaching and Grasping ($r = .46$)
than to any other variables. The correlation between the opportunity to explore objects rich in feedback and the infant's
preference for novel stimuli, although of modest magnitude, is
consistent with some findings of experimental studies. Several
investigators (Rovee & Rovee, 1969; Siqueland, 1969; Watson &
Ramey, 1972) found that changes in auditory and visual stimulation were effective reinforcers of instrumental behaviors. They
found that the rate of varied responses, such as sucking, opening

the eyes, head movement, and kicking, was increased by visual and auditory stimulation that was contingent on these behaviors. In Rovee and Rovee's investigation, the frequency of kicking increased when it produced movement of a mobile; the rate of response also increased when a novel element was introduced in a series of contingent stimuli. Watson and Ramey (1969), in conditioning head activity, compared three kinds of mobiles: a mobile which moved contingently in response to head activity, a noncontingent mobile, and a stabile. They found a significantly higher rate of response to the contingent mobile.

The correlation between Responsiveness and Secondary Circular Reactions is striking because of its conceptual simplicity. Secondary Circular Reactions, a measure of the infant's repeated efforts to elicit feedback from objects, is a type of behavior to which responsive toys lend themselves. The developmental implications of secondary circular behavior are far reaching. According to Piaget, its acquisition is necessary for more complex cognitive activities, such as the use of means-ends relationships in problem solving.

Responsiveness was significantly related to three measures concerned with cognitive-motivational development and also to Fine and Gross Motor development. These relations indicate that this aspect of the inanimate environment affects both motivation and skills. The development of motivation to act on the environment and the development of fine motor skills are reciprocal. The responsive qualities of toys reinforce the infant's efforts at manipulating objects, and this activity in turn helps to improve his fine motor skills. The development of prehensile skills enables the infant to elicit more feedback from objects, further reinforcing his efforts to master the environment.

Complexity of Inanimate Objects

Experimental studies on the role of complexity in humans, as in studies of responsiveness, have concentrated on its effects on the infant's attention. As the infant matures, increasingly complex objects evoke longer periods of attention (Brennan, Ames and

Moore, 1965; Fantz & Nevis, 1967). It is primarily in animal studies that the complexity of inanimate stimuli have shown effects on aspects of development other than attention. Rats raised in "enriched" environments in which complex stimuli are provided show superior learning and problem-solving behavior compared with rats raised in less complex environments (Riesen, 1966; Rosenzweig, Krech, Bennett, & Diamond, 1968).

In this study we were concerned with the complexity of the toys available to the infant, admittedly a small part of the total environment. We found significant relationships with variables which reflect receptivity to stimulation: Reaching and Grasping, Secondary Circular Reactions and the two measures of preference for novel stimuli (Table 12). Fewer significant relationships occurred than with Responsiveness. Contrary to our expectations, Complexity was not correlated with general developmental status, Problem Solving, or Object Permanence. Since theories of the importance of complexity emphasize an optimal level, we checked for curvilinear relationships with the infant variables. Examination of scatter plots showed no evidence of curvilinearity.

These findings suggest that at this early stage of development, complexity may be less significant for general cognitive development than some other dimensions of the inanimate environment. Its effects at this time seem to be to increase the infant's attentiveness to objects and to heighten his interest in novel objects. We would expect that the complexity of materials might become increasingly important for cognitive development at a later period of development.

Future investigations should distinguish Complexity and Responsiveness more sharply; they were rather highly intercorrelated ($r = .70$) in this study (Table 1). In addition, studies should be made of the relation of complexity to variables with which it has a tighter conceptual link. For example, one might measure preference for complexity. An experimental study by Greenberg (1971) suggested that exposure to increasing levels of stimulus complexity in the home promotes the child's subsequent preference for complexity.

Variety of Inanimate Objects

Probably one of the most important indices of an enriched inanimate environment is the degree to which a variety of play materials and household objects are made available to the young child to look at and manipulate. We have discussed the theoretical significance of variety in relation to the social environment. Both Social Variety and Inanimate Variety showed many correlations with developmental outcomes. Of the three measures of the inanimate environment in this study, Variety of Inanimate Objects yielded the greatest number of significant relationships (Table 12). Variety was related to all infant measures except Social Responsiveness and Language, and it correlated more highly with most of them than did Complexity or Responsiveness. These findings lend support to a central tenet of information theory, as well as Piaget's and Hunt's theorizing: varied and changing stimulation arouses the infant and encourages him to orient to the environment; and in adapting to varied stimuli, his sensorimotor skills and cognitive structures become differentiated.

Although few correlations were found between other environmental measures and exploratory behavior and preference for novel stimuli, Variety of Inanimate Objects was significantly related to three of these four measures of exploration and was most highly related to tactile exploration of novel objects ($r = .48$). The implication of these findings is that an infant's natural curiosity is strengthened by the opportunity to see and handle a wide range of objects. This is consistent with Piaget's suggestion that frequent exposure to variety in the environment results in a differentiated capacity for information processing. Both motivation and capacity to assimilate new information increase when an infant's environment is characterized by variety. Our results, in conjunction with the descriptions of the apathy of institutional infants (Provence & Lipton, 1962), support Piaget's view that variety of stimulation is extremely important in the development of an exploratory motive.

The relationships between Variety of Inanimate Objects and exploratory behavior and preference for novel stimuli are also interpretable in terms of Adaptation Level Theory (Helson, 1964). According to this position, experiences with novelty and variety establish an adaptation level in the individual which functions as a motivational anchor point. The degree of variety to which a person becomes adapted defines the range of stimulation that is optimal for, or desired by, that individual. An infant adapted to high levels of variety finds high levels of stimulus input desirable and behaves to maintain those levels. Thus, infants who are accustomed to varied and changing stimulation become more responsive to novel stimuli than do infants who are adapted to lower levels of novel input.

Variety was the one parameter of inanimate objects significantly related to Object Permanence and Problem Solving. At this developmental level, Object Permanence measures primarily the baby's tendency to look for an object that is out of reach and going out of view; Problem Solving measures his efforts and ability to use one object as a means to obtain another that is in view but out of reach and to circumvent barriers to secure objects. The more experience the infant has with a wide variety of materials, the more familiar he becomes with their physical properties and their functional possibilites. Similarly, he will have more frequent encounters with objects that move back and forth from accessibility to inaccessibility. These experiences facilitate the development of the cognitive abilities to deal adaptively with partially accessible objects and with means-ends relationships necessary for object permanence and problem solving.

Although we have interpreted these relationships to be unidirectional, the high relationship between Variety and the Psychomotor Developmental Index ($r = .51$) suggests that this may be an overly simplistic view. Bidirectional relationships are also likely. The correlation may indicate, for example, that the availability of many different objects facilitates motor development; it is also likely that an infant advanced in prehensile skills may be given more objects to handle. Similarly, an infant capable of rudimentary locomotion may bring himself into proximity with more objects. We believe that these data provide support for the importance of environmental influences, but they also illustrate the dynamic interaction between infant characteristics and environmental stimulation.

Our findings on the inanimate environment deserve special emphasis. Much of the research and theoretical discussion of environmental deprivation and enrichment has not made a sharp distinction between stimulation from inanimate sources and from social sources. A clear examination of differential effects was possible in our study because measures of the social and inanimate environments were largely independent of each other. Even measures that are conceptually similar, Social Variety and Inanimate Variety, correlated only .29 with each other (Table 1). In this study, a differentiated analysis of the infant's environment has revealed considerable specificity of environmental effects for some infant functions and generalized effects for others. Two infant measures, Social Responsiveness and Amount of Vocalization, were significantly related only to measures of social stimulation. On the other hand, measures of Exploratory Behavior, Preference for Novel Stimuli, and Problem Solving were related primarily to dimensions of the inanimate environment. Object Permanence and the cognitive-motivational measures—Goal Directedness, Reaching and Grasping, and Secondary Circular Reactions—were significantly influenced by both the inanimate and the social environment.

These findings underscore the importance of differentiated statements about the role of the environment in development. It is not meaningful to label environments grossly as depriving. The same environments may be depriving in some characteristics and enriching in others. Global characterizations of environments probably only hamper our understanding of how the environment affects development, and the mechanisms through which these influences operate.

COMBINATIONS OF
ENVIRONMENTAL VARIABLES

Some Methodological Considerations

The preceding univariate analyses have uncovered many significant and conceptually meaningful relations between maternal behavior and infant functions. Although it is useful to ask whether a given environmental variable makes a contribution to some aspect of infant functioning, ultimately we are interested in understanding how environmental variables act together. In reality, mothers do not simply hold babies or rock them or show them toys. Their behaviors occur in various combinations, and always in a different "mix" from one mother to another. Multivariate techniques permit us to analyze the impact of combined variables. Variables may operate in concert with one another in different ways, often to reinforce or strengthen, sometimes to weaken or negate one another's influence.

The combined effects of two or more variables depend on several factors: the degree and direction of their relationship to each other i.e., whether they are positively, negatively or unrelated to each other, and also the degree and direction of their respective relationships to the dependent variables. The simplest case of summative effects is when two variables are essentially independent of each other, but both are positively correlated with the dependent variable; taken together, the effects of these variables are strengthened. In another case, two variables may be positively related to each other, but one is unrelated or negatively related to the dependent variable. The latter variable may. be a suppressor and mask the effects of the former variable. Controlling for the suppressor variable in a multiple regression equation maximizes the relationship of the first variable. Still another case is one in which two or more variables are so highly related to each other that they are redundant; they neither add to nor diminish each other's impact.

There are other more complex ways in which variables interact. Some variables together facilitate or potentiate each other's influence differently at different points in the distribution of a variable. In a certain range on variable A, an increase in variable B may make little additional contribution, whereas in a higher range on variable A, an increment in variable B may make a substantial difference. We might think of this kind of interaction as similar to a chemical catalyst. Other variables may interact to diminish each other's influence; rather than acting as catalysts, they act as inhibitors. We attempted to study these kinds of additive and interactive effects through stepwise multiple regression and analyses of variance.

At the outset, we were aware that the interactive questions we posed are quite complex. In addition, there are risks involved in doing multivariate analyses with a small sample. The probability of obtaining chance combinations of variables that are meaningless is real. Therefore, we were cautious in interpreting the statistically significant interactions that emerged, being especially sensitive to their theoretical meaning.

Multiple Regression Analysis and Analyses of Variance

There are several statistical strategies for looking at variables operating together. One is to devise composite measures. We reported earlier on some of the relations with the dependent variables of the two composite social measures, Level and Variety of Social Stimulation. Another way is to examine the constituent variables separately, controlling statistically for the effects of one or the other. To do this, we performed stepwise multiple regression analyses, using the discrete environmental measures. The beginning point of this type of analysis involves the selection of the single environmental variable that shows the highest degree of relationship with a given measure of infant functioning. The analysis then proceeds with the selection of additional variables that further contribute to the relationship with the infant measures. Table 13 presents the stepwise multiple regression analyses for each infant measure. The table also includes the univariate and multiple correlations. For each measure, up to five environmental variables are reported. Variables that produced an increment of less than 5% in explained variance were not listed.

Kinesthetic Stimulation and Variety of Inanimate Objects had the highest univariate relationships with 11 of the 16 infant measures. It was not surprising, therefore, that these two environmental variables, which are unrelated to each other, show a pattern of operating in concert to strengthen each other. This combination, Inanimate Variety and Kinesthetic, showed five statistically significant relationships that seem to be conceptually meaningful. In order of magnitude, they were Goal Directedness ($R = .68$), Psychomotor Developmental Index ($R = .61$), Mental Developmental Index ($R = .53$), Object Permanence ($R = .52$), and Fine Motor ($R = .46$). These findings reemphasize the importance of *both* the inanimate and social environment. We have speculated earlier that kinesthetic stimulation maintains the infant in an optimal state of arousal; together, these two dimensions o fstimulation orient the infant to his environment and encourage maximal receptivity to stimuli.

The stepwise multiple regression analysis also led to the identification of a suppressor variable. We had expected that the mother's mediation of objects accompanied by social reinforcement, i.e., presenting or directing the infant's attention to toys while smiling and talking to him, might heighten interest in the environment by reinforcing his attention to objects. This expectation, however, was not borne out by the findings. Although its univariate correlations with the infant variables were consistently around zero, this variable, Social Mediation with Smiles and Vocalizations, when added to a multiple regression equation containing several other environmental variables, had a negative beta weight. The relationship of Kinesthetic Stimulation and Variety of Inanimate Objects to the Psychomotor Developmental Index was enhanced when this variable was statistically controlled (Table 13). In addition, when we controlled for

TABLE 13

Summary of Stepwise Multiple Regression Analyses

Infant Variable	Environmental Variable	Simple r	Multiple R	Significance Level of Multiple R	Percent Increase in Explained Variance	Variate Beta Weight at Last Step	Significance Level of Variate Contribution to R at Last Step
General Status							
Mental Developmental Index	Kinesthetic	.41	—	—	16	.38	.05
	Inanimate Variety	.36	.53	.01	12	.33	.05
Psychomotor Developmental Index	Inanimate Variety	.51	—	—	26	.55	.01
	Kinesthetic	.36	.61	.01	11	.45	.01
	Social Mediation with Smiles and Vocalization	-.11	.70	.01	11	-.37	.01
Social Responsiveness	Auditory Stimulation	.37	—	—	14	.56	.05
	Inanimate Responsiveness	.21	.46	.05	7	.30	.05
	Social Mediation with Smiles and Vocalization	.13	.51	.05	6	-.37	.05
	Kinesthetic	.36	.56	.05	5	.25	N.S.
Language							
Vocalization during Exploration	Social Mediation with Smiles and Vocalization	.49	—	—	24	.67	.01
	Visual Stimulation	-.07	.58	.01	10	-.36	.05
	Social Mediation with Minimal Social Reinforcement	-.16	.63	.01	6	-.25	.05
Language Quality	Kinesthetic	.24	—	—	6	.43	.05
	Tactile	.12	.39	N.S.	9	-.35	.05
Motor Development							
Gross Motor	Inanimate Variety	.42	—	—	18	.47	.01
	Social Mediation with Smiles and Vocalization	.19	.50	.05	7	-.40	.01
	Kinesthetic	.25	.60	.01	11	.35	.01
Fine Motor	Inanimate Variety	.37	—	—	14	.36	.05
	Kinesthetic	.31	.46	.05	8	.40	.01

						r	
Cognitive-Motivational							
Goal Directedness	Social Mediation with Smiles and Vocalization	.10	.58	.01	12	-.39	.01
	Inanimate Responsiveness	.33	.64	.01	8	.27	.05
Reaching and Grasping	Kinesthetic	.57	–	–	32	.54	.01
	Inanimate Variety	.41	.68	.01*	14	.37	.01
	Inanimate Responsiveness	.46	–	–	21	.40	.01
	Inanimate Variety	.38	.54	.01	9	.49	.01
	Social Mediation with Smiles and Vocalization	-.13	.59	.01	5	-.70	.01
	Auditory Stimulation	.01	.68	.01	11	.47	.01
	Tactile	.24	.73	.01	8	.31	.01
Secondary Circular Reactions	Inanimate Responsiveness	.50	.56	–	25	.45	.01
	Kinesthetic	.28	.61	.01	7	.24	N.S.
	Inanimate Variety	.33	–	.01	5	.23	N.S.
Problem Solving	Inanimate Variety	.50	–	–	25	.08	.01
Object Permanence	Kinesthetic	.44	.52	–	19	.32	N.S.
	Inanimate Variety	.30	.57	.01	8	.34	.05
	Play	.40	–	.01	5	.40	.01
	Social Mediation with Smiles and Vocalization	.07	.62	.01	6	-.30	.05
Exploratory Behavior							
Look at Bell	Contingent Response to Positive Vocalization	-.37	–	–	14	-.48	.01
	Play	.20	.50	.01	11	.36	.05
Manipulate Bell	Inanimate Variety	.40	–	–	16	.39	.05
	Play	.35	.54	.01	13	.50	.01
	Auditory Stimulation	-.14	.62	.01	9	-.34	.05
Preference for Novelty							
Look at Novel	Inanimate Variety	.35	–	–	12	.31	N.S.
	Inanimate Complexity	.30	.43	.05	6	.25	N.S.
Manipulate Novel	Inanimate Variety	.48	–	–	23	.37	.05
	Contingent Response to Positive Vocalization	.31	.56	.01	9	.46	.01
	Inanimate Complexity	.34	.63	.01	8	.34	.01
	Visual Stimulation	-.10	.68	.01	8	-.32	.01

Social Mediation in conjunction with other sets of variables, there was an increase in the magnitude of the correlations with Reaching and Grasping, Object Permanence, and Gross and Fine Motor Development. We cannot easily explain why the occurrence of this type of maternal behavior masks the contribution of the other dimensions of stimulation. It may be that affect accompanying the presentation of play materials distracts the infant from giving full attention to objects. The interest value of the mother is probably much greater than that of toys. Still, this is not an adequate explanation of these findings.

A third interesting finding from these analyses is that two infant measures, Problem Solving and Secondary Circular Reactions, were strongly influenced by a single environmental variable. Adding other variables had no effect. Inanimate Responsiveness correlated .50 with Secondary Circular Reactions, and Inanimate Variety correlated .50 with Problem Solving. Additional variables did not produce a significant increment in these relationships.

The stepwise multiple regression analyses, while pointing up some conceptually meaningful combinations, also yielded some combinations that defy meaningful theoretical interpretation. For example, Contingent Response to the Infant's Positive Vocalizations produces a significant increment in the correlation of Variety of Inanimate Objects with Preference for Manipulating Novel Objects. The correlation coefficient increased from .48 to .56. This example is simply given to point up some of the hazards of doing this type of analysis with small samples.

In considering whether statistical *interactions* occur among combinations of environmental variables, two types of analyses were performed. We looked at the significance of interactions with multiple regression analyses, and we also looked at interactions analyses of variance. We were primarily interested in whether a change in one variable had the same effect regardless of the score on the other variable. Since the research design involved the description of naturally occurring behavior rather than the experimental approach of assigning subjects on a random basis to various treatment conditions, statistical evidence of interaction must be interpreted cautiously.

Recognizing the constraints imposed by a small sample and the consequent instability of relationships, we took a conservative approach to these analyses. There were virtually limitless combinations of variables for which one could, with a little reflection, pose some reasonable conceptual justification. To limit the number, we restricted ourselves to the two variables showing the strongest and most pervasive relationships with infant development, Kinesthetic Stimulation and Variety of Inanimate Objects. In addition to our conceptual interest in these variables, there are also technical reasons for the combination. Because these variables were uncorrelated with each other, the sample could be divided at the median on one variable without producing a disproportionate number of cases in a cell on the second variable. No significant sex differences in means existed for either variable, so there was not a disproportionate number of males and females in the respective cells.

Although analysis of variance and multiple regression are accepted procedures for analyzing interactions, we obtained different results from each approach. The multiple regression procedures yielded no significant interactions; the analyses of variance yielded seven. We shall not attempt here to discuss this surprising discrepancy. The methodological and statistical implications of these divergent results are presented elsewhere (Klein, 1974). Klein concluded that the analysis of variance is the more appropriate procedure.

The results of only the analysis of variance are presented in Table 14. There were significant interactions between Kinesthetic Stimulation and Variety of Inanimate Objects and the following infant measures: Bayley Mental Developmental Index, Bayley Psychomotor Developmental Index, Vocalization during Exploration, Social Responsiveness, Goal Directedness, Reaching and Grasping, and Secondary Circular Reactions. Inspection of the cell means shows a similar pattern on all infant measures except Vocalization to Bell. For six of the seven significant interactions, the infant measure was lowest when *both* Kinesthetic Stimulation and Variety of Inanimate Objects were below the median. When one environmental variable was below the median, the position of

TABLE 14

Cell Means and Significance of Interactions of Kinesthetic Stimulation and Inanimate Variety on Infant Functioning

Infant Variable	Inanimate Variety Below Median		Inanimate Variety Above Median		Interaction F	p level
	Kinesthetic Below Median	Kinesthetic Above Median	Kinesthetic Below Median	Kinesthetic Above Median		
General Status						
Mental Developmental Index	86.6	128.2	116.3	117.8	11.4	.01
Psychomotor Developmental Index	90.4	115.1	115.0	115.5	4.3	.05
Social Responsiveness	3.7	6.4	5.1	5.0	6.6	.05
Language						
Vocalization During Exploration	23.0	15.7	12.6	56.9	6.9	.01
Language Quality	2.6	3.8	2.9	3.4	0.5	N.S.
Motor Development						
Gross Motor	5.0	7.4	7.8	7.9	1.3	N.S.
Fine Motor	5.1	9.3	8.1	9.4	1.8	N.S.
Cognitive-Motivational						
Goal Directedness	1.0	4.1	3.1	3.9	7.3	.01
Reaching Grasping	4.4	8.1	7.6	7.9	5.3	.05
Secondary Circular Reactions	0.9	1.9	1.8	1.9	4.7	.05
Problem Solving	1.7	4.3	4.6	5.0	1.4	N.S.
Object Permanence	1.0	3.2	2.4	2.8	3.8	N.S.
Exploratory Behavior						
Looking at Bell	262.7	258.9	250.6	248.8	0.0	N.S.
Manipulate Bell	318.0	283.9	341.4	340.0	0.2	N.S.
Preference for Novel Stimuli						
Look at Novel	224.4	224.7	251.4	275.9	0.2	N.S.
Manipulate Novel	325.4	387.9	457.3	436.4	1.3	N.S.

Note. $df = 1,30$.

the other, whether it was above or below the median, had a substantial effect. When one of the environmental variables was above the median, an increase or decrease in the other had little effect on infant functioning. The results for the Bayley Psychomotor Developmental Index (PDI) illustrate this complex pattern of interaction. When both environmental variables were below the median, the mean PDI was 90.4. When Kinesthetic Stimulation was above the median and Variety below the median, the mean PDI was 115.1. Similarly, when Kinesthetic was below the median and Variety above, the mean PDI was 115.0. When both were above the median there is no marked increase, the mean PDI being 115.5. The one exception to this pattern of findings is the interaction with Vocalization during Exploration. When both environmental variables were above the median, that variable showed the highest score.

One interpretation of these findings is that there is an optimal level of stimulation for these two variables together. If the infant is already receiving a great deal of kinesthetic stimulation. increasing the variety of toys available to him does not further facilitate his cognitive or cognitive-motivational development. Similarly, if he has a great variety of toys, increasing the amount of kinesthetic stimulation does not further stimulate his developmental progress. This does not mean, however, that these two categories of stimulation are interchangeable. Some minimal level of both is necessary for adequate development. Moreover, the optimal level of kinesthetic stimulation will vary with an infant's sensitivity to proprioceptive-vestibular stimulation; and the optimal variety of toys will vary with how rapidly he habituates to stimuli and with his idiosyncratic ways of processing stimulation. Optimal levels of stimulation may also be phase specific; they may differ at different developmental periods. At some stages the infant may be able to use only so much of a particular type of stimulation. This optimal combination may change as the infant matures.

We must remember that none of the infants in this study were grossly deprived of social stimulation, and most had some toys with which to play. "Low" or "high" on either variable, therefore, is a relative term only, and we do not yet know how these environments compare to other child-rearing environments. It should also be noted that as a group these infants are functioning above the means of the standardization group on both the Mental and Psychomotor Developmental Indexes.

By examining several variables in combination, we have extended our understanding of the early environment. Sometimes there are enhanced relationships with infant functioning; sometimes the effects of a variable are masked or obscured by another variable. We also found several significant statistical interactions with a pair of variables from the social and the inanimate environments. These interesting findings would not have emerged from simple univariate analyses.

Multivariate analyses appear on the surface to be promising approaches to the more complex questions regarding the effects of the environment. To our knowledge, there is only one other study of young infants that has used multiple regression analyses in the study of early environmental influences (Clarke-Stewart, 1973). Although this approach may see wider application in the future, it is also necessary to be aware of the risks in making broad generalizations from small samples. There is a reasonable probability of obtaining chance combinations of variables that are meaningless. In interpreting the combinations of variables that emerged in the multiple regression analyses and the interactions in the analyses of variance, we attempted to be sensitive to their theoretical meaning. It is also possible that a particular sample, by virtue of common cultural values and expectations, may show a distinctive range on certain variables, and the interrelationships among the variables may differ from one sample to another. Because of this possibility, conclusions from multivariate analyses may be highly specific to the particular sample studied.

RELATIONS BETWEEN ENVIRONMENTAL
DIMENSIONS AND INFANT FUNCTIONS
FOR MALE AND FEMALE INFANTS

In the preceding analyses of the environment in relation to infant functioning, we have used the total sample of 41 infants. We were also interested in determining whether the early environment operates similarly for boys and for girls. To this end, we analyzed the relations between environmental variables and infant functions separately for boys and girls. We are very much aware of the limitations of the small sample, 20 girls and 21 boys.

Tables E–J in Appendix 1 report the relationships between parameters of the environment and infant functioning separately for male and female infants. The sheer number of relationships make these tables difficult to digest. As in other studies which have analyzed relationships separately for male and female infants, the picture is neither simple nor clearcut. The major finding is that many more significant relationships occur for female infants than for male: 44 significant correlations for girls compared with 6 for boys.

A basic question is whether we are justified in combining the male and female groups and discussing findings without regard to the sex of the infant. There are two reasons why we think it is meaningful to analyze the data for the total group. First, in the total group of male and female infants, there were more correlations that were significant than in either group alone. There were 73 significant correlations in the combined group. Had the relationships with the male infants been entirely random, we would have expected *fewer* significant relationships in the combined group than we found for the girls alone. We concluded that the male group is contributing to the significant relationships in the combined sample; their inclusion increased the prevalence of significant findings. Second, the *direction* of the relationships tended to be the same for both sexes although the size of the correlations was lower for males. Of the 73 correlations that were significant for the total group, the direction of relationship was the same for both boys and girls in 60 instances. Reversals in direction occurred primarily in two variables, Responsiveness of Inanimate Objects and Tactile Stimulation. With the exception of these two variables, the number of significant differences in the magnitude of correlations for the two groups was also less than expected by chance.

We can only speculate why the relationships between environmental variables and the functioning of male infants tended to be of a lower order. One possibility is that these boys and girls received different amounts of stimulation. Table 3 in Chapter 3 presented the means and standard deviations of the environmental variables separately for males and females. Mothers of boys were significantly higher on Level and Variety of Social Stimulation. Although all the other measures were numerically higher for males, the differences fell short of statistical significance. Since there was a tendency for boys to be in a higher range of stimulation, it is possible that this might have affected the prevalence of significant relationships. Our conjecture was that correlations with environmental variables might show up more clearly in the lower ranges of stimulation; perhaps in the higher range of stimulation there is a plateau within which increases make little difference. If this is so, relationships in the male group would be sharply attenuated.

To test this hypothesis, we divided the male group at the median on each of the environmental measures and compared the environment-infant correlations in the upper range with those in the lower range. If the lower range males showed relationships more similar to the females than upper range males, our hypothesis would be credible. There was no evidence, however, of differential relationships between upper range and lower range boys. Thus, although male infants appear to be receiving more stimulation than the females (significantly more on two variables), such an increase apparently has no bearing on the number of statistically significant relationships.

A second factor that may affect the prevalence of significant relationships among female infants is the finding that the environmental variables tended to be more highly intercorrelated for girls than for boys. For example, the median correlation of Contingent Response to Distress with all other stimulation variables was .44 for the girls and .15 for the boys. For girls, the median correlation of Kinesthetic Stimulation with all other environmental variables was .49, compared with .18 for the boys. In most cases, the differences in magnitude of relationships were not statistically significant, but the higher order interrelationships for the females indicates that there is greater overlap among the variables. For each "true" relationship between a specific component of the environment and an infant function, correlations will tend to occur with the overlapping environmental variables. This overlap results in more correlations that are significant, and it also means that less differentiated interpretations of the effects of any single variable are possible. It is important to keep this point in perspective, however. The overlap in environmental variables is only moderate in the female sample; therefore, there is room for substantial differentiated effects. Were the intercorrelations in the .80's or .90's, our analytic procedures and interpretations might legitimately be questioned.

Finally, it appears that there is lower reliability in the measurement of male infant characteristics than female. Although test-retest stability and split-half reliability on infant tests have not been reported separately for boys and girls, one study of boys only (King & Seegmiller, 1973) reported lower reliability scores for the Bayley Scales than appear in the standardization sample in which the data for males and females are combined (Bayley, 1969). This finding led us to compute the split-half reliabilities of the Bayley Mental Developmental Index and Psychomotor Developmental Index separately for male and female infants. We found that male infants had significantly lower reliability scores on the Mental Developmental Index (uncorrected $r = .77$ for boys compared with .94 for girls). Boys were also lower on the Psychomotor scale, although the difference in correlations was not significant ($r = .67$ vs. $r = .79$). Since the infant measures in this study come chiefly from the Bayley Scales, it is likely that the measures were less reliable for boys than for girls.

Although there are some inconsistencies in the literature, some findings indicate that male infants show greater instability in their behavior than do females. Kagan (1971) has reported greater stability in visual fixation and amount of vocalization for girls than boys, especially between 8 and 13 months. Several studies converge in showing higher correlations between infant developmental status and later IQ for girls than for boys (Goffeney, Henderson & Butler, 1971, McCall et, al., 1972; Moore, 1967).

Bayley and Schaefer (1964) have hypothesized that girls' intellectual functioning has a greater genetic component, whereas boys are influenced more by the environment. Research findings on this question, however, are inconclusive, and they are open to different interpretations. Several investigators have found higher relationships between a number of parental characteristics and IQ for girls than for boys (Hindley, 1965; Honzik, 1963; Reppucci, 1971; Werner, 1969). These characteristics—education, socioeconomic status, and parental intelligence—are as likely to be indirect measures of the environment as of genetic factors. Our findings of a higher relationship between the environment and the development of female infants are consonant with these results.

Close inspection of our data suggest that the apparent discrepancy between males and females in the impact of the environment may be due to a greater instability in boys. The fact that measures of infant boys' developmental characteristics are less reliable than those for girls may mean that the day-to-day variation in the behavior of male infants is greater than in female infants. Assessment of mother-child interaction may also be more unstable with male infants because the mother's behavior is partly a response to the infant. We know the reliability of any measure sets limits on the degree of association that can be expected with another variable. In view of this fact, we propose the parsimonious hypothesis that the nature of environmental influences is not fundamentally different for boys and girls. The early environment is significant for both boys and girls; but since boys are more variable and their environment therefore possibly less consistent, it may be more difficult to establish statistical linkages. We do not think it is prudent to emphasize a sex-specific theory of environmental influences until we have a firmer data base.

6

PORTRAITS OF
SOME LIVE INFANTS
AND MOTHERS

Discussion in previous chapters was limited to quantitative relations and abstract theory. Occasionally we have had twinges of regret that in the reduction of our findings to numbers and to statistical indexes, many steps removed from the meaningful associations they represent, we have lost sight of living babies and mothers. Moreover, in our observations we focused on the proximal environment of the infant; deliberately, we described simple behaviors of mothers and simple responses of infants. We thought of these behaviors as the primary components of the infants' early experiences. We are keenly aware that in dissecting the environment, in cutting it up into fine pieces, we have lost the feeling of humanness, the sense of real mothers and infants interacting with each other. The cold statistics we have presented do not give much feeling for the people or for the social context in which they are living. In our concentration on observable behaviors we have essentially ignored the personalities, values, beliefs, aspirations, and broader life orientations of the mothers and fathers and other people who impinge upon the infant. Nor do our categories give us a feel for their homes and neighborhoods or the larger cultural contexts. We have looked at neither the unique individual motivations of these mothers nor the motivations rooted in their experiences as members of a particular ethnic and social group. In this chapter we have tried to redress these deficiencies in a small way. We have reconstructed portraits of some of the mothers and infants whom we came to know and to appreciate as real people.

We chose these six families to give some feeling for the complexity and diversity in the experiences of infants during the first 6 months. These case descriptions are not intended to be intensive studies of these infants or families; rather, they are free impressions that emerged in the course of data collection. In presenting these cases, we tried to shake loose of our categories and our theoretical blinders. These six cases illustrate the diverse experiences of the young infants we have studied. They differ not only in socioeconomic circumstances but also in family structure, in the fathers' involvement with the child, in degree of organization and planning in the care of the child, in the prevailing affective tone, as well as in patterns of stimulation and responsiveness to the infant. We have also described one infant, Angela McCloud, who was not included in the statistical analyses, This case illustrates a caretaking pattern—not unusual in the total sample of 70—in which there were so many changes in caregivers that we felt we did not have an adequate sample of the infant's early experiences.

The bar graphs (Figures 1 and 2) allow us to compare these six infants on selected environmental variables and developmental characteristics: All measures are expressed as standard scores to simplify comparisons among families. These graphs give some feeling for the varied patterns of stimulation. Although in a few cases we see relations between a mother's economic circumstances and how she handles her infant, in others no apparent relationship exists between economic status, living conditions, and patterns of maternal care. Leroy Simmons and Rachel Jeffries lived on the same street under similar impoverished housing conditions, yet the quality of their early experiences was very different. Leroy lived in a crowded, multigenerational family; much of his experience seemed to have an unpredictable quality. He was cared for by his grandmother who inconsistently gave him stimulation and responded to him with equal inconsistency. Leroy was close to the mean on all developmental measures. Rachel, on the other hand, was an extremely active, alert, responsive baby, one of the most advanced in the sample. She received consistently high levels of stimulation and affection from her mother within a well-organized family setting. Angela McCloud, another baby whose living circumstances seemed without clear and predictable patterns, also received affection and highly varied stimulation, but from a wide variety of caregivers. She developed into an alert, well-coordinated baby, but was not extremely responsive socially. Daryl Bradley, although from a family with relatively limited income, had a stable, well-organized life. Like Rachel Jeffries, he was cared for by his mother, who handled him sensitively and was responsive to his needs. She did not give high levels of stimulation, however, nor did she show strong positive affect. Daryl's functioning was depressed in most areas.

Jennifer Ford and Michael Roberts illustrate the contrast in care of two infants from higher socioeconomic backgrounds. Jennifer was cared for by a sitter, Michael by his own mother. The patterns of care contrast sharply. Michael's mother enjoyed playing with him, giving him vigorous kinesthetic stimulation, and expressing warm affect; she was highly responsive to his needs, and provided him with many playthings. Jennifer's caregiver, on the other hand, rarely played with her and did not often respond appropriately to her cries. She had virtually no toys with which to amuse herself, and generally received low levels of stimulation. The development of these two infants strikingly reflect these divergent patterns of care. Michael was bright, alert, and highly responsive to people. Jennifer was a quiet baby who cried and seemed irritable

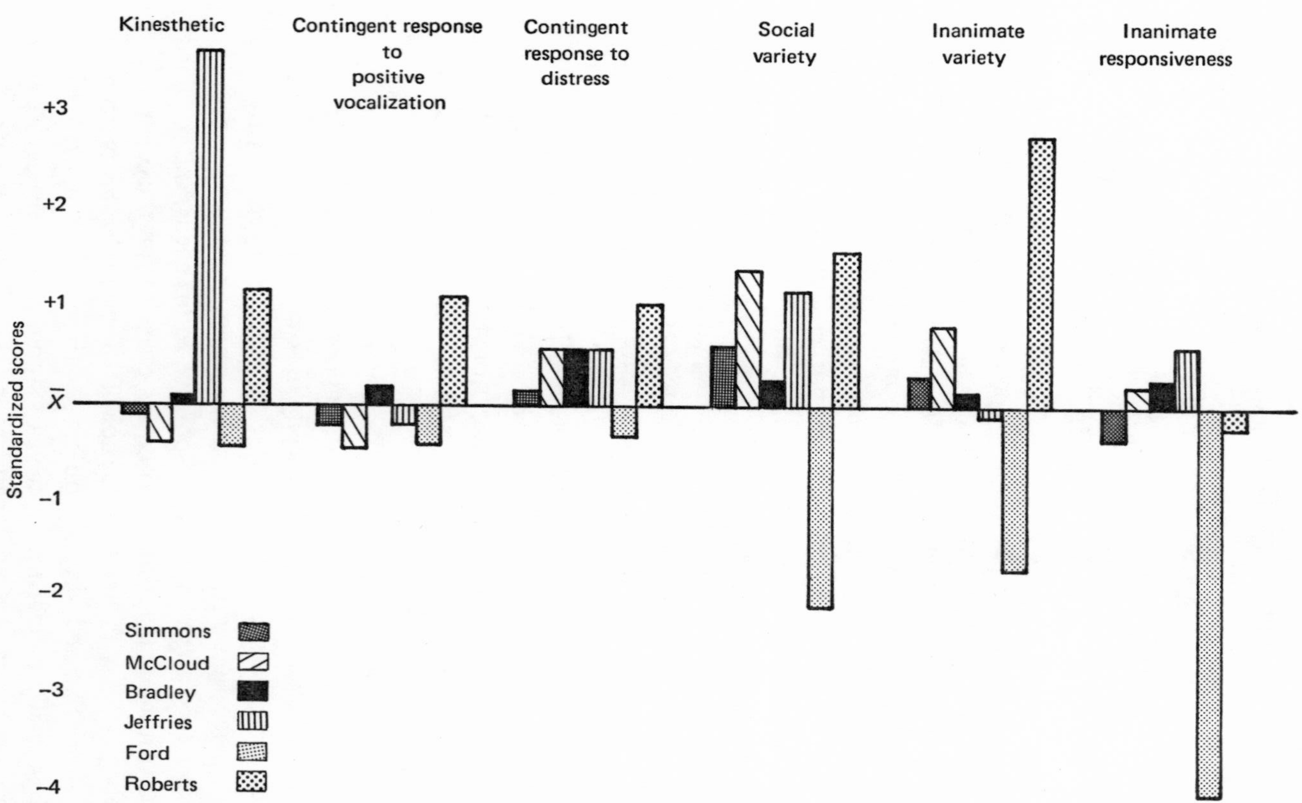

FIG. 1. Independent variables

Kinesthetic

Contingent response to positive vocalization

Contingent response to distress

Social variety

Inanimate variety

Inanimate responsiveness

Standardized scores

+3 +2 +1 X̄ -1 -2 -3 -4

Simmons
McCloud
Bradley
Jeffries
Ford
Roberts

120

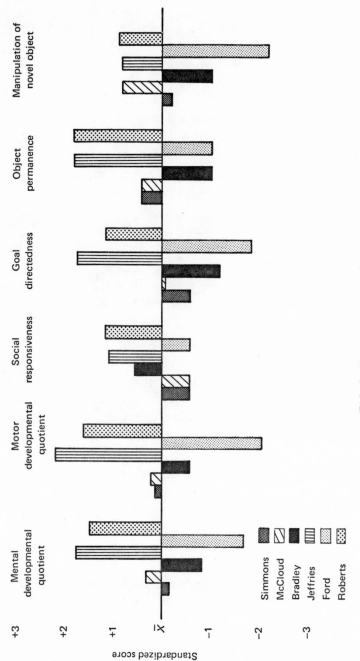

FIG. 2. Dependent variables

121

a great deal of the time. Her functioning level, moreover, was consistently below average.

Presentation of these case studies has several objectives. We want to place these infants and mothers in a larger social context. We also wish to make more vivid, to concretize the maternal and child variables we discussed abstractly in the previous chapters. In some cases we can see illustrations of the statistical relationships between environmental and infant variables clearly; in other cases relationships are less evident. The latter draw our attention to the small percentage of the variance accounted for by the statistically significant relationships.

ANGELA MCCLOUD

Angela McCloud was born into a world full of people, all of whom found "Angel," as they often affectionately called her, entertaining and "fun" to be with. Her mother, Bernice, dropped out of high school several months before Angela was born. For the first 5 months after Angela's birth they lived with the maternal grandparents. Bernice McCloud later reported to the research staff, "It was summer-time and all the kids were home from school. Everybody helped in taking care of Angie. My sister, Mary, who is thirteen, especially liked her and she helped the most."

When Angela was 6 weeks old, her mother took a job as a Neighborhood Youth Worker with the municipal government. This involved spending her afternoons and early evenings interviewing members of the community regarding community problems, and Mary took over complete care of Angela while her mother was out of the home. Mary was "very sad" when, only 3 weeks later, she had to return to school and relinquish afternoon care of the infant to the baby's maternal grandmother. Apparently the grandmother was not happy with this arrangement either because she had a number of young children of her own; therefore, after 6 weeks Angela was taken across the street to a friend's house while her mother worked. A month later, when Angela was 5 months old, Bernice McCloud decided to move out of her own parent's home and join the baby's father, Thomas, who lived with his family. This move appeared to be a fortuitous one in a number of respects. The baby's father, a high school graduate who worked as a filing clerk in a government agency, had maintained a strong tie to both mother and baby since Angela's birth; he was "really crazy about that baby." It was clear that Angela's mother and father enjoyed being together, although, by her account, they had no plans to marry. His 16-year-old sister, who was pregnant and at home awaiting the birth of her baby, was available to take over Angel's care while Bernice continued to work. Thus, by the age of 5½ months, Angela had been exposed to many different people in many different settings. According to her mother, she "loved it."

Bernice McCloud was an attractive, vivacious young woman who was always modishly dressed. Even in Thomas' extended family, Bernice maintained an independent status, buying the food she and the baby ate and contributing to the rent. She did not pay the baby's paternal aunt to care for Angel during the day; there appeared to be a tacit understanding that it was a temporary arrangement that could end at any time. There was no sense of obligation on the part of either young woman. Bernice derived great satisifaction from living in this large, extended family arrangement. When at home in the mornings, she spent most of her time socializing with family members. Although the addition of mother and baby increased the number of people in the six-room apartment to 12, Angela and her mother were not treated as temporary guests. They belonged there in a natural way; despite obvious crowding, they enjoyed the feeling of camaraderie and kinship.

The apartment was located in a World War II vintage housing development that was stark in appearance. The surrounding neighborhood contained other large housing units interspersed with small commercial centers containing grocery stores, taverns, and shops. Streets and grassy areas were littered and presented a trampled, run-down appearance. It was a densely populated area, with considerable trafffic and always many people on the streets. Children played in the streets, often seemingly oblivious to the noise, congestion, and physical danger. The apartment building itself was surrounded by a large asphalt parking lot, fringed with a well-trodden grassy area containing one or two swings and sliding boards. The building doors had several broken windows, and the interior halls were dimly lit, poorly painted, and, in many places, covered with graffiti. Two elevators were not working. All apartment doors were equipped with heavy security locks. The neighborhood children extended their play area from the streets into the building and noisily enjoyed chasing each other down the long, echoing corridors.

The apartment in which Bernice and Angela lived was small and crowded, with the three bedrooms, living room, dining area, and kitchen laid out in a cramped fashion. The rooms had small windows which looked out at the wall of the neighboring building. Upkeep in the apartment was poor, with paint peeling from the walls in some places, cracks in the tile floor, a broken doorbell hanging by exposed wires outside the front door, and dripping faucets in the kitchen. The crowded layout was accentuated by many pieces of dilapidated but comfortable furniture, including large, overstuffed sofas and chairs. The two sofas served as beds for family members at night. The odor of food pervaded the apartment, the window shades were pulled down most of the way, and the television set was on continually. Copies of magazines and comic books were scattered about the apartment. A small corner bookcase housed a large Bible, and several devotional pictures were tacked onto the living room walls. At the time of the home visits in December, a large, brightly decorated Christmas tree took up a great deal of space in the living room.

Family members moved freely about the apartment; there was a general atmosphere of constant activity. The small children used all rooms for play; there were few territorial divisions within the apartment, despite the large number of people living together in elbow-bumping proximity. Although this large family engaged in a large amount of casual social interaction, there was a rather fragmented allocation of responsibility for maintenance of the household and for child care.

Family members cooked their own meals at varying times during the day. Children older than 2 or 3 years were often instructed to "go get something for themselves" when they indicated they were hungry. The tenor of social interaction in this crowded home was a mixture of high-pitched good humor punctuated by outbursts of temper and irritation among family members. The young children appeared to bear the brunt of the negative affect, being disciplined and scolded frequently and sharply by any adult whom they happened to interrupt or displease. In addition, there was considerable disagreement among the adults; the line between vigorous "ribbing" and "joshing," on the one hand, and outright argument, on the other, was sometimes hard for an outsider to discern.

Although there were four children under the age of 5 years living in the household, Angela, as the youngest and only infant, was clearly a favorite of everyone. Much of her day was spent sitting in the living room on the sofa or on a blanket on the floor. Thus located, she was in the center of much of the family activity. Her paternal grandparents were home during the day, and her four aunts and uncles came and went in a rather sporadic fashion, since all but one were either on vacation from school or working irregular hours. She was seldom alone in the room, and she received a great deal of attention from everyone. The young children enjoyed making her laugh by dangling toys and making funny faces for her amusement. The adults carried on a running conversation with her and seemed to enjoy playing with her. Angela responded with great pleasure, becoming thoroughly absorbed in the interaction and delighting everyone with her frequent squeals of laughter. She was an exuberant baby; and when she smiled or laughed, her pretty, rather impish appearance was enhanced.

Angela was provided with many toys and was seldom without something to manipulate and explore. She was adept at handling the toys and at finding them during a game of hide-and-seek, a favorite pastime. She had favorites among the toys, including an old rag doll with a faded and torn dress and a brightly-colored transparent plastic rattle containing "butterflies" that jingled when manipulated. Angela was fascinated by the responsiveness of the latter toy and became absorbed in shaking it, batting it about with her hands, and banging it against any available surface.

Bernice McCloud had no qualms about having other people care for the baby, but when she was home she interacted with her affectionately and often. She was pleased with the baby's sunny disposition and took great pride in her motor competence. When sitting in the living room talking with other members of the family, she sometimes pulled Angela onto her lap and tickled her playfully or participated in the baby's play with objects. The baby reciprocated her mother's pleasure in these activities, actively reaching for toys held just out of reach or searching for objects hidden behind her mother's back. Angela's mother especially enjoyed long, spirited monologues directed to the baby. She also took pleasure in placing the infant in a walker purchased by the baby's father and encouraged her to "run away." The baby was adept at pushing herself about in this vehicle and did so freely.

At times, the lack of restriction on her activities verged on careless disregard for the baby's safety. Once, when she toppled from the sofa onto the floor, her mother retrieved her quickly and admonished her with, "You better grow up quick, Angie; you can't be such a baby." In this way, Bernice verbalized the value which she placed upon the baby's maturity and self-sufficiency, qualities which were effectively encouraged and promoted in many ways by all members of the family. Although "Angel" appeared to be completely accepted by all of the adults, the observer felt that this was partly because she was such an entertaining diversion. Although she seldom cried or demanded caregiving ministrations, it was at those infrequent times that Angel called forth some ambivalence from her mother. When a diaper change or a bottle was required, Bernice affectionately addressed "Angel" as "Little Miss Stinky Pants" or "Pig," although this was said in an affectionate way. Caregiving itself was perfunctory, meals were quickly given, and bottles were usually propped. Thus, in a subtly contradictory way, the mother seemed to appreciate the baby's infantile characteristics (a "cute and amusing toy") and, at the same time, to dislike the burdens they represented for her. This was also exemplified in her father's handling of Angela. Very much the "proud new father," he spent a great deal of time playing with her in an animated fashion and seemed especially to enjoy encouraging her to master new locomotor skills. But, although he responded quickly to any distress she showed by picking her up and cuddling her warmly, he immediately turned her over to another adult for caregiving. As Bernice reported, "He doesn't like the mess and bother."

It was clear that Angela was valued and enjoyed. Bernice, when initially approached by the research staff and asked to participate in the study, had expressed considerable interest and had given her ready and willing consent. She thought it good that people were "trying to find out about babies" and thought that "how you handle a baby makes a difference later on." This attitude of acceptance of the goals of the study was reflected in the ready welcome given the home observer by all members of the family. Although it was the busy holiday season, with most family members at home during the day, the observer was made to feel at ease and was assured that the visits were not an inconvenience. The baby's paternal grandmother, in particular, was most interested in the coding procedure and offered many bits of her own child care wisdom: "You have to talk back to babies when they talk, or else they will stop trying." The observer gained acceptance because she shared the family's investment in the baby and because she reinforced their genuine interest in her development.

In terms of the quantitative categories, Angela's mother showed a definite preference for distal over proximal stimulation. On measures of tactile and kinesthetic stimulation she was slightly below the mean, but she was above the mean on mutual visual regard. The most striking finding emerging from the quantitative analyses was the high amount of verbal stimulation that Angela's mother gave. The total amount of verbal stimulation was one Standard Deviation above the mean, but this stimulation was largely noncontingent. Contingent verbal stimulation was markedly below the mean. This is an example of the special value of highly differentiated measures. Because Angela's mother talked to her so much we would probably have been unaware that only a small proportion of her verbal stimulation was contingent on the infant's positive vocalizations. This fact only became clear because we distinguished contingent from noncontingent verbal stimulation. Moveover, had we not distinguished the type of infant behavior to which the mother responded contingently, we would not have been aware that Angela's mother was selective in her responsiveness. Whereas she was below the mean in her responsiveness to the infant's positive vocalizations, she was somewhat above the mean in response to Angela's discomfort.

In terms of inanimate stimulation, Angela's environment was above the mean on the measure Inanimate Variety. Mrs. McCloud also scored significantly above the mean on Social Variety. This was particularly interesting in view of Angela's tendency to score low on social responsiveness. A closer look at the Social Variety score, a composite of several types of stimulation, revealed that whereas Mrs. McCloud scored very low on amount of social play, she scored very high on the presentation of play materials. This finding points up, again, the usefulness of having differentiated measures of stimulation.

Angela's scores on the Bayley and the Bayley clusters were all close to the mean, except for Social Responsiveness, on which she was slightly below the mean.

MICHAEL ROBERTS

Elaine Roberts took a 2-month leave of absence from her job as an elementary school teacher when her third child, Michael, was born. She told the research staff that they had been a pleasant couple of months. Her two older children, a girl, aged 7 years and a son, 6 years, were both in school, and she had had a great deal of time to devote solely to the baby. "That's not easy, you know, when you work all day and have older children." Having knowledge of child development as a result of her training in education, she enjoyed watching her baby's growth. For those same reasons, she was enthusiastic about the study and asked many questions about the purpose, method of data collection, etc. "I'd like to meet the girls who do the home visits. I think I have Spock memorized, but I'm sure I'll have questions to ask them." She explained that both she and her husband were concerned that they "do their best" for all three children. She confided that they had waited several years before having this third child, since they were concerned about their financial security.

For both Elaine and Franklin Roberts, their marriage and children were central to their lives. Both parents' familes lived in the nearby area and the Roberts' younger sister, 18 years of age, cared for the children on occasion. This was the only family member sharing in child care. The Roberts enjoyed their families, but maintained their independence from them, both social and financial. Both Mr. and Mrs. Roberts held full-time jobs. A college graduate, Elaine Roberts, age 29, had taught in the public schools for several years. Franklin Roberts, 31, had finished 2½ years of college and worked as a social work aide. An egalitarian family, both parents also shared responsibility for the children and they enjoyed mutual activities in the evenings and on weekends. Mr. Roberts spent time with the new baby every day, assisting in all aspects of his care as well as playing with him regularly. He was one of the few fathers who brought the baby to the clinic for his appointment. Like his wife, he expressed great interest in the study and talked with enthusiasm about Michael and his enjoyment of him. He took pride in the baby's accomplishments, and urged Michael to "show off" for the pediatrician. His interaction with the baby appeared warm and sensitive, and he took genuine pleasure in being with him.

Michael was seen at home in mid-July. At that time his mother was caring for him since her summer vacation had begun a month earlier. Michael was cared for by a babysitter when he was between 2 and 4½ months. Mrs. Roberts said she really preferred caring for Michael herself, even though her regular babysitter, a retired nurse, had been very good with the baby; she planned to continue using the same sitter in September when school resumed.

She appeared to enjoy the observer's visits, and appreciated the interest shown in her child. She warmly insisted on the observer's sharing the family's lunch. When the baby napped and the older children were occupied, she enjoyed chatting. These conversations ranged from political issues such as the civil rights movement to her personal feelings about homemaking, child care, and the problems of a working mother. In her comments and questions, Mrs. Roberts conveyed a great deal of sensitivity and concern regarding her children. She was particularly concerned about the issue of sibling rivalry, explaining that, although she had anticipated that it would occur, she sometimes felt anxious about how best to handle it. She also expressed concern about the pros and cons of leaving a small infant with a babysitter during the day, although she felt that Michael had shown no adverse effects. She mused that it would be "nice to be able to stay at home all year round. When you work all day, you're tired in the evenings and that causes tensions. Franklin helps a lot, but he's tired, too. I sometimes worry that we can't spend enough time with each of them . . . that's why I don't work in the summer-time, although the money would be nice." She explained that she and her husband "worried" about having the money to send the children to college and "help them out." In general, however, she seemed to feel that things were going well for all of them and she was pleased. "We've been lucky in many ways."

An attractive, vivacious, poised woman, Elaine appeared to derive great enjoyment from her role as a mother. She structured her day so that all three children were included in ongoing activities, and she was adept at distributing her own time and attention among them. An energetic person, she initiated activities designed especially to amuse the older children and often carried the baby with her as she moved about. Possessed of a wry sense of humor, she took pleasure in the baby's antics and especially enjoyed the play between the baby and the older siblings, which she skillfully encouraged and carefully monitored. Although she had relatively little time to devote solely to the baby, she interacted with him in a variety of ways and provided him with a broad range of experiences. With three active children, there was an air of constant activity and noise in the household, but Mrs. Roberts still exercised control over the children's behavior in an understated and subtle but firm way. With equanimity, she set limits within which play was encouraged. Only occasionally did she become exasperated and raise her voice, "banishing" the older children to their bedroom while she "pulled herself together."

The Roberts lived in a large, modern, well-maintained high-rise apartment building. Attractively landscaped, the building was located in a neighborhood containing other apartment buildings and private homes. Set back from any major roads, the complex contained a number of shops, professional offices, and service facilities in the basement of the building; a swimming pool and sun deck; and a large, well-equipped playground for the younger children. Many families with young children lived in the building, and in the summer the recreational areas were used extensively by mothers and their children. Elaine Roberts spent several hours each day out of doors, socializing with friends as they watched their children on the swings and in the pool. In this way, Michael was exposed to a wide variety of people. Some of the preteenage girls enjoyed holding him and taking him for a "swim" in the wading pool. Mrs. Roberts appeared to encourage this, yet she kept a careful eye on the baby's whereabouts and safety.

The Roberts' apartment consisted of two bedrooms; a large combined living/dining room; a well-equipped, modern kitchen; and bath. A small balcony, containing comfortable deck chairs and a charcoal grill, opened into the living room through sliding glass doors. The floors throughout the apartment were wooden parquet, there were large ample windows letting in a great deal of light, and all the rooms were painted in light, airy colors. The family owned a large color television set, and there were several shelves of books, including an encyclopedia set. Although the apartment was stylishly furnished and contained a number of fragile decorative items, all rooms were made accessible to the children for their play as long as they did not climb on the living room furniture or touch anything in the bookshelves. On this point, Elaine was firm and the two older children appeared to   respect her wishes.

On first appearances, Michael was rather a homely little boy, but he had a wide, engaging grin that invariably elicited smiles from his mother or siblings. Small and wiry, he was extremely active and spent most of his waking time in motion. The family owned much infant equipment, including a jumper and a walker. Michael appeared to enjoy the walker, which moved about easily on the apartment's wooden floors. He was adept at locomoting in it and could be found in many different places in the apartment during the course of the day. His mother was particularly proud of his motor development and encouraged practice, often calling for the baby to "come over" from across the room. Mrs. Roberts often placed Michael on the rug in the living room because she felt that it was important that he learn to crawl efficiently. He spent a good deal of time exploring the furniture in the living room; sometimes attempting to pull himself up on the couch or coffee table. Mrs. Roberts seemed relaxed about this exploration, although she kept a careful eye on breakable items and reprimanded the baby sternly when he attempted to touch them. Elaine Roberts appreciated the importance of toys for children's play, and there were many age-appropriate toys in the home. These included a cradle gym, a number of soft, stuffed animals, dolls, several picture books, a complex mobile, and a few noise-producing, manipulable toys. Michael's sister and brother also left numerous toys lying about the apartment, so Michael was usually within reach of several playthings. These he explored with interest, although usually for only moderate lengths of time.

Michael appeared to be primarily a socially-oriented infant and when other people were within view, he concentrated his attention on them. At these times, he might hold an object passively, mouthing it. Quick to laugh, he appeared to enjoy his siblings' playful overtures, responding with squeals of glee and intense bursts of activity. His favorite game was being tickled, and he sometimes responded with a brief whimper when brother or sister walked away after a playful interlude. Mrs. Roberts monitored the play between her children. Occasionally, she took a few minutes out of her own busy schedule to play exclusively with Michael, scooping the baby into her lap for a hilarious game of tickling or peek-a-boo. The baby responded to these overtures with delight and often fussed his mother put him down. His mother ignored this distress, explaining to the observer that "he has to learn that I have a lot of things to do."

During summer vacation, Mrs. Roberts felt that the children benefited from a certain amount of discipline and basic structure to their day. She thought that this training should start early, and although she fed Michael on a flexible schedule, she put him down for two regular naps, regardless of whether he was sleepy. His crib had been placed in the second bedroom, where the other children also slept. Delightfully decorated, with colorful pictures on the walls and bright rugs and bedspreads, this room contained a great variety of toys. The two older children's bicycles were stored in one corner of the room, and there was a large toy chest and roomy bookshelves for storing the other items. Mrs. Roberts felt that the baby enjoyed being in this room and explained that he could "just look around at everything if he doesn't want to fall asleep." When he was put in the crib, Michael was always given several toys to play with until he fell asleep.

As the third child, Michael was required to share his parents' time and affections. Despite their busy lives, however, he was provided with a great deal of warmth and attention and a diversity of meaningful experiences. His development was carefully monitored and his individual needs respected. Michael was an excitable baby and Mrs. Roberts felt that his intense involvement in play often shaded into overexcitement. Therefore, Mrs. Roberts tried to tailor Michael's exposure to stimulation to his capacity to handle it, often telling the older children to "slow down . . . play with the baby more gently." At the same time, the demands the baby made upon the family were carefully coordinated with the needs of the family as a whole. Although she discriminated sensitively the baby's distress signals, picking him up and carrying him about for a few moments when he was truly "frazzled," on other occasions Mrs. Roberts provided only an encouraging word or perhaps a change of position. As she put it, "Michael's a lively baby and we all like to see that, but he is one of three, and he can't stay on center stage all day." Mrs. Roberts skillfully managed her family without appearing harassed or overburdened. The observer gained the impression that she was a warm and responsive mother who felt competent and had a clear sense of direction in her life.

On the quantitive measures, Mrs. Roberts stands out among the six mothers in the amount of stimulation she gave. There was a lively animated quality to her interactions that was reflected in her high scores on kinesthetic and auditory stimulation and in expression of positive affect. The varied quality of her stimulation is indexed by high scores on Variety of Social Stimulation and Variety of Inanimate Stimulation, both of which were well above the mean. Mrs. Roberts was also above average in the immediacy of her response to the infant's distress. Finally, she was highly responsive to Michael's positive behavior, as indicated by the amount of her speech that was contingent on his positive vocalizations. Reflecting this highly stimulating and responsive environment, Michael scored above the mean on all dependent variables.

LEROY SIMMONS

Susan Simmons, a pretty, shy young woman, gave birth to her first child, Leroy, when she was 17 years old. She dropped out of high school during the middle of her sophomore year when her pregnancy became apparent. Unmarried, she was totally dependent financially on her parents, and she lived with them until the baby's delivery. She said that she spent the time watching television in their apartment and visiting with friends. When first seen by the research staff, the baby was 2 months of age. At that time, Susan was still living with her parents, but confided to the pediatrician that she hoped to return to school "very soon." In the meantime she was planning to find a job, preferably one where she could work in the evenings. She hoped to be able to bring home some money so that she and the baby's father could move into an apartment together. His income as a parking lot attendant was not sufficient to support the three of them. Despite her expressed interest in school and job, her plans seemed vague and unrealistic, and she conveyed a mood of apathy and resignation. The pediatrician described her reaction to participation in the study as "interested, but stand-offish." The financial reimbursement to participants appeared to be an important factor in her consent. A reserved attitude toward the research staff continued during the home visits.

Susan Simmons was still living with her parents when seen 3 months later. She was working 5 days a week as a waitress at a local carry-out. Her mother, Mrs. McKnight, cared for Leroy while she worked. Susan still expressed some interest in returning to school, but pointed out that the current school year was almost over, "so I probably won't go till next year some time." When asked about her plans to establish a household with the baby's father, she now seemed uncertain. She reported that he saw the baby only two or three times a week and "liked" him, but played with him only briefly during these visits and never helped with caregiving tasks. She said that she would like to "get away" from her present living arrangements "soon." She rather vaguely mentioned the possibility of moving in with her "sister-in-law" who lived alone with her three children, but added that it was improbable because she lived "clear across town."

There was considerable confusion and difficulty in arranging for the home observations. Susan was not sure her mother would want the observer to come. Although she agreed to approach her mother on the subject, she repeatedly failed to do so. It was finally suggested that the observer come to explain the coding procedure on a day when Susan could be at the home. At that time the observer could request the maternal grandmother's cooperation. Susan's position in the home was apparently a subordinate one; she was anxious about imposing on her mother.

Leroy's grandmother was most cooperative when approached and expressed interest in the idea of a study of babies. She proudly pointed out Leroy's accomplishments and invited the observer to come "anytime. . . . He's a good baby! We'd be glad for you to look at him."

The McKnight's apartment occupied two floors over a store on a busy commercial street in the inner city. The surrounding neighborhood was dirty, run-down, rat-infested and had one of the highest crime rates in the metropolitan area. During spring 1968, violent civil disturbances had centered in this area, and many buildings and stores were burned and looted. The apartment itself was in a state of serious disrepair. The stairway leading directly from the street into the living room was dimly lit, and the bannister swayed as one walked up the stairs. One overhead light, which ordinarily illuminated the steep climb, was broken at the time of the visits. Furnishings in the apartment were sparse. Most items appeared to be old, the sofa and armchairs sagged, and the upholstery was faded and torn. Only the television set appeared to be new. The walls were chipped and soiled, with remnants of wallpaper appearing in some places; they were adorned with religious pictures and three or four calendars, some out of date. There were a few rugs on the floor, and the floor itself was dirty and scuffed. The door to the one bathroom was off its hinges and rested against the wall and the toilet was backed up during the 2 days that the observer was there. In the kitchen, scraps of food were scattered on the floor. Although there were windows in every room, only the kitchen appeared light and bright. In all other rooms the shades were drawn and lights were turned on during the day. Throughout the apartment, children's toys, bottles, and occasional articles of clothing were scattered on the floor. Roaches scuttled about in some of the rooms. The apartment was hot and dry, and the smell of foods lingered in the air.

The household was a large one. In addition to her mother and stepfather, Susan's two older brothers and three sisters shared the apartment. One of her sisters, aged 19, had two young children of her own, and another sister was only 4 years old. Thus, it was a family consisting of 11 people divided among three generations, ranging from Leroy, aged 6 months, to the maternal grandfather, only 42 years. Members of the family came and went frequently, but Leroy's grandmother appeared to function as a sort of pivot around which this activity revolved. She spent most of her time in the home, caring not only for her youngest child but for her grandchildren as well. She was in charge of the household and appeared to be the final authority in matters concerning child care. On the other hand, adult members of the family seemed to be responsible for buying their own food and preparing it. The kitchen was the "communal" room in the house. Parents were responsible for feeding their own children in the evenings and they slept with them. The bedrooms of the apartment were divided along sub family lines, with Leroy sharing a small room with his mother. Delegation of responsibility within the household was a complex affair and, not surprisingly, Susan's relationship to her mother was ambiguous.

Mrs. McKnight, a large, tired-looking woman, spent most of her time moving about the apartment, cleaning and "minding" the children. She spent a considerable amount of her time disciplining, speaking to the children in a weary, irritated fashion, but she still managed to convey gentleness and affection. The children in turn appeared to like her. The older children were very active and occupied much of her attention and time. She did not encourage them to play with Leroy because she did not want him to "get hurt."

Although Leroy was able to sit up by the time he was 5½ months old, he was usually placed on his back or stomach on the living room sofa or on the floor for long periods of the day. During the morning, he was usually given several toys and left in the bedroom alone. Frequently these objects fell out of his reach or were taken by the older children when he was not looking, so that he spent moderately long periods of time having nothing with which to play. This did not seem to bother him greatly. He was ordinarily in a position to watch the other people as they moved about, and he seemed to enjoy observing the social ebb and flow around him. He followed passersby closely, with an alert, animated expression and frequently smiled or cooed when he caught another person's eye. During these encounters, he often reacted with a burst of motor activity, but he did not fuss when contact was broken. Playful interludes with the children or with Mrs. McKnight occurred sporadically and were typically geared to the other person's inclination to play rather than to Leroy's indications of readiness. He especially seemed to enjoy being taken onto his grandmother's lap, and reacted by snuggling into her arms and then reaching out to grasp her clothing or touch her face. At these times, Mrs. McKnight was at her most relaxed. Her worried expression faded as she stroked and patted Leroy, smiling at him and talking to him gently. He clearly occupied a special place in her affections.

An even-tempered baby, Leroy seldom cried. When he did, his grandmother would pop a bottle of milk into his mouth. A partially filled bottle was usually near him. He was adept at locating it and sucked on it sporadically throughout the day.

The toys available to him—several small rattles, blocks, a deflated balloon, a small wooden doll—were simple in nature and appeared to be hand-me-downs from previous infants. They were not highly stimulating toys, and he gave them only passing attention. He preferred to manipulate household objects, such as a piece of newspaper or a small transistor radio. Despite the paucity of play materials, he was adept at manipulation, incorporating a number of different schema into his play, such as tearing, banging, and patting. Occasionally he maintained interest for as long as 5 minutes. With the exception of the bottles, Leroy made only truncated efforts to regain an object that had fallen out of reach.

Mrs. McKnight's interest in Leroy's developmental advancement was selective. He was encouraged to feed himself with the bottle, but at no time during either home observation did he receive a meal of solid food. This heavy reliance upon bottles for both nutrition and pacification appeared to meet the needs of his caregiver. Being a quiet baby, he tolerated intermittent attention;

he conveniently faded into the background. Once during the visit, for example, he managed to inch himself to the edge of the sofa without being observed and fell onto the floor. Even then he did not cry. Possibly because of this unobtrusiveness, he was seldom the target of his grandmother's irritation, as were the older children. Occasionally he was told to "Stop that fussing or you'll be sorry." His cheerful nature and quiet passivity were rewarded; he was appreciated and "liked" by his grandmother even though he was not the center of her attentions.

Leroy's scores on all of the infant variables hovered around the mean. Leroy's grandmother provided him with average amounts of both social and inanimate stimulation. She was slightly above the mean of the sample on the composite social stimulation measure, Variety, and in the amount of time she spent talking to him and holding him. She was close to the mean in the expression of positive affect. She was slightly above the mean in contingent response to distress, but slightly below in contingent response to positive vocalizations. In spite of her impoverished circumstances, she provided him with a fair variety of play materials, but these were somewhat low on responsiveness.

DARYL BRADLEY

Danette and Charles Bradley lived with their four children on the second floor of an old, well-preserved house in a primarily residential section of the city. Located only two blocks from a busy commercial north-south artery leading from the suburbs into the downtown area, the neighborhood was nonetheless relatively quiet, with old frame houses on tree-lined streets. The streets and modest front yards were, for the most part, clean and neat. Although not affluent in character, the neighborhood bore the signs of care and attention on the part of the residents. The Bradleys shared the house with Mrs. Bradley's sister and brother-in-law, one family living on each floor. The Bradleys maintained daily contact with their in-laws and felt that the neighborhood was an acceptable one in which to raise their children, but they dreamed of saving enough money to buy a single-family house in the suburbs. Both parents shared this goal, one toward which they had been working for 5 years.

Danette Bradley, 24 years old, left school to give birth to her first child when she was 17 years old. During the next several years, a daughter and two more sons were added to the family. Her husband, 10 years older than she, left high school to enlist in the Army, then finished his education while in the service. He supported his growing family from his modest earnings as a construction worker. Danette sometimes contributed to the family's income by working as a domestic at one of the large Washington hotels. While she found this work "hard and tiring," she liked being able to bolster the family's income. She told the research staff that "My husband and I want the very best for Daryl and his brothers and sister. I stopped working when Daryl came along, but I would like to start again as soon as I can. We just hope we'll have enough money to get them through college and pay for it ourselves. Sometimes it just doesn't seem possible . . . there are so many expenses with four children. Sometimes we worry that one of us won't be able to work. That would make a big difference. I don't like to think about it."

The Bradley's home reflected both the necessity of living on a tight budget and the parents' desire to provide the family with comfortable, pleasurable surroundings. The apartment was small for six people, consisting of two small bedrooms, a living room, kitchen and bath. Despite being cramped, it was furnished and decorated in a cheerful, pleasant manner, with care taken in many small decorative touches. The furniture was comfortable and adequate with one or two quite new pieces. Mrs. Bradley kept the window shades pulled three-quarters of the way down most of the time, regardless of the weather, giving the rooms a somewhat dimly lit atmosphere. This was offset somewhat by the bright colors used in decorating and by the light from the television set and lamps. Every room in the apartment was neat and tidy. Danette Bradley was proud of her home, and it was an inviting place to visit.

At home during the day with her three youngest children, she spent her time cleaning the apartment, preparing meals for the family, relaxing in front of the television set, and, occasionally, visiting with her sister downstairs. In her relationship with the observer, she was an energetic, talkative, and warm-natured young woman. She seemed to take pleasure in her children, although, on occasion, she grew restless in the absence of more adult companionship. She said that she ordinarily kept the television on for the greater part of the day "to keep me company." She was sensitive to each of her children's demands, quick and generous of her time and attention in responding to them, and adept at monitoring all three simultaneously. Although she expressed some anxieties to the observer about discipline problems, she appeared to be well in control of the children, and "good behavior" was highly valued. With her firm manner, she was able to maintain a reasonable level of order in the crowded household, although this required her almost constant attention. On several occasions, she rather wistfully conveyed some frustration with her living circumstances, "Children need more room. They need a big yard to play in."

Mrs. Bradley's concern for her children's welfare was reflected in her spontaneous comments regarding their health. She mentioned that the baby had a cold recently and that she had begun to take him to a private pediatrician, rather than to the neighborhood clinic, because "they don't do anything for a baby with a cold at that clinic." A number of her comments indicated that both she and her husband understood that a healthy developmental course in a child was not an automatic thing. Included among the few books in the home was a paperback on child care. "You have to take good care of your kids. You have to let them know that you care." She reported that her husband tried to spend some time in the evenings with the children, although "He's really very tired when he comes home. He likes to put his feet up and relax, and he doesn't like them to run around and make noise." Reported to be "very fond" of Daryl, he had relatively little time to spend with him, although he managed to play with him occasionally.

The Bradley's interest in Daryl's well-being was also reflected in their interest in, and compliance with the goals of the study. After asking a number of questions of the contacting pediatrician, Mrs. Bradley agreed, "Of course, you can come look at Daryl any time. Anything that will help you."

A handsome baby, Daryl was a regular "participant-observer" in the family's activities. He was able to sit adeptly by himself at 5½ months of age, so he was usually placed on the sofa in the living room with a large pillow propped behind his back. From this central vantage point, he spent most of his waking hours watching the social activity around him. Although he was sometimes provided with objects to play with—a rattle, or a small, easily manipulable household object, such as a spool of thread—he sustained only moderate interest in them. He perfered to attend to the people around him. Although he was not a motorically active infant, Daryl spent a great deal of time cooing and babbling to himself, especially when focusing on the activity going on in the room. He seldom, however, fussed or cried. He appeared to be a very self-sufficient baby, making few overt demands on his mother for time and attention.

Daryl responded with enthusiasm to his mother's overtures, watching her face, cooing, smiling and occasionally reaching out to touch her clothing or face. Compared with other mothers in the study, Mrs. Bradley spent only a moderate amount of time interacting with Daryl, perhaps in part because of the claims the other children made upon her. She handled Daryl confidently, looking and speaking to him from across the room and frequently approaching him to adjust his position or to retrieve his pacifier. She was adept and efficient in feeding him and in other caretaking activities. However, she was notably reserved in expressing positive feelings and spent little time in leisurely forms of contact such as social play. In many subtle ways, she appeared to cater to Daryl's immature qualities and needs. For example, she rarely allowed him to experience the slightest discomfort, usually responding rapidly but with little spirit or animation. She did not seem to resent the demands he made upon her, perhaps because he required relatively little attention. She seemed to appreciate his self-sufficiency, while, at the same time, she did not actively encourage independent functioning. Thus, her mothering combined an easy and sensitive acceptance of the baby with a relative neglect of more intensely stimulating forms of interaction. Mother and baby seemed to suit each other well.

On the other hand, Daryl received a fair amount of playful attention from his brother and sister, aged 3 and 4 years. They enjoyed teasing him by dangling toys in front of him and then snatching them away as well as playing more social games like tickling. Daryl welcomed these overtures, often holding his arms out toward his brother and sister, smiling and laughing loudly. He appeared not to mind the teasing, reacting with pleasure to the social aspects of the encounter rather than with frustration at the abrupt disappearance of the toy. His mother approved of his pleasurable response; at the same time, she monitored his reactions for any indications of distress.

Thus, Daryl's experience was characterized by concerned parenting largely in the form of sensitive and efficient caregiving with little "extra" added stimulation. His world was organized and monitored by his mother with an eye toward his comfort, but was somewhat limited in the variety of input specifically directed to him. He was a centrally located observer of the family's activities. He watched everything around him with absorbed interest, and reacted to social approaches, especially by his siblings, with delight.

Quantitatively, Mrs. Bradley was close to the mean on all measures. She was low in expressing positive feelings, and physical contact with Daryl was primarily passive; she scored above average on tactile and below average on kinesthetic stimulation. She was a mother who talked to her baby rather infrequently, but a high proportion of her verbalizations were contingent. Her contingent responsiveness was more marked in relation to the baby's distress than to his positive vocalizations. She was slightly above average on variety of social stimulation, and the variety of play materials she made available to Daryl was also slightly above average.

On the whole, Mrs. Bradley seemed to be a mother who was trying her best to give the baby what he needed, but the quality of her interaction was muted. Daryl's functioning was below average on most measures, particularly on the cognitive-motivational clusters, but he was above average in social responsiveness. This is an example of a case in which it would be interesting to have differentiated quantitative measures of the amount of stimulation provided by siblings. Such information might help clarify the incongruity between Daryl's levels of functioning in the cognitive-motivational and social spheres.

JENNIFER FORD

Jennifer Ford's parents were committed to an upwardly mobile lifestyle for their family. The young couple rented a pleasant, spacious house in the Northwest section of the city, a primarily residential area. They were proud of the financial independence and relative security that they had achieved for themselves and their three small children. A college graduate, Beverly Ford, 29, taught elementary school in the District of Columbia. Her 31-year-old husband, Richard, who had completed 2 years of college, worked as a salesman in a local department store. Both parents had worked full time throughout their childbearing years, since they hoped and planned to buy a home of their own some time in the future. When initially approached about participating in the study, Mrs. Ford had been interested and eager to do so, even though she had already returned to full-time employment, and the baby would have to be seen at the babysitter's home.

The Fords had thought carefully about day care arrangements for Jennifer and had found a sitter whom they felt was competent and reliable. Mrs. White, an elderly retired schoolteacher, owned her own home, which she shared with a niece. She supported herself by caring for young children. The Fords began leaving Jennifer with her during the day when the baby was just over 2½ months old and this arrangement had continued uninterrupted throughout the course of the study. On weekday mornings at about 8, one parent or the other left Jennifer at Mrs. White's home. When she had finished at school in midafternoon, Mrs. Ford picked Jennifer up on her way home.

Because Mrs. White cared for Jennifer during most of the daytime hours, the baby was observed with her as caregiver. During the initial contact with the pediatrician on the research staff, Mrs. Ford reported that Jennifer had considerable contact with her mother and father and with her two older sisters. Mr. Ford helped diaper, bathe, and feed the baby; and he enjoyed playing with her. Her 7-year-old sister also occasionally helped in feeding and bathing her. Mrs. Ford expressed pleasure and pride in the baby, although her statements about Jennifer's development tended to be rather undifferentiated, e.g., "She's a good baby," or "She seems like a happy child." The interviewer felt that because Mrs. Ford had such a strong need to continue working and because of her confidence in Mrs. White, she was comfortable with the child care arrangements.

For her part, Mrs. White had clearly articulated beliefs about child rearing to which she adhered strongly. At the same time, she seemed to be sensitive to possible criticism. She was extremely reluctant to allow the observer to come to her home for an observation. When first approached by Mrs. Ford regarding the visits, Mrs. White had flatly refused to allow them. When the baby's mother, at her own initiative, offered her extra money, she agreed reluctantly. Both home visits were nonetheless late because Mrs. White repeatedly put off the observer, telling her that suggested times were "inconvenient." The observer was concerned that the data might be grossly distorted because of this extreme reluctance. However, at the end of the first visit, Mrs. White smiled, invited the observer back and said that she had enjoyed her company. She admitted that, "because of all the modern regulations," she had feared that the observer was coming to judge her caregiving. Although she seemed reassured at the end of the home visit, she still asked, "Now, what do you think?"

Mrs. White's style of caregiving focused almost exclusively on the physical needs of the three children in her care. She handled the routines of feeding, bathing, and diapering competently; but she seemed insensitive to Jennifer's signals. Although Jennifer was considerably more demanding of attention than was the other infant, she was careful to provide both babies with equal amounts of stimulation. While feeding or changing diapers, she talked to them in a matter-of-fact way. Beyond these brief and relatively perfunctory encounters, she gave little stimulation. Both were kept in carbeds during most of the day, each baby placed on the floor in a corner of the dining room out of sight of each other and of visitors to the house. A toddler, who was also being cared for by Mrs. White, was not allowed near either infant. Both babies spent a considerable amount of time dozing or sleeping, and Mrs. White did not want them to be "disturbed." Jennifer was provided with only one toy, a stuffed animal, which was placed beyond reach so that she could do nothing but look at it. During both visits she had a pacifier, although she only occasionally handled or sucked it.

Mrs. White also valued discipline in child rearing. Feeding, for example, was rigidly scheduled with no deviations even if Jennifer screamed with hunger. During the first home visit, she told the observer that she had recently argued with the mother of the toddler in her care, insisting that he should be toilet trained by the time he was 2½ years. The mother, feeling that training should be postponed until a later age, had taken the baby out of Mrs. White's care for a short time. At the time of the visits, however, he was back and training was proceeding on a determined schedule.

Jennifer was a pretty infant, small, compact, and rather "impish" in appearance, with a shock of curly hair. Perhaps because she spent many of her waking hours lying in the small carbed, her activity level was low. She was never observed to turn over. On the rare occasions when Mrs. White sat her up, she quickly toppled over again. Perhaps most striking was her difficulty in grasping and picking up objects, although when she was offered a pacifier, she would occasionally reach toward it. This fumbling approach to the inanimate world was not, however, matched by her social responsiveness. She readily smiled and cooed when the caregiver approached and appeared to enjoy being picked up, held, and talked to.

Perhaps because these social interludes were infrequent and of short duration, Jennifer spent a good bit of her time fussing and crying. Although Mrs. White usually responded quickly to the baby's cries, her responses were often inappropriate. On one occasion, for example, when Jennifer had been lying in the carbed crying for a long time, Mrs. White finally took her from the bed and sat her in the corner of the sofa. Jennifer immediately stopped crying and looked around the room with interest, but a few moments later, because she had not been propped, she toppled over onto her side and resumed crying. Hearing her cries from the other room, Mrs. White decided that Jennifer did not want to sit up and returned her to the carbed. As Jennifer continued to cry, she changed her diaper and gave her water to drink and then seemed perplexed and impatient when the baby continued to cry. She told the observer that Jennifer could not be hungry, since lunch was still 30 minutes away and concluded that she must be sleepy. Left alone, Jennifer cried herself to sleep and was then awakened 15 minutes later for a feeding.

The care provided by Mrs. White was highly consistent with the tidiness and order of her home. Her house was located on a pretty, well-maintained street. She had planted a lovely garden, which she tended faithfully with the help of her niece. The spotless, modern kitchen was equipped with appliances which had all been carefully chosen to match the yellow decor. Several pieces of furniture in the house appeared to be new, and all were in excellent condition. Armchairs and the sofa were neatly provided with lace anamacasters. During both visits, a bouquet of fresh flowers from her garden adorned the living room coffee table. All shades in the house were drawn even though the weather outside was bright and sunny. Asking the observer if she had enough light to write by, Mrs. White confessed that, although it might seem strange to keep the house darkened, she felt it was more comfortable that way. Her pride in her orderly home was reflected in her courtesy to the observer. At both visits, she served coffee on a tray set with a lace doily.

Mrs. White guarded her lifestyle vigilantly. The babies in her care were treated as extensions of this carefully controlled environment. The children were expected to be seen and not heard, to behave "neatly," within defined limits. If the baby did not conform, as in the case of Jennifer's continued crying, Mrs. White seemed at a loss and reacted with subdued expressions of irritation. For Jennifer, who showed a need for stimulation and a capacity for responding to the people around her, this environment proved to be stifling and debilitating.

This environment is one of the most extreme in the sample in its low level of stimulation. Mrs. White's profile is striking in its virtual absence of variation in her interaction with the infant. In addition, Jennifer had no objects to play with other than a pacifier, which was relatively low in responsiveness. On some measures like contingent responsiveness and kinesthetic stimulation, Mrs. White was less extreme, but still below the mean. Jennifer's development reflected this high degree of sensory deprivation.

The fact that she was confined to a carbed during much of the day and had few opportunities to exercise her limbs or to practice fine motor skills, together with the fact that she had no toys to manipulate, resulted in few opportunities for her to practice fine or gross motor skills. Since the only "plaything" she was given was a pacifier, she recieved minimal scores on both Variety of Inanimate Objects and Responsiveness of Inanimate Objects.

In all respects, Jennifer was functioning below the mean of the sample. Her scores were particularly depressed in fine and gross motor development, in cognitive-motivational development, and in general cognitive functioning. Her ability to reach and grasp objects was most severely affected; her score fell two standard deviations below the mean. Her scores on the exploratory behavior measures and preference for novel objects were also low. Jennifer is a vivid example of the debilitating effects on a young infant of an environment low in both social and inanimate stimulation.

RACHEL JEFFRIES

Rosie Jeffries, an attractive, retiring young woman of 22, was eager to participate in the study after hearing about it from the pediatrician at the clinic where she took her three young children for their regular checkups. She explained that, although she had worked briefly in a restaurant upon completing high school, she had been a "housewife" at home for the last 3 years, since her first baby had been born. Although her husband, Anthony, aged 24, was currently working only 4 days a week as a delivery man for a local department store, she felt it was important that she stay with her children "at least until they go to school." "I guess they need to have me around," she volunteered. "Besides, I like small babies, and Rachel is such a good baby." Admitting that the family had a hard time making ends meet, she, nonetheless, said that she did not plan to seek work in the foreseeable future.

The Jeffries rented a large, rather cavernous, dark apartment located over a store in a busy commercial area just six blocks down the street from Leroy Simmons' family. The young couple lived alone with their children, although Mrs. Jeffries volunteered that both of their extended families lived in the immediate area. The street, which would be almost totally burned out during the violence of 1968, was dirty, congested, and rat-infested. The stairs and hallway leading to the apartment were poorly lit and shabby. The plaster was cracked, and the paint was peeling in the hallway and in the interior of the five-room apartment. The family had clearly made an attempt, using their limited income, to furnish and equip the apartment attractively. Even though the overall effect was of five sparsely furnished, strung-out rooms lacking color and light, everything was clean and tidy. The living room contained one overstuffed sofa, enhanced by two brightly colored pillows, one armchair, one wooden folding chair, two lamps, a television, and a small coffee table. Clean curtains hung at the window overlooking the roof of an adjoining building; and several pictures, taken from magazines, were tacked to the wall. A

TV Guide, several magazines, and old newspapers were neatly stacked on the coffee table.

Mr. and Mrs. Jeffries shared one bedroom with the infant; and the two older boys, 18 months and 3 years of age, shared the second. At the time of the visits, both beds were neatly made and covered with clean, faded cotton spreads. The children's bed had no pillows. A small table in the parents' bedroom was used for changing the baby's diapers. The kitchen, at the end of the hallway, looked out over an adjoining rooftop. It had an old gas stove, a sink whose faucet dripped continually, a refrigerator with a broken handle on the door, a metal-topped table, and three straight-backed chairs. But in spite of the dirty paint and cracked plaster it had a tidy look.

Mrs. Jeffries was careful to identify the observer before opening the apartment door. "We have to be careful here," she explained. "That's why the children and I spend most of our time inside when Anthony is at work." On his days off, however, the family often went out to visit relatives or to the zoo. During the week, the apartment served as the children's playground, where the two older ones raced about actively inventing games of chase and playing with an old tricycle and the few other toys available to them.

Mrs. Jeffries spent much of her time in the living room, watching television, playing with the baby, and entering into the older children's activities in a gentle, good-humored way. Their consistently high activity level did not seem to irritate her; she laughed at their antics and, on occasion, when wishing to redirect or moderate their energies, picked one or the other up, cuddled him, and suggested a change of pace. Her approach was consistently positive and she frequently praised them. On the rare occasions when she scolded, she did so in a firm but pleasant manner. Despite the paucity of toys, the two little boys were exuberant, curious, and outgoing and demonstrated a clear affection for their mother.

Rachel was handled in a similar fashion. Always extremely gentle with her, Mrs. Jeffries spent long periods of time holding her, talking to her, or playing games such as peek-a-boo. She often kept Rachel beside her, rocking her back and forth in a stroller while she watched television or talked on the telephone. Rachel was usually near her mother and in the center of her brothers' activities; her world in the dark, sparse apartment was cheerful, characterized by varied, changing stimulation.

An alert, chubby baby, she responded to the people around her in an exuberant, bubbly fashion. Although she did not vocalize very often, her face was usually wreathed in smiles as she followed her brothers' moves and as she monitored her mother's activities. Frequently, she smiled to herself as she observed two other family members smiling at each other. Commenting on her baby's happy expression, Rosie told the observer that "She's like that with her Daddy, too. I think that's why he plays with her so much when he's at home. He seems to be partial to her." When approached by her mother or a brother, Rachel characteristically held her arms out and wiggled with excitement. When a person walked away from her, she did not cry, but continued to watch with interest. She seldom cried unless hungry or fatigued. When distressed, she responded to her mother's quick interventions by cuddling into Rosie's arms, grasping her mother's dress, and quieting. At these times she cooed with pleasure as her mother talked soothingly to her. The attentions of her brothers did not calm her when she cried; she visually sought out her mother and responded only to her ministrations.

An active, sturdy baby, Rachel enjoyed sitting in her stroller or on the sofa, a posture which she could maintain for as long as 10 minutes without falling. When placed on the floor, she seemed to enjoy waving her arms and kicking her legs, rolling from back to stomach, and hunching herself up unto all fours, after which she would take a few clumsy crawling steps backward. When her mother encouraged her to crawl forward to reach a roll of twisted newspaper, a favorite game between them, Rachel would smile broadly and make repeated, lunging movements toward the paper. Rosie watched her daughter with gentle amusement, and praised and encouraged her efforts. Then, after several moments, she would slide the paper to just within the baby's reach. Grasping it, Rachel explored the paper with relish each time this game occurred, tearing off bits of paper, crumpling them in her fist, and banging the entire roll against the floor. On occasion she was observed to smile as she explored.

Throughout the course of the two visits, Rachel was provided with four different toys, all rather simple in nature. These she explored only briefly and the observer was left with the impression that she had long since exhausted their interesting possibilities. Perhaps realizing this, during each visit, Rosie gave her several household objects to play with—a match box with matches inside, several crumpled, brightly colored playing cards, a large piece of cellophane, and an empty grocery sack. Rachel turned her full attention to each as it was given to her and played with it for sustained periods of time. She became fussy only when an object fell out of her reach, a situation usually quickly remedied by her mother. When she tired of the objects near her, Rachel usually resumed watching the social activity in the room around her; infrequently she simply sat quietly and stared at the television screen.

It was clear to the observer that Mrs. Jeffries took pride in her children. A solicitous mother, she responded to the children in a consistently positive fashion. Perhaps because she chose to stay indoors during the day, she filled her hours by immersing herself in their care and amusement. Relaxed in her caregiving, she fed Rachel on a flexible schedule and arranged for a quiet place for her to nap when she became tired. She set up a gently structured, highly contingent schedule of caregiving and, within an overtly dreary environment, managed to create a home filled with warmth, spontaneity, and good humor.

Mrs. Jeffries, although clearly a highly stimulating mother, was somewhat inconsistent on the quantitative measures. She scored well above the sample mean on measures of Kinesthetic Stimulation and on Level and Variety of social input. Her high score on Kinesthetic Stimulation reflects the frequency with which she rocked the baby in the buggy. Her observed warmth toward

Rachel is seen in her score on Expression of Positive Affect, which was one standard deviation above the mean. She was above average in the immediacy of her response to distress, although she fell somewhat below the mean on contingent responsiveness to the baby's positive vocalizations. Although she did not provide Rachel with a great variety of toys, those she gave her were somewhat above the mean in responsiveness. The quantitative profile, thus, confirms the observer's impression that Mrs. Jeffries was a mother who managed to provide her baby with a richly stimulating environment despite her very limited means. Reflecting this high level of stimulation, Rachel was one of the most advanced babies in motor, cognitive, and social development. She scored at least 1 standard deviation above the mean on all measures of infant functioning.

These case descriptions illustrate how proximal stimulation variables operate in a larger social context. They give one some feeling for the complex relations between maternal care and infant development. One gains a glimpse of the varieties of physical settings in which families thrive and have difficulties and, in addition, one obtains occasional insights into the myriad motivations that influence a mother's behavior with an infant. We believe that theoretical understanding of human development is often sharpened by coming back to reality, that by getting closer to the lives and feelings of people we increase our depth of understanding of the environment and its complexities.

7

OVERVIEW

The early environment of the infant is not simply warm or cold, responsive or unresponsive, depriving or stimulating. These global characterizations mask the richness and complexity of the infant's experiences. We have analyzed the natural environment and have differentiated it on many dimensions. We found significant relations between these dimensions of early experience and infant characteristics at 6 months. We believe that we have taken some small steps in elaborating our understanding of early experiences.

We found this research alternately exciting and sobering, challenging and frustrating. In every phase of the study we were impelled to examine our fundemental assumptions and methodologies. In the development of methods, in the choice of environmental and infant variables, in the course of data collection and statistical analysis, and especially in the process of attempting to give meaning to the findings, we became increasingly aware of the limitations of the concepts and methods available. We were forced again and again to examine and then question certain basic theoretical and methodological preconceptions. Many of the questions raised could not be resolved in this study; but in identifying them, we think we have gained some conceptual clarity. We believe that articulating the issues and setting them out for examination is a first step toward more adequate conceptualization and design.

A recurrent problem centered around the appropriate level at which to describe the early environment. From the beginning we were convinced that global characterizations of the environment were inadequate. To understand the role of early experience, we felt we had to look at discrete behaviors of mothers and properties of the environment.

In the analysis of the environment the first distinction we made was between stimulation from people and stimulation from inanimate objects. Within the social environment we distinguished the sensory modalities in which a mother provides stimulation—visual, auditory, tactile, and kinesthetic stimulation; her expression of positive affect; and the extent to which she is responsive to the infant's positive vocalizations as well as his cries and frets. Some discrete behavioral measures were conbined into higher order categories, Level and Variety of Social Stimulation. In the inanimate environment we delineated several attributes of objects: the variety of playthings available and their complexity and responsiveness.

We found that few of these variables were highly interrelated, a confirmation of the value of differentiating the environment. Rather, the characteristics of the inanimate and the social environments were highly independent. There was less independence among the variables of the social environment, but few variables were so highly related that they could be considered redundant. One mother may talk to her infant a great deal and yet be relatively unresponsive to his distress signals; another may hold or rock her baby for long periods of time, but respond infrequently to his vocalizations. A provocative finding, never previously reported, was that the degree of relation among the environmental variables was affected by the sex of the child. On the whole, there is more independence among the measures of the environment for boys than for girls.

Consistent with our conviction as to the importance of differentiating the environment, we felt it necessary to analyze infant characteristics and functions. Our image of the young infant has changed strikingly in the past decade. We no longer see him as an undifferentiated organism who responds globally and diffusely to stimulation, but we see him as an individual with some degree of differentiation in his response repertoire. Therefore, we broke down the global developmental quotient into a variety of functions, distinguishing gross and fine motor skills, vocalization and language, social responsiveness, object permanence, and such cognitive-motivational functions as goal-directedness and secondary circular reactions. We also measured the infant's visual and manipulative exploratory behavior and his preference for novel objects.

RELATIONSHIPS BETWEEN THE
ENVIRONMENT AND THE INFANT

The fundamental significance of this study lies in the findings that differential relationships exist between specific dimensions of the environment and specific dimensions of infant development. These findings have major implications for theories of early enviornmental influence. We found that some enviornmental variables are more highly related to certain infant characteristics than other variables and that certain variables show highly specific effects, while others have more pervasive relationships with infant development. Especially striking are the different orders of relationships of near and distance receptor stimulation with the infant variables. Visual and auditory stimulation are related only to social responsiveness, while kinesthetic stimulation is related significantly to social and cognitive-motivational characteristics. Kinesthetic Stimulation and Variety of Inanimate Objects also show important differences in relation to the dependent variables. Although they both influence many aspects of infant development, the magnitude of the correlation varies with specific variables. The variables with which Kinesthetic Stimulation is most highly related are Goal Directedness and Object Permanence; Variety of Inanimate Objects is most highly related to Problem Solving and Manipulation of Novel Objects.

A pointed example of the specificity of relationships is the high correlation between Responsiveness of Inanimate Objects and Secondary Circular Reactions. This finding is noteworthy because of its congruence with theoretical expectations and because of its implications for the development of more complex cognitive skills. Secondary circular reactions are precursors of cognitive skills such as problem solving. Through repeated encounters with objects that provide feedback as a result of his manipulations, the infant learns about means-ends relationships.

The importance of distinguishing different kinds of maternal responsiveness was emphasized by our finding of low correlations between two contingency measures, the mother's contingent response to the infant's positive vocalizations and the mother's contingent response to the infant's distress. Mothers who are responsive to the infant's coos and vocalizations do not necessarily respond rapidly to him when he is crying. Moreover, these two aspects of maternal responsiveness have very different effects. Contingent responsiveness to the infant's vocalizations has a selective effect. It facilitates the infant's positive vocalizations. Rapid response to the infant's frets and cries shows more pervasive effects. It was positively associated with both fine and gross motor development and three of the four cognitive-motivational variables.

Both Kinesthetic Stimulation and Variety of Social Stimulation are highly related to the early manifestations of object permanence. Our interpretation is that each makes a distictive contribution. Varied experiences, occurring in different contexts, may help the infant develop an elaborated schema of the mother, which in turn is associated with the growing realization that she exists independently of his immediate interactions with her. It is probably equally important for the development of object permanence that the infant give up the symbiotic view of himself and his mother and define the boundaries of his own body, a process which may be facilitated by kinesthetic stimulation.

There is a long-standing belief that motor development is primarily maturationally determined and is not significantly influenced by the environment. We found, however, several environmental variables related to motor development. The amount of kinesthetic stimulation, the extent of the mother's responsiveness to the infants's indications of distress, and the variety of play materials available to the infant were all significantly related to the Bayley Psychomotor Index. These findings indicate that motor development is not totally independent of the infant's experiences.

Exploratory behavior and preference for novel stimuli showed the strongest relationships with the variety and complexity of play materials. Rubenstein (1967) in a previous study emphasized the social antecedents of exploratory behavior and preference for novelty. She found that these infant behaviors were related to a general index of social stimulation, any maternal attentiveness. In that sample, however, mothers who were more attentive also made a variety of toys available to their babies. It was not possible in that study to sort out the relative importance of social and inanimate stimulation because these two components of the environment were positively interrelated. In the present sample, amount of social and inanimate stimulation are largely unrelated, and we find that inanimate stimulation has a stronger relationship with exploratory behavior and preference for novelty than does social stimulation.

The cognitive-motivational variables—Goal Directedness, Reaching and Grasping, Secondary Circular Reactions, and Problem Solving—have special theoretical significance. The term "cognitive-motivational" was chosen with some deliberateness to express our conviction that these two domains of infant behavior have close interdependence. We thought of these activities as expressions of the infant's motivation to learn about and to master the environment, as early manifestations of effectance motivation (White, R. W., 1959).

These cognitive-motivational variables reflect a similar quality of reaching out, acting on, and evoking some response from the environment. Although several theoretical formulations converge in asserting the importance of this kind of motivational construct, it has been treated at an abstract level, and no adequate measures of this concept have been developed. In this study we have identified specific behaviors to index cognitive-motivational variables. Lewis and Goldberg (1969) have formulated a "generalized expectancy model" emphasizing contingent mother-infant interaction in the development of the child's belief that he can affect his environment, that he can obtain reinforcement through his own actions. Watson (1966) speaks of "contingency awareness" as a precondition for later learning. Hunt (1965) has used the concept of "intrinsic motivation," contending that interactions with the environment are self-reinforcing. The common thread in these formulations is the active, information-processing infant, initiating and in turn being influenced by his transactions with the environment. We have singled out dimensions in the natural environment that show substantial relationships with early manifestations of these cognitive-motivational characteristics.

A complex and controversial issue is the relative importance of the human and inanimate environment. Some investigators have maintained that the provision of varied and stimulating playthings could substitute for warm interaction with a mother figure. Experimental studies have found relationships between infant attention and certain characteristics of inanimate stimulation, but there have been no studies of inanimate stimulation in the natural environment. The independence of the inanimate and the social environment in our study, in conjunction with relationships found between social stimulation and social responsiveness and language, on the one hand, and between properties of inanimate stimulation and exploratory behavior, on the other, indicate that both inanimate stimulation and social stimulation make a distinctive contribution. They are not interchangeable; one cannot be easily substituted for the other.

MULTIVARIATE ANALYSES

In the real world, variables operate together in different ways, sometimes to enhance each other's impact, sometimes to diminish or negate each other. Our awareness of the limitations of univariate analyses—of analyses of relationships between single, isolated dimensions of experience and single measures of the infant's functioning—led us to undertake several types of multivariate analyses, stepwise multiple regression analyses, and analysis of variance. In theory, multivariate analyses enable one to examine the summative effects of several independent variables; they allow control for the action of suppressor variables; and they enable analysis of interactions among variables.

Although multivariate analyses are not strictly comparable to the experimental manipulation of several variables simultaneously, and statistical control differs from experimental control of variables, we had hoped that these analyses would yield insights about the complexities of the environment that did not emerge from the univariate analyses. We found that the results of the stepwise multiple regression analyses and analyses of variance complemented the univariate results and enhanced our understanding of the environment. For example, in the multiple regression analyses, the two variables, Kinesthetic Stimulation and Variety of Inanimate Objects, which singly had strong and pervasive relationships with infant functioning, when looked at together, had even stronger effects. In the analyses of variance, these same variables had significant interactions with each other, affecting several infant variables. The effects of these environmental variables operating in combination were not simple, nor were they apparent from the univariate analyses.

We believe that different approaches to the analyses of multiple variables might be useful in future investigations. Multivariate analyses provide statistical control for the effects of one variable on another at the level of the relationships that exist in the total sample. Regardless of the correlation between two variables, the likelihood of two types of stimulation occurring together may differ from one mother to another. Perhaps statistical control at the level of the total sample is too remote from the realities of the individual mother-infant interaction. It may be necessary to discriminate and compare the effects of *individual patterns* of stimulation, i.e., several types of stimulation occurring simultaneously. For example, one might distinguish those caregivers who characteristically hold, smile, and engage in eye-to-eye contact while talking with their infants from those who interact in more isolated patterns such as talking from a distance without any accompanying behavior. In this way one might be able to determine whether multiple modalities of contingent behavior have different effects than do single-modality interactions. We are suggesting that units of description involving patterns of behavior may capture the effects of several variables operating together more faithfully than the statistical controls of multivariate procedures.

ENVIRONMENTAL INFLUENCES ON BOYS AND GIRLS

There is a vast literature comparing males and females on various cognitive, temperamental, and personality characteristics. In this investigation we asked several questions regarding sex differences. First, we were interested in whether there are experiential differences between boys and girls early in life and, second, whether the impact of the enviornment is similar or different for boys and girls during infancy.

In regard to experiential differences, as noted earlier, boys and girls were exposed to different amounts and patterns of stimulation. Boys received more varied and more intense social stimulation than did girls. We also found that there is somewhat greater interrelatedness among the environmental variables for girls. The fact that they were more highly intercorrelated may mean that girls experience greater consistency and predictability in interaction with their mothers than do male infants.

A close look at the literature on experiential differences reveals many inconsistencies, and some of the findings are of marginal statistical significance. There is reason to believe that there are more *similarities* than differences in the experiences of male and female infants. Because some of the variables on which differences have been reported involve interactions with other variables, clear generalizations cannot be made. Perhaps there has been such a strong cultural bias to look for differences between males and females that some investigators have overlooked similarities.

With regard to the magnitude of correlations between environmental variables and infant functioning, we have found differences for boys and girls. The correlations for the girls are consistently higher; however, the direction of the relationships are similar for boys and girls. These findings suggest that male infants are less malleable than girls; that is, there is stronger evidence that girls are influenced by the environment early in infancy. There are several possible explanations for these differences. They might be related to the fact that boys mature at a more uneven rate or to the fact that the early infancy of boys is marked by greater instability in functioning. They might also be related to differences in level, patterning, and consistency of maternal stimulation and responsiveness. These are merely speculations in need of evidence. As in most studies, our findings on sex differences are incidental to the major purposes of the study. Clearly these questions can be answered only with more systematic attempts to test these hypotheses directly.

TOWARD BETTER CONCEPTUALIZATION AND METHODOLOGY

When we take a critical look at our methods and findings from a respectful distance, we can see some of the limitations of the study. This awareness has led to some fresh ideas for future studies. These ideas evolved gradually from our immersion in the data, prompted in part by feelings of frustration about unclarities, in part by the theoretical meaningfulness of our findings.

Although we observed and recorded many varieties of maternal behaviors, certain aspects of the mother-infant relationship need to be explored further, e.g., the affectional relationship and contingent interactions between mother and infant. In recent years there has been a tendency to stress cognitive stimulation and to ignore the affective components of the infant's experience. If we look at this issue in historical perspective, we realize that the de-emphasis on affective influences has come about partly in reaction to preoccupation with variables, such as maternal warmth, which have been difficult to define with any degree of precision. Because of the difficulties in devising measures of these distinctive aspects of human interaction, there has been an inclination to deny their importance. This research utilized three measures of positive affect: a rating of the Expression of Positive Affect and frequency counts of Smiling and Play. These measures probably have no simple direct relation to the degree of affectional involvement of mother and child or the mother's basic acceptance of the infant. Only to a limited extent can we interpret them as reflections of basic warmth. Some of our other measures, such as the mother's responsiveness to the infant's positive vocalizations and the speed with which she responds to his distress, might also be indirectly related to the depth of her feelings towards the child. Future studies must investigate the ways in which warmth in its various aspects is communicated by the mother to the infant. We need to clarify the concept and then develop behavioral measures that index different aspects of the mother's expression of warmth. We need to articulate the behavioral cues used to infer the depth of the affectional relationship and then define these indicators as precisely as possible.

We have noted that the mother's responsiveness to the infant can be taken as an index of her sensitivity; contingency measures are also important from an operant learning perspective and from the perspective of expectancy theory. There is a great need for interactive techniques with which to capture the dynamic interplay between the infant and the environment. An ideal method of studying contingencies is through continuous recording of sequences of interaction between mother and infant. This approach poses enormous methodological difficulties, however, both in recording and in data reduction. Rather than attempt to reconstruct contingencies from continuous records of behavior, we found it more feasible to develop categories of specific contingent interactions. This procedure does not give identical information as sequential records of the behavior of the mother and of the infant because it does not handle chains of responses, but it simplifies tremendously the observational process and the treatment of results. In our analyses we used only two interactional categories: (*a*) a time-sampling measure of maternal vocal responses to the infant's positive vocalizations and (*b*) a rating of the latency of her response to the infant's distress signals. In future studies we would want to look in a more differentiated way at maternal contingencies. We would try to see whether there are differential effects of responses to the infant in different modalities and of different intensities. For example, we would distinguish coming within view of the infant, picking him up, smiling, vocalizing, touching him, or rocking him. It would also be desirable to code more subtle signals from the infant than crying or vocalizing, such as smiles, coos, mild fussy vocalizations, burps, hiccups and coughs, and various forms of motor restlessness. More refined categories of infant signals and maternal responses should yield a richer picture of the complex network of social exchanges between mother and infant. Measures of the number and subtlety of the infant signals to which the mother responds should also give us a more differentiated index of the mother's sensitivity and responsiveness to the infant.

The impact of any behavior is often modified by the setting in which it occurs and the state of the infant at the moment of stimulation. Therefore, we think it important to distinguish the various contexts in which stimulation is given, the organismic contexts of stimulation in addition to physical contexts of feeding, play, and rest. We need to be sensitive to the interaction between maternal behavior and infant states, such as drowsiness, quiet alert state, and active alert state. Awareness of infant states also helps us understand better the meaning to the infant of specific maternal behaviors. Vigorous kinesthetic stimulation when the infant is drowsy might have different significance than the same stimulation when he is alert.

Although we have obtained a highly differentiated picture of variations between primary caregivers, our study has been limited to one sociocultural context. Moreover, our focus has been on the microsystem of mother and infant; we have not attempted to see the meaning of mother-infant interaction within its cultural context. Maternal behaviors such as contingent response to distress, the amount of kinesthetic stimulation, and the encouragement of gross motor activity, undoubtedly are influenced by the modal values of a society or subculture and its idealized image of the young child. Cultures that value self-sufficiency or stoicism may encourage mothers to ignore the young infant's cries for long periods of time. Cultures that see infants as fragile may develop exaggerated means of protecting them from exposure to stimulation. Studies in other social and cultural contexts should help us gain greater understanding of how particular cultural values, sanctions, and prohibitions interact with maternal behaviors and influence development.

MODELS OF STIMULATION

In thinking about existing models of stimulation, we are struck by the extent to which there is an implicit assumption that more is better—that more stimulation, either greater frequency or intensity, by itself facilitates development. While some justification exists for this model, there are a number of reasons why it is undoubtedly simplistic. There are subtle qualitative differences among environments that are not reflected in frequency measures. Moreover, high frequencies of a particular kind of stimulation or in a given modality may result in less varied stimulation. It is known that even very young infants habituate to repetitive, unvarying stimulation. Giving the infant more stimulation may at the least be ineffective; if it is repetitive, at the worst, it may hinder developmental progress. Still another problem with a frequency and intensity model is that the effects of some variables may be nonlinear. An increment in stimulation at one point in the distribution may be facilitative; at another point, it may be inconsequential or even disruptive. This problem is a common one, often unrecognized in the quantitative treatment of psychological variables.

Studies of severe deprivation have emphasized that infants require a minimum amount of stimulation, but perhaps more pertinent to understanding variations in normal development is the concept of optimal amounts and optimal intensities of stimulation. Several theorists have stressed the importance of optimal stimulation, a view supported by experimental work with animals. The concept of optimal levels of stimulation enormously complicates measuring the impact of stimulation. We must take into consideration the basic differences among infants in sensory thresholds, in habituation rates, and in modes of processing stimuli. Thus, any stimulus configuration cannot simply be defined in terms of its external properties, independently of the organism. Its impact is not uniform for every infant; it will vary with an infant's neurophysiologically based sensitivities and thresholds as well as with the baby's state at the moment of stimulation.

The concept of optimal levels of stimulation must be seen from a developmental perspective also. There are periods when the organism is ready for the development of specific functions. If appropriate stimulation is given at this time, it is most likely to enhance the development of that particular characteristic. The same environmental variable may have some influence at an earlier or later point, but its impact at these times is diminished. Thus, the finding that kinesthetic stimulation is so strongly related to goal directedness and object permanence may mean that these *functions* are especially susceptible to environmental influences at this time. It may also mean that at this developmental period, the *infant* is especially sensitive to kinesthetic stimulation. At a later point in development, visual or auditory stimulation might be more effective in facilitating symbolic capacities.

BIDIRECTIONAL INFLUENCES

This study has essentially limited itself to the conventional, unidirectional model of the environment acting on the infant. We recognize that the environment does not simply act *on* the infant. The infant and the environment are an interactive system; the infant not only elicits different kinds of responses from his mother and others, but also his characteristics and changing states mediate or buffer the impact of stimuli. Aside from casual observations based on commonsense hunches, we know very little about the infant's effects on his environment. We know that a sensitive mother responds to a variety of signals from her baby. It is likely that an alert, vigorous infant elicits many more and different responses from his mother and other people than does a lethargic one. There is a cyclical pattern of reciprocal interactions; his responses to maternal stimulation encourage more stimulation.

It is also likely that the infant's orientation to objects and people very early becomes part of a feedback system with the environment. His smiling, vocalizing, and reaching out to people, his visually attending to and manipulating objects tend to be self-reinforcing and thus, to some extent, self-perpetuating. These behaviors become part of a system of reciprocal interactions which may characterize an infant's transactions with the environment over a long period of time. This orientation to the world may be a consistent and very significant characteristic of the young child that adds to the continuity of his experience. If we see the infant and young child as a changing organism, and the environment as a dynamic system in interaction with this changing organism, then new formulations of questions on long-term effects and new research designs are needed.

When we look at bidirectional influences in a broader time perspective, we realize that the question of whether early experiences are significant for later personality and cognitive development is too simple. From an interactional viewpoint, this question would be formulated very differently. We would ask two distinct but related questions, which have different implications for our research designs. First, we would ask, as we did in this investigation, what aspects of the early environment are associated with which developmental characteristics in early infancy. A second question, which is a logical elaboration of the first, is how these developmental characteristics influence later interactions with the environment. This formulation distinguishes between the remote influence of early experiences on later functioning ("sleeper effects") and successive contemporaneous influences. We would hypothesize a chain of influences in which the environment affects contemporaneous functioning and these functions, in turn, influence subsequent interactions with the environment. In the latter case, changes in early cognitive or personal-social characteristics may have implications for the child's subsequent sensitivities and continuing interactions with his environment. For example, if the development of object permanence is a necessary precursor for some of the symbolic operations required in problem solving, then the earlier acquisition of this cognitive capacity may accelerate the next stage of cognitive development. Thus, if having a variety of playthings at 6 months facilitates object permanence at that time, it is not a remote influence on a later development; it is a contemporaneous effect which is part of a sequence of influences. Similarly, environmental factors related to the development of locomotor skills may have no direct relationships to later cognitive development, but the early appearance of independent locomotion may still be significant for later problem-solving capacities. The child who has acquired the ability to crawl and walk early may have more opportunities to explore his environment and experiment with means-ends relationships. The infant who has developed a feeling of mastery through his experiences with reponsive objects may subsequently show more initiative in exploring his environment, and this activity will further enhance his problem-solving capacities. We would suggest then that longitudinal study of the effects of early experiences should look not only at remote influences across time, but also attempt to understand the sequential chain of mutual interactions between the child and the environment over time.

IMPLICATIONS FOR INTERVENTION

One of our hopes in this study was to develop some theoretical and empirical bases for optimizing the environments of young children. We hoped that our findings might have implications for prevention and intervention. Underlying intervention programs is the assumption that the environment can be manipulated to enhance the development of children. Many attempts at intervention were first made during the preschool years. When these efforts produced only modest and short-lived gains in cognitive functioning, it was concluded that earlier intervention might be necessary. Operating on the assumption that early experiences are crucial, it was hoped that intervention during early infancy might prove more effective and more lasting.

Although many intervention programs made an effort to use the best theoretical knowledge available, most programs have been predicated on the assumption that home environments are deficient, that they are lacking in elements essential for healthy personality and cognitive development. In their concentration on modifying childrearing conditions and in supplementing infants' experiences, almost no attempt has been made to study the environments of poor children. We have been struck by the paucity of ethologically oriented studies in the natural environment. We have no norms on what are adequate child-rearing conditions and what are depriving amounts and patterns of stimulation. It is extremely difficult to define the limits of the normal range because no investigations have systematically described the full spectrum of maternal behavior and the inanimate environment. We feel that an ethological approach with detailed descriptions of infants' experiences is necessary to develop effective intervention programs. Moreover, it is important that investigators be open to the stimulating aspects of environments and competent patterns of family interaction, and not be oriented solely to their deficiencies. To develop effective intervention programs we must be sensitive to and build on strengths as well as redress deficiencies.

In our sample we included infants from economically disadvantaged backgrounds to gain descriptive data on the environments of children similar to those that have been identified for intervention efforts. We found a wide variation in these economically similar environments. We have identified a number of dimensions of mothering and of the inanimate environment that are related to the developmental progress of infants during the first 6 months of life. Thus, our findings seem to have implications for intervention programs. We must remember, however, that although there were many statistically significant correlations, most were only of moderate magnitude. We believe that application of these findings to intervention programs should not be done in a simple-minded way. Infants in our investigation showed a wide range in functioning; the important point is that differences in functioning were systematically related to specific dimensions of the mother-infant relationship. We cannot make sweeping generalizations about these infants or mothers as a group, nor can we make any facile recommendations. The overriding implication of our findings is that intervention must be *selective*. Economically disadvantaged families are not homogeneous with regard to the experiences they provide their infants, nor are they all in need of intervention programs.

On one characteristic, the continuity of maternal care, we feel confident that the experiences of many infants in this sample were different from typical middle-class infants. Approximately 40% of our sample had multiple primary caregivers at some time or had several changes in caregivers during the first 6 months of life. We do not know the long-term effects of this degree of discontinuity in caretaking. It is generally assumed that any form of discontinuity is harmful; there is a possibility, however, that warm primary mothering associated with some discontinuity may not be detrimental to the child. In fact it may help the infant to become more adaptable. Perhaps in learning to relate to multiple mother figures, the strength of the infant's attachment to one person is diluted, but his basic capacity to establish close relationships may not be seriously affected. We may have underestimated the infant's capacity to form strong attachments to several adults. The possibility exists that a child is more open to multiple relationships at some developmental periods; during others continuity with a single caregiver may be more important.

The multifaceted character of the environment highlighted in our findings has other implications for intervention efforts. We know very little about how variables work in combination with one another. What appears to be an isolated relationship between a form of stimulation and some outcome may in fact be part of a larger complex of variables. Modification or alteration of a single variable may so change the stimulus gestalt that their combined effects may be radically altered. Similarly, the modification of one component of the environment may inadvertently affect other dimensions which are also important. For example, if a mother is encouraged to give an infant more opportunity to explore toys on his own, she may engage him less often in active play.

The degree of independence we found in different dimensions of the environment suggests that mothers may have preferred modes of interacting with infants. Some mothers may be exquisitely responsive to particular infant sensitivities; others may be completely unaware of these same sensitivities. If we glibly propose that a mother act in ways not in accord with her readings of what the infant needs, we may invite very antagonistic and discordant interactions. Similarly, to advocate that she handle the infant in a manner that is not consonant with her culturally based beliefs may also disrupt smooth interactions between mother and infant.

These findings have a relevance that goes beyond intervention programs; they have broad relevance for child rearing and for designing environments for all children. It may be possible to mold the infant according to precisely defined specifications by manipulating the relative balance of stimulation in the various modalities, in the patterns of contingent response, and in the dimensions of inanimate stimulation. We believe, however, that there are no simple recipes for child rearing. Interacting with an infant is an art in which general principles of child development must be sensitively adapted to human individuality.

CONCLUDING COMMENTS

Although we are very much aware of the limitations of an overly analytic approach and of remaining too close to the level of univariate relationships, we believe that differentiated analysis of the environment has value. In addition to its methodological neatness, establishing relations between carefully defined maternal behaviors and characteristics of inanimate stimuli with sectors of infant development has led to clarification of conceptual issues. Moreover, it is possible to combine discrete behaviors into psychologically meaningful larger units by developing higher order variables and by combining variables with multivariate techniques. These procedures enable us to be more sharply aware of the components of higher order abstract variables. A differentiated analysis of the environment helps us see the distinctive contributions of specific components of experience and increases our understanding of the processes by which these distinctive elements influence development. This level of analysis is heuristic and should stimulate more precise theories regarding the action of the early environment.

We have been troubled by the unnatural isolation of variables in the natural environment. We can look at variables independently as if they are operating in isolation, but in real life stimuli do not function in isolation. We have treated our measures as if they are discrete variables, but in fact many stimuli occur simultaneously. For example, a common everyday behavior such as reaching out to the infant in the crib and picking him up may simultaneously involve mutual regard, talking, smiling, touching him, and moving him. The influence of any of these stimuli might be affected by the total configuration. Experimental studies which in theory manipulate single variables also have not given adequate consideration to the larger stimulus context.

We recognize that the isolation of variables in the natural environment distorts reality. Each of these discrete elements of the infant's experience, while having a statistically significant and theoretically meaningful relationship with some aspect of infant development, nevertheless accounts for only a small part of the variance; these elements do not permit predictions with a high order of accuracy. It seems clear that any single variable alone cannot explain the development of any single infant ability or characteristic. No one variable is decisive for any particular infant function.

Developmental research still seems to be asking complex questions in oversimplified form. We have been limited by our simple theoretical models and statistical techniques in trying to deal with very complicated issues. Although it is meaningful to ask to what extent a given environmental variable makes a contribution to some aspect of infant functioning, we also need to ask more complex questions about how environmental variables interact with each other and how organismic and environmental variables interact. We need integrative models to consider the larger environment, to take into account many variables acting together on the infant, to consider contextual variables as well as direct influences. Such a conceptual model must deal not only with additive effects in which two variables contribute an additional fraction to the relationships; it should also be able to handle the ways in which several variables interact with each other, perhaps in the manner of catalysts, to enhance each other's effects, or as inhibitors to dilute or diminish each other's influence.

Our models must also take into account the basic differences that exist among infants in sensory thresholds, in habituation rates, and in modes of processing stimuli. Such fundamental differences mean that any stimulus configuration cannot be defined only in terms of its external properties, independently of the organism. Its impact is not uniform for every infant—it will vary with a particular infant's neurophysiologically based sensitivities and thresholds. Thus, after dissecting the components of the environment and of infant characteristics, we must put the pieces together and look at the whole infant and environment as an interactive system. Ultimately, we need a conceptual model able to handle many variables, both environmental and organismic, interacting with each other in many complex ways.

CORRELATIONS OF ENVIRONMENTAL AND INFANT VARIABLES FOR BOYS AND GIRLS

TABLE A

Interrelations Among Environmental Measures: Boys

	Modalities			Contingencies		Affect			Social Mediation		Composite Variables		Inanimate Stimulation		
	Kinesthetic	Visual	Auditory	Contingent Response to Positive Vocalization	Contingent Response to Distress	Positive Affect	Smiling	Play	With Minimal Social Reinforcement	With Smiles and Vocalizations	Level	Variety	Responsiveness	Complexity	Variety
Modalities															
Tactile	.47	.31	.21	.27	—	.29ᵃ	—	—	.42	.33	.47	.43	—	—	-.22
Kinesthetic		—	.30	.29	—	—	.32	.26	—	—	.49	.47	-.39	-.28	—
Visual			.61	.41	—	.47	.61	.52	—	.44	.69	.51	—	—	—
Auditory				.73	—	.70	.55	.62	-.33	.70	.75	.70	—	—	—
Contingencies															
Contingent Response to Positive Vocalization					.23	.52	.30	.39	—	.55	.68	.50	—	—	—
Contingent Response to Distress						—ᵃ	—	—	.46	—	.27	.35	—	—	.25
Affect															
Expression of Positive Affect							.43	.69	-.32	.49	.48	.49	—	-.26ᵃ	—
Smiling								.21	-.39	.23	.42	.27	—	—	—
Play									—	.49	.65	.77	—	-.28	—
Social Mediation															
With Minimal Social Reinforcement										—	.20	—	.36	.24	—
With Smiles and Vocalizations											.56	.72	—	—	.22
Composite Variables															
Level												.78	—ᵃ	—ᵃ	—ᵃ
Variety															
Inanimate Stimulation															
Responsiveness														.42ᵃ	—
Complexity															—
Variety															

Note. Dashes represent correlation < .20.

ᵃSignificant difference in correlation between boys and girls, $p < .05$.

TABLE B

Interrelations Among Environmental Measures: Girls

	Modalities			Contingencies		Affect			Social Mediation		Composite Variables		Inanimate Stimulation		
	Kinesthetic	Visual	Auditory	Contingent Response to Positive Vocalization	Contingent Response to Distress	Positive Affect	Smiling	Play	With Minimal Social Reinforcement	With Smiles and Vocalization	Level	Variety	Responsiveness	Complexity	Variety
Modalities															
Tactile	.53	.51	.27	.44	.57	.78[a]	.49	.41	.21	.43	.65	.61	.39	.39	—
Kinesthetic		.30	.42	.37	.51	.61	.19	.67	.49	.56	.78	.65	—	—	—
Visual			.48	.46	.54	.65	.69	.47	-.22	.22	.63	.51	—	.25	-.27
Auditory				.61	.44	.34	.52	—	—	.54	.72	.31	-.20	—	-.30
Contingencies															
Contingent Response to Positive Vocalization					.43	.44	.68	.08	-.23	.30	.69	—	—	—	—
Contingent Response to Distress						.64[a]	.28	.44	—	.42	.67	.52	—	—	.35
Affect															
Expression of Positive Affect							.43	.70	.20	.50	.78	.82	.41	.52[a]	—
Smiling								—	-.20	—	.54	—	.20	.31	—
Play									.38	.52	.54	.82	.40	.41	—
Social Mediation															
With Minimal Social Reinforcement										.39	.24	.42	.31	.22	.26
With Smiles and Vocalizations											.58	.63	—	.33	—
Composite Variables															
Level												.67	.54[a]	.55[a]	.26
Variety															
Inanimate Stimulation															
Responsiveness														.83[a]	.33
Complexity															.27
Variety															

Note. Dashes represent correlation < .20.

[a] Significant difference in correlation between boys and girls, $p < .05$.

TABLE C

Intercorrelations Among Dependent Variables: Boys

Infant Variables	General Status		Social	Language		Motor Development		Cognitive-Motivational					Exploratory Behavior		Preference for Novelty	
	MDI[a]	PDI[b]	Responsiveness	Vocalization during Exploration	Language Quality	Gross	Fine	Goal Directedness	Reaching and Grasping	Secondary Circular Reaction	Problem Solving	Object Permanence	Look at Bell	Manip. Bell	Look at Novel	Manip. Novel
General Status																
MDI[a]		.54	.70	–	.56	.51	.55	.80	.67	.45	.45	.83[c]	–	.26	–	.32
PDI[b]			–	–.29	–	.94	.77	.58[c]	.56	.44	.56	.48	.30	.32	–	.36
Social Responsiveness				–	.78	–	–	.54	.30	.23	.20	.51	–	–	–.21	–
Language																
Vocalization during Exploration					.22	–.35	–	–	–	–	–[c]	–	–	–	.28	–
Language Quality						–	–	.37	–	–	–	.43	–	–	–.28	–
Motor Development																
Gross							.78	.60	.59	.50	.47	.48	.26	.33	–	.28
Fine								.68	.78	.36	.52	.52	.27	.51	.27	.28
Cognitive-Motivational																
Goal Directedness									.71	.46	.40	.67	.24	.40	–	–
Reaching and Grasping										.62	.32	.56	.28	.26	.24	.33
Secondary Circular Reaction											.30	.42	.37	.20	.27	.25
Problem Solving												.52	.40	.32	.35	.47
Object Permanence													.25	–	–	.20
Exploratory Behavior																
Look at Bell														.34	.24	–.34
Manipulate Bell															.49	–
Preference for Novel Stimuli																
Look at Novel																.50
Manipulate Novel																

Note. Dashes represent correlation < .20.
[a]MDI = Mental Developmental Index.
[b]PDI = Psychomotor Developmental Index.
[c]Significant difference in correlation between boys and girls, p < .05.

TABLE D

Intercorrelations Among Dependent Variables: Girls

Infant Variables	General Status		Social	Language		Motor Development		Cognitive-Motivational				Object Permanence	Exploratory Behavior		Preference for Novelty	
	MDI[a]	PDI[b]	Responsiveness	Vocalization during Exploration	Language Quality	Gross	Fine	Goal Directed-ness	Reaching and Grasping	Secondary Circular Reaction	Problem Solving		Look at Bell	Manip. Bell	Look at Novel	Manip. Novel
General Status																
MDI[a]		.85	.72	-.53	.40	.63	.85	.90	.82	.76	.69	.49[c]	—	.31	.30	.43
PDI[b]			.49	-.43	.20	.91	.91	.89[c]	.80	.72	.75	.45	.26	.59	.38	.64
Social Responsiveness				-.23	.39	.40	.43	.56	.35	.68	.29	.41	—	—	—	—
Language																
Vocalization during Exploration					-.29	-.38	-.52	-.44	-.58	-.44	-.65[c]	—	—	-.22	—	—
Language Quality						—	.23	.40	—	.28	.25	—	.39	—	—	-.29
Motor Development																
Gross							.77	.71	.66	.65	.72	.41	.22	.61	.31	.71
Fine								.81	.91	.71	.68	.46	.25	.53	.38	.52
Cognitive-Motivational																
Goal Directedness									.79	.81	.72	.54	.21	.38	.35	.59
Reaching and Grasping										.75	.66	.42	—	.48	.48	.64
Secondary Circular Reactions											.46	.41	—	.26	.34	.48
Problem Solving												.36	—	.30	—	.53
Object Permanence													.21	.35	.27	.44
Exploratory Behavior																
Look at Bell														.61	.54	—
Manipulate Bell															.57	.52
Preference for Novel Stimuli																
Look at Novel																.48
Manipulate Novel																

Note. Dashes represent correlations <.20.
[a]MDI = Mental Developmental Index.
[b]PDI = Psychomotor Developmental Index.
[c]Significant difference in correlation between boys and girls, $p < .05$.

TABLE E

Relations Between Modalities of Social Stimulation and
Infant Functioning: Boys and Girls

Infant Variable	Near Receptor Stimulation				Distance Receptor Stimulation			
	Tactile		Kinesthetic		Visual		Auditory	
	Boys	Girls	Boys	Girls	Boys	Girls	Boys	Girls
General Status								
MDI[a]	—	.35	.20	.46*	—	—	.20	—
PDI[b]	-.21	.43^c	—	.51*	-.23	—	—	—
Social Responsiveness	—	.34	—	.44*	.41	—	.24	.51*
Language								
Vocalization during								
Exploration	—	—	.26	—	—	—	.35	—
Language Quality	-.23	—	—	.32	—	-.25	—	—
Motor Development								
Gross	-.31	.41^c	—	.37	-.25	—	-.25	—
Fine	—	.33	—	.32	-.29	—	—	—
Cognitive-Motivational								
Goal Directedness	—	.46*	.37	.62**	—	—	—	—
Reaching and Grasping	—	.30	.25	—	—	—	—	—
Secondary Circular								
Reactions	—	.53*	—	.36	—	.21	—	—
Problem Solving	—	.23	—	.31	—	-.34	.29	—
Object Permanence	-.32	.34^c	.25	.47*	—	—	—	—
Exploratory Behavior								
Look at Bell	.21	—	.29	.36	—	.21	-.25	—
Manipulate Bell	—	—	—	.35	—	.22	—	-.21
Preference for Novel								
Stimuli								
Look at Novel	—	—	—	—	—	—	—	—
Manipulate Novel	-.28	.36^c	-.25	.28	—	—	.41	—

Note. Dashes represent correlation < .20.
[a]MDI = Mental Developmental Index.
[b]PDI = Psychomotor Developmental Index.
[c]Significant difference in correlation between boys and girls, $p < .05$.
*$p < .05$.
**$p < .01$.

TABLE F

Relations Between Contingent Social Stimulation and
Infant Functioning: Boys and Girls

Infant Variable	Contingent Response to Positive Vocalization		Contingent Response to Distress	
	Boys	Girls	Boys	Girls
General Status				
Mental Developmental Index	—	.29	—	.45*
Psychomotor Developmental Index	−.30	—	.26	.43
Social Responsiveness	—	.44*	—	.24
Language				
Vocalization during Exploration	.39	−.20	−.22	—
Language Quality	—	—	−.28	—
Motor Development				
Gross	−.38	—	.30	.22
Fine	—	—	.24	.36
Cognitive-Motivational				
Goal Directedness	—	.24	—	.54*
Reaching and Grasping	—	—	—	.31
Secondary Circular Reaction	−.22	.27	—	.33
Problem Solving	—	.21	—	.23
Object Permanence	−.20	—	—	—
Exploratory Behavior				
Look at Bell	−.33	−.32	—	—
Manipulate Bell	—	—	.40	—
Preference for Novel Stimuli				
Look at Novel	.20	—	—	—
Manipulate Novel	.47*	—	.32	.25

Note. Dashes represent correlation $< .20$.

$*p < .05$.

TABLE G

Relations Between Maternal Affect and Infant Functioning:
Boys and Girls

Infant Variable	Expression of Positive Affect		Smiling		Play	
	Boys	Girls	Boys	Girls	Boys	Girls
General Status						
Mental Developmental Index	—	.33	—	—	.29	—
Psychomotor Developmental Index	—	.42	—	—	—	.31
Social Responsiveness	.21	.30	.30	—	.36	—
Language						
Vocalization during Exploration	.28	—	—	—	—	—
Language Quality	—	−.23	—	—	—	—
Motor Development						
Gross	−.24	.38	—	—	−.25	.27
Fine	—	.35	—	—	—	.23
Cognitive-Motivational						
Goal Directedness	—	.51*	—	—	.22	.33
Reaching and Grasping	—	.35	—	—	—	—
Secondary Circular Reactions	—	.50*	.26	.30	—	—
Problem Solving	—	—	—	—	.24	—
Object Permanence	—	.53*	—	—	—	.64*
Exploratory Behavior						
Look at Bell	—	—	—	—	—	.50*
Manipulate Bell	—	.41	−.21	—	.26	.57*
Preference for Novel Stimuli						
Look at Novel	.24	—	—	—	.26	.22
Manipulate Novel	.21	.51*	—	—	—	.27

Note. Dashes represent correlation $< .20$.

*$p < .05$.

TABLE H

Relations Between Social Mediation of Play Objects
and Infant Functioning: Boys and Girls

Infant Variable	Social Mediation with Minimal Social Reinforcement		Social Mediation with Smiles and Vocalizations	
	Boys	Girls	Boys	Girls
General Status				
Mental Developmental Index	—	.23	−.22	.21
Psychomotor Developmental Index	—	.25	−.37	—
Social Responsiveness	—	—	—	.28
Language				
Vocalization During Exploration	−.20	—	.55**	.27
Language Quality	—	.52*	—	—
Motor Development				
Gross	—	—	−.46*	—
Fine	—	.22	−.37	—
Cognitive-Motivational				
Goal Directedness	—	.46*	—	.31
Reaching and Grasping	—	—	−.31	—
Secondary Circular Reaction	—	.23	—	.20
Problem Solving	—	.22	—	—
Object Permanence	—	—	—	.23
Exploratory Behavior				
Look at Bell	.32	.31	—	—
Manipulate Bell	.26	—	—	—
Preference for Novel Stimuli				
Look at Novel	—	—	.22	—
Manipulate Novel	—	.21	—	.27

Note. Dashes represent correlation $< .20$.
*$p < .05$.
**$p < .01$.

TABLE I

Relations Between Level and Variety of Social Stimulation
and Infant Functioning: Boys and Girls

Infant Variable	Level		Variety	
	Boys	Girls	Boys	Girls
General Status				
Mental Developmental Index	—	.34	.25	.34
Psychomotor Developmental Index	—	.25	—	.42
Social Responsiveness	.21	.42	.31	.32
Language				
Vocalization During Exploration	—	—	.36	—
Language Quality	—	—	—	—
Motor Development				
Gross	—	—	—	.37
Fine	—	—	—	.31
Cognitive-Motivational				
Goal Directedness	.27	.47*	.31	.50*
Reaching and Grasping	.30	—	—	.27
Secondary Circular Reaction	—	.35	—	.43
Problem Solving	.21	—	.28	—
Object Permanence	—	.38	.25	.52*
Exploratory Behavior				
Look at Bell	—	—	—	.37
Manipulate Bell	—	—	.43*	.50*
Preference for Novel Stimuli				
Look at Novel	—	—	—	.26
Manipulate Novel	—	.26	—	.43

Note. Dashes represent correlation < .20.

*p < .05.

TABLE J

Relations Between Dimensions of Inanimate Stimulation
and Infant Functioning: Boys and Girls

Infant Variable	Inanimate Stimulation					
	Responsiveness		Complexity		Variety	
	Boys	Girls	Boys	Girls	Boys (N=18)	Girls (N=18)
General Status						
Mental Developmental Index	−.21	.45*a	—	.23	.20	.44
Psychomotor Developmental Index	−.39	.51*a	—	.34	.46*	.54*
Social Responsiveness	—	.28	—	—	—	—
Language						
Vocalization to Bell	—	—	—	—	.24	−.24
Language Quality	—	—	—	—	—	—
Motor Development						
Gross	−.26	.47*a	—	.36	.27	.51*
Fine	−.23	.52*a	—	.33	—	.51*
Cognitive-Motivational						
Goal Directedness	−.21	.49*a	—	.37	—	.56**
Reaching and Grasping	—	.60**	—	.47*	−.17	.60**a
Secondary Circular Reaction	.27	.56**	.44*	.54*	.24	.36
Problem Solving	−.27	—	—	—	.45	.52*
Object Permanence	−.22	.23	—	.25	.25	.29
Exploratory Behavior						
Look at Bell	—	.22	—	—	.28	—
Manipulate Bell	—	.38	−.21	.35	.42	.47*
Preference for Novel Stimuli						
Look at Novel	—	.42	—	.50*	.22	.50*
Manipulate Novel	—	.43	—	.53*	.31	.73**

Note. Dashes represent correlation < .20.
[a]Significant difference between correlation coefficients, $p < .05$, for boys and girls.
*$p < .05$.

MANUAL FOR OBSERVATION OF THE HOME ENVIRONMENT AND MOTHER–INFANT INTERACTION

The coding system presented in this manual was designed to describe selected experiences of 5-month old infants observed in the course of a day in their homes. This time-sampling procedure provides scores for a variety of aspects of the infant's environment and some aspects of infant behavior, as well as for selected sequences of events, e.g., infant cries . . . mother offers toys.

The categories in this manual are listed in the order in which they appear on the time-sampling form (see Figure A, Sample Recording Sheet, pp. 192–193). To look up the definition of a code, one should refer to its column number on the time-sampling form, and look for the corresponding column number in the manual.

Observation Categories	Column/s on Time-Sampling Form	Page/s in Coding Manual
I. Context	1	194–195
II. Proximity of Primary Caregiver	2	196
III. Infant Behavior		
A. Eats	3	196
B. Focused Exploration	4–9	196–197
1. Toy		
2. HO/CO		
3. Person		
4. Self		
5. Other		
C. Vocalization	10–11	197–198
1. Nondistress		
2. Distress		
D. Looks at Person	12–13	198
1. Primary caregiver		
2. Other person		
IV. Description of Sources of Stimulation		
A. Visual Focus, PC	14–15	198
B. Sources of Attentiveness	16–18	199–201
V. Social Stimulation		
A. Attentiveness I	19–23	201
1. Looks at baby		
2. Mutual regard		
3. Holds		
4. Touches passively		
5. Touches passively with an object		
B. Attentiveness II	24–31	202–203
1. Vocalizes to baby		
2. Vocalizes contigently to nondistress vocalization		
3. Vocalizes contigently to distress vocalization		
4. Vocalizes in imitation of baby vocalization		
5. Touches actively		
6. Touches actively with an object		
7. Moves baby		
C. Animation	32–33	203–205
1. Smiles broadly within reach of the baby		
2. Personal-Social play		
D. Response to Distress	34–40	205–206
1. Social soothing alone		
2. Provides play object		
3. Feeds		
4. Other caretaking		

Observation Categories	Column/s on Time-Sampling Form	Page/s in Coding Manual
D. Response to Distress (*continued*)		
5. Pacifier		
6. Checks or acknowledges		
7. Other		
E. Encouragement of Emergent Gross Motor Responses	46–47	208
1. Posture		
2. Locomotion		
F. Social Mediation–Encouraging Attentiveness to Stimuli	41–45	206–208
0. Separates infant from object		
1. Position within view		
2. Position within reach		
3. Position in hand		
4. Enticing, highlighting		
G. Salient Verbalization Not Directed to Infant	48	209
VI. Change in Container or Room	49–51	209
VII. Inanimate Stimulation		
A. Number of Objects within Reach	52–55	209–210
1. Toys		
2. HO/CO		
B. Variety of Objects within Reach		211

GENERAL INSTRUCTIONS FOR OBSERVERS

1. The time-sampling cycle is 90 seconds in length and consists of a 30-second observation period and a 60-second recording period. A home observation consists of 120 units (3 hours) each day.

2. Coding is discontinued when the baby falls asleep. The observer should stop coding after scoring three consecutive time-sampling units during which the following criteria are met:

   a. Infant's eyes are closed.
   b. Breathing pattern is regular.
   c. The infant is not eating or drinking.

SUBJECT						BEGAN		AWAKE
OBSERVER						ASLEEP		ASLEEP

	CONTEXT	PROX-PC	EATS	FOC EXPL	VOC	LOOKS AT	VISUAL FOCUS PC ONLY	SOURCES ATT	ATT-I
	1-Non CA 2-CA 3-Mixed 4-No Att Scored	1-WR 2-Int 3-R-WV 4-R-OV		1-Toy 2-HO/CO 3-Person 4-Self 5-Other	1-Non Dis 2-Dis	1-PC 2-Per 0	1-PC-MFB 2-PC-FE	1-PC 2-OA 3-Child	1-Look 2-MR 3-Holds 4-T-Pass 5-T-Pass/obj
	1	2	3	4-9	10-11	12-13	14-15	16-18	19-23
1									
2									
3									
4									
5									
6									

FIG. A. Sample recording sheet

3. Identifying the Primary Caregiver (PC). A primary caregiver is a person who is reported to provide a major proportion of care for the infant from 9 a.m. to 5 p.m., Monday–Friday. A baby may have more than one primary caregiver, although only one PC is sampled during an observation. On the basis of information obtained from the mother, the observer decides in advance the identity of the PC to be observed on that day. This decision is not made during or after the observation.

4. In order to remain as unobtrusive as possible while coding, the observer sits or stands quietly near the baby, does not move quickly when she changes position or location; does not speak to, smile at or otherwise interact with the infant; and, to the extent that it is possible, does not interact with

AWAKE				OBSERVATION NO.				PAGE	
END				DATE				SUBJECT NO.	
			PC				LOCATION		

ATT-II	ANI	R TO DIS	ENC ATT STIMULI	ENC EM GROSS MOTOR RESP	SAL VOC $\overline{B}$	CHANGE C/R	NUMBER WR		OBJECTS WR
							Toy	HO/CO	
1-Voc to B 2-Voc C ND 3-Voc C Dis 4-Voc-Imit 5-T-Act 6-T-Act/obj 7-Mov B	1-Br Sm 2-Pl	1-S Soo al 2-Pl obj 3-Feeds 4-Oth CA 5-Pacif 6-Ch/A 7-Other	0-Sep 1-PosWView 2-PosFReach 3-PosIHand 4-Ent,Hi	1-Post 2-Loc					
24-31	32-33	34-40	41-45	46-47	48	49-51	52-53	54-55	
						.			

the primary caregiver. Behavior directed to the observer by either the PC or the infant is not scored.

5. The following general rules apply when coding a time-sampling unit:

a. Certain columns are coded in every time-sampling unit:
   (1) Context (Column 1)
   (2) Proximity of primary caregiver (Column 2)

b. Certain columns are coded only in time-sampling units in which relevant behaviors occur, and these columns are scored independently of all other columns:
   (1) Infant behaviors (Columns 3-13)
   (2) Background vocalization (Column 48)
   (3) Change of container or room (Columns 49-51)

(4) Aspects of the inanimate environment (Columns 52–55)

c. The remaining columns are scored only when some person is attentive to the infant. If the primary caregiver is attentive, she is scored in Column 16, Sources of Attentiveness, and her visual focus is scored in Column 14. If any person other than the primary caregiver is attentive, regardless of whether or not the primary caregiver is also attentive, that person is scored in Columns 16–18. The behavior of one of the people scored in Columns 16–18 is coded in detail in Columns 19–47. Preemption rules for making this choice are listed in Sources of Attentiveness.

DEFINITIONS OF CATEGORIES

COLUMN 1: CONTEXT

This column describes the setting in which the infant is being observed. Only one Context category is coded in each time-sampling unit. If any person is attentive to the baby in the unit, Noncaretaking, Caretaking or Mixed is scored. If both caretaking and noncaretaking behavior are directed toward the baby in the same unit, Caretaking should be scored. If no person is attentive during the unit, No Attentiveness is scored.

1. *Noncaretaking (Non C)*. Attentiveness occurring in any context other than one in which the baby's physical needs are being met. This category also includes preparations for caretaking events, and transitions between caretaking events.
2. *Caretaking (CA)*. Attentiveness to the infant directed toward meeting his physical needs. Includes activities such as feeding, burping, diapering, bathing, dressing, wiping his face. Also includes attentiveness to the infant in units during which the primary caregiver is not directly responsive to the

physical needs of the infant, but the meeting of these needs is the primary concern, e.g., when the infant is eating a meal, falling asleep, or waking up.

3. *Mixed*. A brief caretaking act interjected into an essentially noncaretaking context, e.g., wiping the baby's nose while playing with him or checking briefly to see if his diaper is wet.

4. *No Attentiveness (No Scored Att)*. No person is attentive to the baby.

Rules

1. *Onset of Caretaking*. Coding of caretaking does not begin until the baby has been involved in a caretaking procedure, e.g., the diaper is being removed, the first spoonful of food has reached his mouth. If the baby is simply placed on the changing table or seated in a high chair, caretaking is not scored.

2. *Interruptions of Caretaking Procedures*. If a caretaking procedure such as a meal or bath has begun and is interrupted for further preparations, score Caretaking throughout the interruption. If a social interlude occurs within a caretaking context, i.e., the caretaking is discontinued briefly and purely social interaction occurs, score three time-sampling units of Caretaking and then change to Noncaretaking for the duration of the interlude.

3. *Transitions between Caretaking Procedures*. If one caretaking procedure ends, score Noncaretaking until the baby's body is positioned and actually involved in the next caretaking procedure, regardless of the length of time elapsing before the onset of the second procedure.

4. *Self-feeding*. If attentiveness is scored in a time-sampling unit in which the baby feeds himself any foods except a bottle, score Caretaking at mealtime and score Mixed at all other times. If attentiveness is scored in a time-sampling unit in which the baby is feeding himself a bottle, score Caretaking.

COLUMN 2: PROXIMITY OF THE PRIMARY
CAREGIVER (PROX-PC)

This column describes the physical and visual accessibility of the primary caregiver to the infant. One code, describing the closest proximity during the observation unit, is scored.

1. *Within Reach (WR)*. The primary caregiver is able to reach the baby by stretching her arm forward, backward or to the side, by bending over or by stooping down.
2. *Intermediate (Int)*. The primary caregiver cannot reach the infant but is less than 10 feet from him.
3. *Remote—within View (R—WV)*. The primary caregiver is 10 feet or more from the baby and can see him or could if she turned in his direction.
4. *Remote—out of View (R—OV)*. The primary caregiver is 10 feet or more from the baby and cannot see him even when facing in his direction.

COLUMN 3: EATS

The baby is ingesting fluids from the bottle or breast or is eating solid foods. Sucking on a bottle without ingesting fluid is not scored as eating. Ingesting medicine is not scored unless the medicine is mixed into a full bowl of food or a full bottle of liquid.

COLUMNS 4-9: FOCUSED EXPLORATION
(FOC EXPL)

Focused Exploration is the simultaneous visual and haptic exploration of an object or person by the infant. Haptic exploration is holding or manipulating the object. Focused Exploration is scored only when the baby's hand is involved in manipulation, although other parts of his body may also be involved. Merely resting the hand on or against the object is not sufficient. Persistent reaching for an object beyond reach is not scored unless the infant succeeds in touching the object at least once.

The categories below define the types of objects with which focused exploration may occur. These categories are not mutually exclusive. Score all objects which are explored.

1. *Toy*. An object made for children to play with. Detailed definition in Columns 52–55.
2. *Household Object/Caretaking Object (HO/CO)*. Objects in the environment which may serve as toys although they are primarily for adult or caretaking purposes. Detailed definition in Columns 52–55.
3. *Person*. Simultaneous looking at and manipulating the same part of the body of a person. Manipulating one body part while looking at another is not scored. Simultaneous visual and haptic exploration of clothing or jewelry being worn by a person is scored.
4. *Self*. Simultaneously looking at and manipulating the same part of the infant's own body or clothing. Hand regard, the infant moving his hand while looking at it, is scored.
5. *Other*. Simultaneously looking at and manipulating an inanimate object that is not a toy, HO/CO, or something worn by a person. Play with water is an example.

COLUMNS 10–11: INFANT VOCALIZATION (VOC)

All sounds, positive, neutral, and negative, by the infant except vegetative (burps, choking) or respiratory (coughs, heavy breathing) sounds are scored. If there is doubt about whether a vocalization is positive or negative, Nondistress should be coded. A single fragile peep is not scored.

1. *Nondistress Vocalization (Non D)*. Coos, gurgles, and grunts. Vocalizations other than whimpers, fusses or cries which are not accompanied by an unhappy facial expression.

2. *Distress Vocalization (Dis)*. Whimpers, fusses, and cries, and vocalizations that are accompanied by an unhappy facial expression.

COLUMNS 12–13: LOOKS AT PERSON (LOOKS AT)

The infant looks directly at a person's face, at any other part of a person's body, or at the clothing or jewelry worn by a person. Fleeting glances are not scored. There must be a pause during which the baby's eyes fix on a person.

1. *Primary Caregiver (PC)*. The infant looks at the primary caregiver.
2. *Person Other than Primary Caregiver (Per O)*. The infant looks at a person other than the primary caregiver, or the infant looks at himself in a mirror.

Rule

1. If the infant looks at a group of people which includes the primary caregiver, but it is not clear whether the infant looked at the primary caregiver or at another person, neither person is scored.

COLUMN 14: VISUAL FOCUS OF PRIMARY CAREGIVER (VISUAL FOCUS, PC)

The length of time that the primary caregiver looks at the baby's face or at any part of his body is scored in this column.

1. *Major Focus on Baby (MFB)*. The primary caregiver looks at the baby for half of the time-sampling unit or longer (15–30 seconds).
2. *Focus Elsewhere (FE)*. The primary caregiver looks at the baby for less than half of the time-sampling unit (0–14 seconds).

COLUMNS 16–18: SOURCES OF ATTENTIVENESS (SOURCES ATT)

Any person who is attentive to the infant beyond merely looking is recorded in Columns 16–18. Three sources of attentiveness are distinguished.

1. *Primary Caregiver (PC)*. The person who is reported to have primary responsibility for the infant's care on Mondays through Fridays between 9 a.m. and 5 p.m.
2. *Other Adult (OA)*. A person 17 years of age or older, other than the primary caregiver.
3. *Child*. A person 16 years of age or younger, other than the primary caregiver.

Rules

1. *Multiple sources of attentiveness.* Each category of persons attentive to the infant is scored only once during a time-sampling unit, regardless of how many individuals actually stimulated the infant. For example, if the primary caregiver, two other adults and four children are all attentive to the baby in one time-sampling unit, Columns 16–18 are scored with a 1, a single 2, and a single 3.
2. *Choice of the person whose behavior is coded in Columns 19–47.* When there are multiple sources of attentiveness scored in Columns 16–18, the behavior of only one person is scored in Columns 19–47. The code number for that person is entered in Column 16. Criteria for selecting the primary source of stimulation are:

   a. *Primary caregiver.* If the primary caregiver is attentive, her behavior is coded, regardless of whoever else is attentive.
   b. *Person other than the primary caregiver who most actively stimulated the infant.* If the primary caregiver is not attentive to the baby, but several other people are,

the person who most actively stimulated the baby, as defined by the following rating scale, is scored. If several people are stimulating the baby at an equally high level, the person who is holding the baby is chosen. If more than one person holds the baby, the person holding him the longest is scored. If two or more people hold him equal lengths of time, the last person to hold him is scored. The rating scale for determining level of stimulation follows:

(1) *Minimal: Passive contact.* Passive contact between person and infant, without trying to direct the infant's attention and activities, e.g., looking at baby without mutual regard; passive holding or touching.

(2) *Very low: Passive physical contact with brief, perfunctory stimulation.* Sustained passive physical contact between person and infant with a brief and perfunctory active stimulus, e.g., a pat or two, shifting the baby's position, saying a few words.

(3) *Low: Brief active stimulation without sustained physical contact.* The attentive person actively stimulates the baby briefly without mutual visual regard.

(4) *Intermediate: Active stimulation without attempted elicitation.* The stimulation involves a substantial degree of stimulus change (active touching, talking to, moving the baby), but there is no obvious attempt to elicit a response from the baby.

(5) *High: Active elicitation.* The attentive person actively attempts to elicit a response from the infant in any of the following ways:

(a) Engaging the baby's visual attention socially or with a toy.

(b) Active encouragement of motor skills.

(c) Responding to the infant's vocalizations, i.e., sustained imitation of the baby's vocalization; any response to distress except Check/Acknowledge, Columns 34–40.

(d) Active encouragement of social responsiveness, i.e., broad smiling and play.

COLUMNS 19–23: ATTENTIVENESS I (ATT-I)

Two classes of attentiveness are distinguished: passive and active. Passive attentiveness describes situations in which there is no rapid onset-offset or stimulus change. The passive attentiveness codes are Looking, Holding, Touching Passively and Touching Passively with an Object. Active attentiveness involves stimulus change. The active attentiveness codes are Mutual Regard and all of the codes in Columns 24–31.

1. *Look*. The person looks at the infant's face or at any part of the infant's body for any period of time, regardless of whether or not the infant looks back.
2. *Mutual Regard (MR)*. The person and the infant have direct eye-to-eye contact.
3. *Holds*. The person wholly or partially supports the infant's weight or maintains the infant's balance. Do not score if the baby is held just long enough to move him from one place to another.
4. *Touch Passively (T-Pass)*. Some part of a person's body is resting, at that person's initiative, against the baby without moving. This person is not supporting the baby's weight or balancing him. Do not score a touch initiated by the baby.
5. *Touch Passively with an Object (T-Pass/obj)*. A person is resting some object on or against the baby's body or in his mouth for at least five consecutive seconds, without moving it, e.g., holding a bottle quietly in the baby's mouth.

Rule

1. Holds preempts Touch Passively if they occur simultaneously. However, if they occur at different times in the same time-sampling unit, score both.

COLUMNS 24–31: ATTENTIVENESS II
(ATT-II)

Active attentiveness is stimulation in which stimulus change or movement is a principal feature. Active attentiveness codes are Mutual Regard in Columns 19–23 and all codes in Columns 24–31.

1. *Vocalization to the Baby (Voc to B).* The person speaks or sings to the baby or directs a non-speech sound (whistling, laughing, other sounds such as "ouch" related to interaction with the baby) to him. All contingent and imitative vocalizations directed to the baby (defined below) are also scored Vocalization to the Baby (Code 1).

2. *Vocalization to the Baby Contingent upon the Baby's Nondistress Vocalization (Voc C ND).* The person vocalizes to the baby following a nondistress vocalization by the baby in the same time-sampling unit. Both infant and adult vocalization must occur in the same observation unit. The contingent vocalization need not be logically related or apparently in response to the infant's vocalization; it need only follow the baby's vocalization in time.

3. *Vocalization to the Baby Contingent upon the Baby's Distress Vocalization (Voc C Dis).* The person vocalizes to the baby following or during a distress vocalization by the baby in the same time-sampling unit. Both infant and adult vocalization must occur in the same observation unit. The contingent vocalization need not be logically related or apparently in response to the infant's vocalization; it need only follow the baby's vocalization in time.

4. *Imitative Vocalization (Voc-Imit).* The person imitates the sounds made by the infant. Spontaneous baby talk, such as "goo-goo," is not scored.

5. *Touch Actively (T-Act).* The person touches the infant actively, with movement, but without moving the infant's whole body and without an inanimate object, e.g., pats,

rubs, tickles, kisses. The touching may occur through clothing such as rubbing the baby's back when he has a shirt on.

6. *Touch Actively with an Object (T-Act/obj)*. The person touches the infant actively, with movement, with an inanimate object. Examples include giving the baby an object or taking an object from the baby; dressing, diapering, moving a bottle or spoon in and out of the baby's mouth; jiggling the nipple of the bottle when it is already in the baby's mouth.

7. *Moves Baby (Mov B)*. The person moves the baby's whole body or at least half of it. Examples include picking the baby up, raising the baby's lower trunk for diapering, changing the baby's position, righting the baby when he falls over from a sitting position, rocking, bouncing, jiggling.

Rule

1. If Touch Actively and Touch Actively with an Object occur simultaneously, score only Touch Actively with an Object. If they occur at different times in the same time-sampling unit, score both.

COLUMNS 32–33: ANIMATION (ANI)

The face of the person attentive to the baby is lively and spirited. There may be high activity of other parts of the person's body as well.

1. *Broad Smile within Reach (Br Sm)*. A person who is within reach of the baby smiles broadly while looking at the baby, in response to something the baby has done, or as a result of interaction with the baby. The smile must be clear and full. Half smiles, little smiles and ambiguous smiles are not scored.

2. *Personal-Social Play (Pl).* The person engages in animated play that has a "fun" quality, where the apparent object is to amuse the baby, to play a game with recognizable rules or to act out a fantasy situation. To score the code, one of the following criteria must be met:

   a. Facial-vocal play
      (1) Smiling or laughing in one of the following contexts: the person is trying to amuse the infant; the person and the infant are amusing each other in a reciprocal play situation; there is a game acted out; or there is a fantasy situation acted out.
      (2) Making fun-like sounds, e.g., boo, tsk-tsk-tsk; singsong sounds accompanying a game.
      (3) Making faces in a playful context.

   b. Fine body play. Limb movement, as in patticake when the hands are patted together; tickling.
   c. Gross body play. The infant's whole body is moved in play, e.g., jiggling, bouncing on the knee, throwing the baby in the air, holding the baby overhead, rolling him on the bed.

Rules

1. *Smiling during Play.* If the person smiles broadly in the context of Personal-Social Play, only Personal-Social Play is scored.
2. *Inanimate Objects Involved in Play.* Personal-Social Play should be distinguished from Encouragement of Attentiveness to Inanimate Stimuli, Columns 41–45, which describes how inanimate objects are presented to the baby. The major element of Personal-Social Play is the personal aspect of it. The person playing with the baby is not primarily presenting a toy, but is presenting herself or part of herself in a playful fashion. Although an inanimate object may be involved in Personal-Social Play, it is not a criterion for scoring the

interaction as playful. If an object is presented during the course of play, both Personal-Social Play and the relevant codes in Columns 41–45 should be scored.

COLUMNS 34–40: RESPONSE TO DISTRESS (R TO DIS)

Response to Distress is scored if a person attempts to soothe the baby following a distress vocalization by the infant in the same time-sampling unit. Score only those adult responses which are clearly elicited by infant's fussing and crying.

1. *Social Soothing alone (S Soo al)*. An individual tries to soothe the infant by social stimulation. One of the following criteria must be met:

   a. Vocalizing to the baby (more than minimal acknowledgement of distress).
   b. Holding the baby (exclude transitional holding or carrying to a new position).
   c. Rocking or jiggling the baby.
   d. Encouraging the baby to look at mother or sibling, or otherwise trying to focus the baby's attention on a person.
   e. Encouraging the baby to sit up or crawl as a means of diverting his attention from his discomfort.

   If any of the categories listed below (2 to 6) occur simultaneously with Social Soothing, they are scored rather than Social Soothing.
2. *Play Object (Pl Obj)*. The person attempts to divert the infant by giving him an object to play with or by highlighting an object to catch his attention.
3. *Feeds*. The person feeds the baby in order to soothe him.
4. *Other Caretaking Response (Oth Ca)*. The person changes the baby's diaper or engages in some caretaking activity other than feeding.

5. *Pacifier (Pacif)*. The person gives the baby a pacifier.
6. *Checks and/or Acknowledges the Baby's Distress Minimally (Ch/A)*. The person checks with a brief glance to see why the infant is crying or acknowledges verbally and briefly the fact that the infant is crying, e.g., "Oh, you're hungry," or "Wait a minute, I'm coming."
7. *Other*. The person responds with any clear response other than those listed above, e.g., changes the baby's location or position.

Rule

1. *Multiple responses*. All discrete responses occurring in the time-sampling unit are scored, with the following exception. When Social Soothing accompanies a change of position or location, Social Soothing is scored instead of Other if the social components are the principal means by which the person is trying to soothe the baby. Other is scored, however, if the change in position or location is the primary means of effecting the soothing and the accompanying social soothing is incidental.

COLUMNS 41–45: ENCOURAGEMENT OF ATTENTIVENESS TO STIMULI (ENC ATT STIMULI)

These columns describe behavior in which the primary intent of the attentive person is to encourage or discourage the infant's visual and tactile exploration of objects.

0. *Separating Infant from Object (Sep)*. The person either purposefully or accidentally separates the infant from an inanimate object, part of another person's body, or part of the infant's own body. The infant must be actively reaching for or exploring the object when the separation takes place. Separation is not scored if the infant is only mouthing the object.

1. *Positioning an Object within View (Pos W View)*. The person purposefully positions the infant or an object so that the object is within view but not within reach of the baby.
2. *Positioning an Object within Reach (Pos F Reach)*. The person purposefully positions the infant or an object so that the object comes within the baby's reach.
3. *Positioning an Object in the Baby's Hand (Pos I Hand)*. The person purposefully puts an object directly into the baby's hand.
4. *Enticing, Highlighting (Ent-Hi)*.

   a. *Enticing*. The person purposefully directs the infant's attention to an object to which he is not attending by making the properties of the object salient to him, e.g., banging a rattle on a surface.
   b. *Highlighting*. When the infant is attending to an object, the person manipulates the object in such a way as to bring specific properties of the object (visual, tactile, auditory) to the infant's attention, e.g., rattling a rattle, winding up a music box, showing the clapper of a bell.

Rules

1. *Positioning*.

   a. The positioning codes are scored more than once if the behavior continues into succeeding time units.
   b. Positioning includes: placing the baby so that he can see himself in a mirror (because positioning of the mirror, an inanimate object, is involved); moving parts of the baby's own body to bring his attention to them, e.g., wiggling the baby's toes; placing a pacifier within view, within reach, or into his hand.
   c. Do not score any positioning where the primary intent is other than to encourage attentiveness to the object. Examples: positioning of caretaking objects in use, such as spoon of food, bottle of milk; placing a pacifier directly in the baby's mouth; moving the baby or another

person so that the person is within the baby's view, his reach or in his hand.

2. *Enticing, Highlighting*

a. Highlighting includes moving parts of a person's body other than the face, if the purpose is clearly to bring the baby's attention to them.

b. Do not score highlighting parts of the person's face, such as wrinkling the nose, covering the face during peek-a-boo, or highlighting parts of the infant's body, e.g., clapping his hands together.

COLUMNS 46–47: ENCOURAGEMENT OF EMERGENT GROSS MOTOR RESPONSES (ENC EM GROSS MOTOR RESP)

The person directly encourages the baby to engage in behaviors involving control of posture and locomotion. Simply verbalizing to encourage postural or locomotor responses, if unaccompanied by a gesture or other nonverbal communication, is not scored. Hovering in the vicinity of the baby merely to prevent him from falling is not scored.

1. *Posture (Post)*. The person actively encourages the baby to develop postural control, e.g., sitting, standing. Placing the baby in a sitting position is scored when there is active encouragement of his continuing to maintain that position partially by himself and when the focus is primarily on his motor performance. Holding the baby in a standing position is scored when there is some weight supported by his legs and feet, although focus on the infant's performance in supporting his weight is not required.

2. *Locomotion (Loc)*. The person encourages the baby to develop independent locomotion by helping him to walk, coaxing him to move in his walker by himself, pushing him in his walker, encouraging him to crawl.

COLUMN 48: SALIENT VERBALIZATIONS NOT
DIRECTED TO THE BABY (SAL VOC B)

This column describes verbalizations directed to someone other than the baby when either the speaker or the person spoken to is within 10 feet of the baby. Human voices emanating from a television or radio are not scored.

COLUMNS 49-51: CHANGE IN CONTAINER
OR ROOM (CHANGE C/R)

Change is scored when the infant is in a new container or room, one he was not in during the previous time-sampling unit, or if he is in two containers or rooms in the same time-sampling unit. Containers include an infant seat, a crib, a playpen, a person's lap, etc.

Rule

1. *Transitions*. Transition points are not scored, such as a room passed through on the way to another room. Arms or lap are not scored if the infant is picked up and held just long enough to be carried to another container.

COLUMNS 52-55: NUMBER OF OBJECTS
WITHIN REACH (NUMBER WR)

An object is within reach if the infant can touch it with his hand by moving his arm forward, up or to the side. The number of objects within reach of the infant is counted and recorded for each time-sampling unit. Each object within reach is counted separately, whether or not it resembles or is a duplicate of another object within reach.

1. *Toy (Columns 52–53)*. A toy is an object made for children of any age to play with, including teething rings, but excluding pacifiers and toy-like parts of infant furniture. Broken-off pieces of toys are scored as separate toys, e.g., a detached wing of a bird is scored as a separate toy. A toy with a string attached, when both toy and string are within reach or when only the toy is within reach, is scored as one toy. A toy with the string attached, when only the string is within reach, is scored "string" (see HO/CO, below).

2. *Household Object/Caretaking Object (HO/CO) (Columns 54–55)*. Household Objects are objects in the environment which may serve as toys although they are primarily for adult use. Caretaking Objects are objects made or bought to meet the physical needs of the baby. Examples of objects included in the category, HO/CO, are newspapers, ashtrays, cigarette cartons, wallets, telephones, telephone wire, pets, string, jewelry, pots and other utensils used to prepare and store food. Excluded from the HO/CO count are objects which are so common in our culture that infants are likely to habituate to them.

Objects excluded are:

a. Food and bottles.
b. Table utensils (silverware, cups, plates, baby food jars).
c. Other caretaking objects when they are in use, e.g., a powder can from which powder is being shaken, a comb being used to comb the infant's hair, a tissue used as a bib. When not in use, these items are scored.
d. Linen (bedclothes, tablecloths, facecloths, towels, etc.) and all similar fabric items.
e. Clothing.
f. Structural features of the room, e.g., windows, sills, floor.
g. All adult and infant furniture, including toy-like parts of the furniture.

VARIETY OF OBJECTS WITHIN REACH
(OBJECTS WR)

In the blanks on the right of the observation sheet, the observer records each toy or HO/CO by name. Each object is listed only once, regardless of the number of time-sampling units in which it is within reach of the baby. The measure, variety, refers to the number of different objects within reach of the baby during the home observation.

Rules

1. *Identical Objects.* Items identical in appearance are listed only once, e.g., two yellow kleenexes are listed only once.
2. *Parts of Objects.* If a part of an object is not the same as the whole in appearance, texture, or functional possibilities, e.g., wing of bird and bird, score two different objects. If part and whole are essentially the same except for size, score one object.
3. *Essentially Identical Objects except for Minor Variation.* If two or more objects are alike except for minor variations, score one object, e.g., playing cards; pastel pink tissue and white tissue. If, however, there is a major color difference, score two different objects.
4. *Differences in Configuration.* An object seen under different conditions, e.g., a hard cover book open and closed, is considered as one object.
5. A single giant plastic bead is scored separately from a strand of two or more beads.

3

MATERNAL RATINGS

1. *Expression of Positive Affect.* The extent to which positive affect is expressed in an intense, demonstrative manner.

   0. *No positive affect noted.*
   1. *Very low*   —Quiet, subdued, low keyed through-out—but suggestive of positive feeling tone.
   2. *Low*   —Quiet, subdued expression with occa-sional moderate expression of positive feeling. Strong expression of feeling is absent.
   3. *Moderate*   —Moderate expression of feelings throughout the time period—"pleas-ant" smiles, warm speaking tones.

Intense positive expression is rare or absent.

4. *High*   —Somewhat demonstrative expression of positive feelings (less intense than 5) is fairly frequent.

5. *Very high*   —Demonstrative, exuberant, intense expression of positive feelings is frequent.

2. *Contingency of Maternal Responses to Distress.* The extent to which mother's response is *immediate* and *specific* to the infant's signal.

0. *Not applicable* —Infant manifests no distress, or others respond instead of mother.

1. *Very low*   —Infant cries for several minutes before distress is acknowledged or acted upon.

2. *Low*   —Soon after distress is manifest, mother may acknowledge it, but usually does not act directly to reduce it for several minutes.

3. *Moderate*   —At times mother responds to distress quickly, but at times not for several minutes.

4. *High*   —Mother usually responds almost immediately to infant's cry.

5. *Very high*   —Mother usually responds to minimal cues, e.g., increased motor activity, change to mouthing or finger sucking, borderline distress vocalization, without overt crying developing.

CHARACTERISTICS OF THE INANIMATE ENVIRONMENT

I. *Responsiveness of Objects Within Reach.* This is a rating of changes in stimulation that can be produced by the *average* 5 month old interacting with the object. The essential element of "responsiveness" is the object's capacity to respond contingently to the infant's manipulation, so that the infant receives feedback in the form of changes in visual, auditory or tactile stimulation. Thus, the structure of the object, as well as its size, are considered in relation to the average 5 month old infant's fine motor skills as these limit his ability to manipulate, retrieve, and control the object.

Four dimensions of responsiveness have been distinguished: Moving Parts, Reflected Image, Change in Shape and Contour, and Noise Production. Each should be rated independently of the other.

A. *Moving Parts.* The extent to which the object consists of distinct parts which can be moved (independently of each other) by the infant.

Three major classes of Moving Parts are distinguished:

1. Exterior parts which can be manipulated independently of each other by the infant; the parts in motion can be both seen and touched by the infant, e.g., cradle gym.
2. Interior parts which move when the infant manipulates the object; the distinct parts in motion can be seen but not touched by the infant, e.g., a ring filled with particles floating in fluid.
3. Objects which are weighted, suspended or affixed by suction so that they return to the infant after he moves them, e.g., a "battable" roly-poly clown.

   (Objects which may or may not be affixed by suction are rated in the state in which they are observed; ratings for objects which are affixed by suction part of the time and free part of the time are averaged.)

   Moving parts which can be both touched and seen by the infant (class 1) are rated higher on responsiveness than are parts in motion which can be seen only (class 2). Class 3 objects are given a rating of 3 for the characteristic of "battableness"; any additional moving parts on the object may serve to raise the overall rating for the object. The moving parts must be visible to be scored at all. Whether or not the moving parts produce noise is not relevant for this rating; this property is rated separately under Noise Production.

Moving Parts (*Ratings*):

1. *Very Low Responsiveness*

    no moving parts, e.g., cup, block, string, paper, ashtray.

    a part capable of minimal movement, with little likelihood of the infant's discovering this movement, e.g., trigger of pistol.

2. *Low Responsiveness*

    Class 1

    a. one minor part that moves freely, e.g., clapper of bell.

    b. several minor parts that move slightly, e.g., ears and tail of stuffed animal.

    Class 2

    c. internal parts that are not salient when in motion, e.g., small plastic duck with beads, saltshaker with salt.

3. *Moderate Responsiveness*

    Class 1

    a. one major part that moves freely, e.g., blue-head rattle with ruffled collar, red ring with string.

    b. several parts, some major, that move moderately, e.g., beads on a stroller, pages of magazine.

    Class 2

    c. internal parts that are very salient while in motion, e.g., hourglass.

    Class 3

    d. a "battable" object, e.g., roly-poly clown, object suspended in a transparent ball.

4. *High Responsiveness*—several parts that move freely, e.g., 4-duck ferris wheel with visible marbles,

3 plastic balls on chain, and large fabric clown.

5. *Very High Responsiveness*—many major parts that move very freely, e.g., mobile, cradle gym, plastic keys or disks on a chain.

B. *Reflected Image.* The extent to which the object reflects an image clearly visible to the infant and contingent upon his action.

1. *Low Responsiveness*—reflects no image, or hardly any, e.g., plastic rattle.
2. *Moderate Responsiveness*—reflects hazy or distorted image, e.g., window glass, metal pencil sharpener, aluminum foil.
3. *High Responsiveness*—reflects clear, sharp undistorted image, e.g., mirror.

C. *Change in Shape and Contour.* The extent to which changes in the configuration of the contour or geometric shape or boundary of the object are responsive to the infant's manipulation. These changes in contour, shape and boundary exclude those due to "Moving Parts." They are produced primarily by bending, crumpling, squashing, crumbling.

1. *Very Low Responsiveness*

no change e.g., ceramic mug, beads on a stroller, hourglass.

minimal change: either the object as a whole is quite, but not completely, resistant, or only a relatively minor part is responsive, e.g., white plastic imitation coke bottle, suction cup on free suction toy, small ears of a large stuffed animal.

2. *Low Responsiveness*—limited change

a. The object as a whole is subject to limited change, e.g., rubber teether, clothespin, squeaker toy, empty Marlboro flip-top box.

   b. parts of the object are subject to some change, e.g., long string on taut cradle gym.

3. *Moderate Responsiveness*
   a. object as a whole is moderately responsive, e.g., long strand of giant plastic beads (5-11 beads).
   b. one major part is responsive, e.g., string attached to non-responsive object (red ring with string); keys on 6-in. chain.
   c. several secondary parts are very responsive, e.g., strings of umbrella mobile.

4. *High Responsiveness*
   a. object as a whole is highly responsive, e.g., very long strand of giant plastic beads (12 beads or more).
   b. a major proportion is very responsive, e.g., large fabric clown, 3 plastic balls on 12-in. chain.

5. *Very High Responsiveness*—very highly responsive, e.g., newspaper, magazine, string, ribbons, tissue, empty Tarryton pack, soft cookie.

D. *Noise Production.* The extent to which the object has intrinsic or structural noise-making potential which can be activated by the infant's manipulation. The potential for noise must be inherent in the construction of the object, and not the result of banging the object against another object.

1. *Low Responsiveness*—produces no noise in response to the infant's manipulation, e.g., pacifier, telephone wire, teaspoon.
2. *Moderate Responsiveness*—may produce noise on occasion, but not consistently, because the required manipulation is difficult for a typical 5-month-old, e.g., most squeaker toys, telephone with dial.
3. *High Responsiveness*—easily produces significant

distinct sounds, e.g., rattle, cradle gym, giant beads, disks on chain, newspapers, beads on stroller.

II. *Complexity of Objects Within Reach.* The extent to which the object provides "information" to the infant via his various modalities.

    A. There are five components in this rating:

        1. *Number of Colors*—the extent to which the object is multicolored.

        2. *Amount of Pattern*

            a. *Visual Pattern*—amount of pattern printed on the surface of the object, e.g., pictures, lettering.

            b. *Tactile Pattern*—small scale variation in the contour, usually decorative in purpose, e.g., closely spaced ridges, ruffles, etc.; or variation in texture, e.g., plastic with areas of fur.

        3. *Number of Different Shapes*—number of different geometric shapes comprising the object; also large-scale variation in contour, usually defining the object, e.g., small sphere (head) plus large sphere (torso) plus narrow cylinders (limbs) comprise stringdoll.

        4. *Size*—amount of area to be looked at or touched before the infant can identify or recognize the object.

        5. *Extent of Responsiveness*—extent to which feedback in the form of changes in stimulation can be produced by a 5 month infant interacting with the object (see "Responsiveness of Objects Within Reach" for details); responsiveness comprises the number of dimensions (of the 4 rated) on which the object is responsive, and the extent to which it is responsive on each dimension.

B. Scoring Criteria:

1. *Very Low*
    All the following apply:
    a. Monochromatic.
    b. No visual or tactile pattern.
    c. One or two different shapes, or one or two "turns" in the contour defining the object.
    d. Small.
    e. Lowest scores on all responsiveness dimensions or quite responsive on only one dimension.

Examples: One smooth giant bead, a plastic doughnut, yellow block, pink plastic cup, telephone cord, ribbon, Kleenex.

2. *Low*
    Class a:
    1. Small.
    2. Basically monochromatic.
    3. May or may not have minor color or tactile accents.

Must have at least one, may have as many as two of the following:
    4. Fairly responsive but on one dimension only.
    5. Has a good deal of repetitive *tactile*, but not *visual* pattern.
    6. Several different shapes, or some large scale variation in contour.

Examples: Fork, hammer, telephone & barbell rattles, pacifier, pretzel teether, pink key teether, textured fruit with ridges, blue rubber keyhole teether.

Class b: All the following apply:

1. Medium to large.
2. Basically monochromatic.
3. Small amount of visual or tactile pattern.
4. Minimally responsive on all dimensions.
5. Very few different shapes; very little large scale variation in contour.

Examples: White imitation coke bottle, brown glass ashtray, Johnson's Baby Powder, aluminum ashtray.

3. *Moderate*—Only *one* of the following applies:

   a. Multicolored—at least two major colors with strong color accents, or three or more major colors.
   b. Highly patterned—much visual and/or tactile pattern; (must have some of both visual and tactile pattern; must have high degree of at least one of them).
   c. Many different geometric shapes and/or much large scale variation in contour.
   d. Moderate to high responsiveness.*

Examples: Doll with diaper, ceramic mug, small plastic duck.

4. *High*—Any *two* of the following apply:

   a. Multicolored—at least two major colors with strong color accents, or 3 or more major colors.

*Responsiveness should not be the major criterion for moderate complexity. If the object is utterly "simple" except for its responsiveness (i.e., if it is very low on the other 3 criteria, e.g., plain sheet of paper), its complexity rating is 2 rather than 3. Only if the object just misses meeting the other 3 criteria is "Moderate to high responsiveness" sufficient to score 3 on Complexity.

    b. Highly patterned—much visual and/or tactile pattern; (must have some of both visual and tactile pattern; must have high degree of at least one of them).

    c. Many different geometric shapes and/or much large scale variation in contour.

    d. Moderate to high responsiveness.

    (The components not meeting the above listed criteria are present to a *lesser* degree or not at all.)

Examples: Disks on a chain, keys on a chain, blue face rattle on collar, lamb squeaker, tiger squeaker, Bozo, face rattle on clear handle, balls and rings on suction stick, telephone with coiled wire, colorful magazine.

5. *Very High*—All the following apply:

    a. Multicolored—at least two major colors with strong color accents, or three or more major colors.

    b. Highly patterned—much visual and/or tactile pattern (must have some of both visual and tactile pattern; must have high degree of at least one of them).

    c. Many different geometric shapes and/or much large scale variation in contour.

    d. Medium to large in size.

    e. Moderate to high responsiveness.

Examples: Umbrella mobile, doll with patterned dress, cradle gym, ducks on wheel, large red clown.

SUPPLEMENTARY INFANT MEASURES– PROBLEM SOLVING

1. *Overcoming an Obstacle*

Description: A transparent plastic obstacle is positioned within easy reach of the infant with its long axis horizontal to the table and its lower edge resting against the table. It is held by the tester with a thumb and two fingers on each lateral edge so that the infant's view of an attractive rattle lying on its side behind the obstacle is not obscured. The tester notes whether the infant looks, touches, pulls, pushes, mouths, or reaches over and around the obstacle to get the suction rattle. The obstacle is not released by the tester unless the infant uses considerable force to push or pull it over.

Scoring:

_____ 0. Shows no interest in obstacle or object behind obstacle by not looking or giving a brief glance.

Shows interest by looking at object and/or obstacle.

Shows interest by touching, mouthing or pulling obstacle but does not secure object. (Primary interest in obstacle.)

_____ 1. Tries unsuccessfully to secure object by pulling, pushing or reaching around obstacle.

_____ 2. Forcefully pushes or pulls obstacle and secures object.

_____ 3. Reaches over or around obstacle and gets object.

2. *Finding a Partially Hidden Object*

Description: An attractive rattle is partially covered by a white cloth in such a fashion that approximately one-third of the rattle is exposed and within easy reach of the infant. It is noted whether the infant's primary interest is in the cloth or in the partially hidden rattle.

Scoring:

_____ 0. No interest shown in cloth or object by not looking or by giving a brief glance.

Looks at cloth but does not touch or pull it.

Interest in cloth but not object—may pull, mouth, or push it.

_____ 1. Looks intently at partially hidden object, but makes no move to secure it—may activate cloth but makes no effort to get object.

_____ 2. Attempts to secure object either by reaching for it directly or by pulling cloth away but is unsuccessful.

_____ 3. Secures object by pulling cloth away or by reaching for it directly.

3. *Using a Support to Secure an Object*

Description: A white cloth is placed on the table in front of and within easy reach of the infant. An attractive rattle is then placed on its side on this cloth out of the infant's reach but easily within his view. To reach the rattle he would have to first pull the cloth toward himself. In this way he would be using a support (cloth) to secure the object.

Scoring:

_____ 0. No interest shown in cloth or object by not looking or by giving a brief glance.
Looks at cloth but does not touch or pull it.
Interested in support but not object—may pull, mouth, or push it.

_____ 1. Interested in object but does not use support to get object—may look at object intently and try to reach out for it but does not use cloth as support.

_____ 2. Uses support by pushing or pulling it, but is not successful in getting object.

_____ 3. Uses support to get object successfully.

4. *Using a String to Secure a Ring*

Description: The red ring is placed directly in front of but out of the infant's reach, however, the gimp (plastic string) which is attached to the ring is within easy reach. It is noted whether the infant looks, pulls, or plays with the gimp alone, or if he pulls the ring within his reach with the gimp. The inference of purpose-fullness is partly determined by the time that elapses between pulling the ring within reach and actually picking up the ring.

Scoring:

_____ 0. Not interested in ring or string. May glance at them briefly.
Looks at string and ring but makes no effort to reach out for them.

_____ 1. Plays with string or pulls ring accidentally. May touch ring but does not pick it up.

_____ 2. Pulls string questionably, not purposefully to get ring. Long latency between pulling the ring within easy reach and actually picking it up.

_____ 3. Pulls string purposefully to get ring. Picks up ring soon after it is within easy reach.

BIBLIOGRAPHY

Ainsworth, M. *Infancy in Uganda: Infant care and the growth of love.* Baltimore: Johns Hopkins, 1967.

Ainsworth, M., Bell, S., & Stayton, D. Individual differences in strange-situation behavior of one-year-olds. In H. R. Schaffer (Ed.), *The origins of human social relations.* New York: Academic Press, 1971.

Ambrose, A. (Ed.) *Stimulation in early infancy.* New York: Academic Press, 1969.

Anderson, S., & Messick, S. Social competency in young children. *Developmental Psychology,* 1974, **10,** 282–293.

Bayley, N. Comparisons of mental and motor test scores for ages 1–15 months by sex, birth order, race, geographical location, and education of parents. *Child Development,* 1965, **36,** 379–411.

Bayley, N. *Bayley scales of infant development.* New York: Psychological Corporation, 1969.

Bayley, N., & Schaefer, E. S. Correlations of maternal and child behaviors with the development of mental abilities: Data from the Berkeley Growth Study. *Monographs of the Society for Research in Child Development,* 1964, 29(6, Serial No. 97).

Beckwith, L. Relationships between infants' vocalizations and their mothers' behavior. *Merrill-Palmer Quarterly,* 1971, **17**, 211–226.

Bell, S., & Ainsworth, M. Infant crying and maternal responsiveness. *Child Development,* 1972, **43**, 1171–1190.

Bergman, T., Haith, M., & Mann, L. Development of eye contact and facial scanning in infants. Paper presented at the biennial meeting of the Society for Research in Child Development, Minneapolis, April 1971.

Berlyne, D. *Conflict, arousal and curiosity.* New York: McGraw-Hill, 1960.

Bishop, B. M. Mother-child interaction and the social behavior of children. *Psychological Monographs,* 1951, 65(328).

Bloom, K., & Erickson, M. The role of eye contact in the social reinforcement of infant vocalizations. Paper Presented at the biennial meeting of the Society for Research in Child Development, Minneapolis, April 1971.

Bowlby, J. Maternal care and mental health. *Monograph Series,* No. 2, Geneva: World Health Organization, 1951.

Bowlby, J. *Attachment and loss.* London: Hogarth Press, 1969.

Brackbill, Y. Extinction of the smiling response in infants as a function of reinforcement schedule. *Child Development,* 1958, **29**, 115–124.

Brennan, W., Ames, E., & Moore, R. Age differences in infants' attention to patterns of different complexities. *Science,* 1966, **151**, 354–356.

Brody, S. *Patterns of mothering: Maternal influences during infancy.* New York: International Universities Press, 1956.

Bronson, W. C. The growth of competence: Issues of conceptualization and measurement. In H. R. Schaffer (Ed.), *The origins of human social relations.* New York: Academic Press, 1971.

Brossard, L. M., & Décarie, T. G. Comparative reinforcing effect of eight stimulations on the smiling response of infants. *Journal of Child Psychology and Psychiatry*, 1968, 9, 51–59.

Brossard, L. M., & Décarie, T. G. The effects of three kinds of perceptual-social stimulation on the development of institutionalized infants. *Early Child Development and Care*, 1971, 1, 111–130.

Caldwell, B. M. The effects of infant care. In M. Hoffman & L. Hoffman (Eds.), *Review of child development research*, Vol. 1. New York: Russell Sage Foundation, 1964.

Cameron, J., Livson, N., & Bayley, N. Infant vocalizations and their relationship to mature intelligence. *Science*, 1967, 157, 331–333.

Casler, L. Maternal deprivation: A critical review of the literature. *Monographs of the Society for Research in Child Development*, 1961, 26(2, Serial No. 80).

Casler, L. The effects of extra tactile stimulation on a group of institutionalized infants. *Genetic Psychology Monographs*, 1965, 71, 137–175.

Casler, L. Perceptual deprivation in institutional settings. In G. Newton & S. Levine (Eds.), *Early experience and behavior*. Springfield, Ill.: Charles C Thomas, 1968.

Chomsky, N. A. Review of B. F. Skinner, *Verbal behavior*. *Language*, 1959, 35, 26–58.

Clarke-Stewart, K. A. Interactions between mothers and their young children: Characteristics and consequences. *Monographs of the Society for Research in Child Development*, 1973, 38 (6–7, Serial No. 153).

Corman, H. H., & Escalona, S. K. Stages of sensorimotor development: A replication study. *Merrill-Palmer Quarterly*, 1969, 15, 351–361.

Dember, W. N. Motivation and the cognitive revolution. *American Psychologist*, 1974, 29, 161–178.

Deutsch, C. P. Social class and child development. In B. M. Caldwell & H. N. Ricciuti (Eds.), *Review of child development research*. Vol. 3. *Child development and social policy*. Chicago: Univ. of Chicago Press, 1973.

Escalona, S. K. *The roots of individuality.* Chicago: Aldine, 1968.

Escalona, S. K., & Heider, G. M. *Prediction and outcome: A study in child development.* New York: Basic Books, 1959.

Etzel, B. C., and Gewirtz, J. L. Experimental modification of caretaker-maintained high rate operant crying in a 6- and 20-week-old infant: Extinction of crying with reinforcement of eye contact. *Journal of Experimental Child Psychology,* 1967, 5, 303–317.

Fantz, R. L. Visual experience in infants: Decreased attention to familiar patterns relative to novel ones. *Science,* 1964, 146, 668–670.

Fantz, R. L., & Nevis, S. Pattern preferences and perceptual-cognitive development in early infancy. *Merrill-Palmer Quarterly,* 1967, 13, 77–108.

Fiske, D., & Maddi, S. A conceptual framework. In D. Fiske & S. Maddi (Eds.), *Functions of varied experience.* Homewood, Ill.: Dorsey, 1961.

Foster, M., Vietze, P., & Friedman, S. Visual attention to noncontingent and contingent stimuli in early infancy. Paper presented at the annual meetings of the American Psychological Association, Montreal, Aug. 1973.

Fraiberg, S., & Friedman, D. A. Studies in the ego development of the congenitally blind child. *The Psychoanalytic Study of the Child,* 1964, 19, 113–169.

Frank, L. K. Tactile communication. *Genetic Psychology Monographs,* 1957, 56, 209–225.

Freedman, D. G. Smiling in blind infants and the issue of innate vs. acquired. *Journal of Child Psychology and Psychiatry,* 1964, 5, 171–184.

Fries, M. The formation of character as observed in the well-baby clinic. *American Journal of Diseases of Children,* 1935, 49, 28–42.

Geber, M. The psycho-motor development of African children in the first year and the influence of maternal behavior. *Journal of Social Psychology,* 1958, 47, 185–195.

Gewirtz, J. L. A learning analysis of the effects of normal stimulation privation and deprivation on the acquisition of social motivation and attachment. In B. M. Foss (Ed.), *Determinants of infant behavior.* New York: Wiley, 1961.

Gewirtz, J. L. Mechanisms of social learning: Some roles of stimulation and behavior in early human development. In D. Goslin (Ed.), *Handbook of socialization theory and research.* Chicago: Rand-McNally, 1969.

Gewirtz, J. L., & Gewirtz, H. B. Stimulus conditions, infant behaviors, and social learning in four Israeli child-rearing environments: A preliminary report illustrating differences in environment and behavior between the "only" and the "youngest" child. In B. M. Foss (Ed.), *Determinants of infant behavior III.* New York: Wiley, 1965.

Goffeney, B., Henderson, N. B., & Butler, B. V. Negro-white, male-female eight-month developmental scores compared with seven-year WISC and Bender test scores. *Child Development,* 1971, 42, 595–604.

Goldberg, S. Infant development and mother-infant interaction in urban Zambia. In P. H. Leiderman & S. Tulkin (Eds.), *Cultural and social influences in infancy and early childhood.* Stanford: Stanford University Press, 1975.

Goldfarb, W. Effects of psychological deprivation in infancy and subsequent adjustment. *American Journal of Orthopsychiatry,* 1945, 15, 247–255.

Gray, S. W., & Klaus, R. A. The early training project: A seventh year report. *Child Development,* 1970, 41, 909–924.

Greenberg, D. J. Accelerating visual complexity levels in the human infant. *Child Development,* 1971, 42, 905–918.

Greenberg, D. J., Uzgiris, I. C., & Hunt, J. McV. Attentional preference and experience: III. Visual familiarity and looking time. *Journal of Genetic Psychology,* 1970, 117, 123–135.

Guilford, J. P. Intelligence, 1965 model. *American Psychologist,* 1966, 21, 20–26.

Harlow, H. F. Love in infant monkeys. *Scientific American,* 1959, 200, 68–74.

Harlow, H. F., & Harlow, M. K. The affectional systems. In A. M. Schrier, H. F. Harlow, & F. Stollnitz (Eds.), *Behavior of nonhuman primates,* Vol. 2. New York: Academic Press, 1965.

Haugan, G. M., & McIntire, R. W. Comparisons of vocal imitation, tactile stimulation, and food as reinforcers for infant vocalizations. *Developmental Psychology,* 1972, 6, 201–209.

Hebb, D. O. *The organization of behavior.* New York: Wiley, 1949.

Helson, H. *Adaptation-level theory: An experimental and systematic approach to behavior.* New York: Harper & Row, 1964.

Hindley, C. Stability and change in abilities up to five years: Group trends. *Journal of Child Psychology and Psychiatry,* 1965, 6, 85–99.

Hollingshead, A. B. *Two factor index of social position.* New Haven: Yale University Press, 1956.

Honzik, M. A sex difference in the age of onset of the parent-child resemblance in intelligence. *Journal of Educational Psychology,* 1963, 54, 231–237.

Hunt, J. McV. *Intelligence and experience.* New York: Ronald Press, 1961.

Hunt, J. McV. Motivation inherent in information processing and action. In O. J. Harvey (Ed.), *Motivation and social interaction.* New York: Ronald Press, 1963.

Hunt, J. McV. Intrinsic motivation and its role in psychological development. In D. Levine (Ed.), *Nebraska symposium on motivation.* Lincoln: University of Nebraska Press, 1965.

Hunt, J., & Bayley, N. Explorations into patterns of mental development and prediction from the Bayley Scales of Infant Development. In J. P. Hill (Ed.), *Minnesota symposium on child psychology,* Vol. 5. Minneapolis: University of Minnesota Press, 1971.

Jones, S. J., & Moss, H. A. Age, state, and maternal behavior associated with infant vocalizations. *Child Development,* 1971, 42, 1039–1051.

Kagan, J. *Change and continuity in infancy.* New York: Wiley, 1971.

Kagan, J., & Lewis, M. Studies of attention in the human infant. *Merrill-Palmer Quarterly*, 1965, **11**, 95-127.

Kaila, E. Die reactionen des sauglings auf das menschlichte gesicht. *Annales Universitatis Aboensis*, Ser. B. Humaniora, 1932, **17**, 1-114.

Kessen, W., Marshall, M. H., & Salapatek, P. H. Human infancy: A bibliography and guide. In P. H. Mussen (Ed.), *Carmichael's manual of child psychology*, Vol. 1. (3rd ed.) New York: Wiley, 1970.

Kilbride, J. E., Robbin, M. C., & Kilbride, P. L. The comparative motor development of Baganda, American White, and American Black infants. *American Anthropologist*, 1970, **72**, 1422-1428.

King, W., & Seegmiller, B. Performance of 14- to 22-month old black, firstborn male infants on tests of cognitive development: The Bayley Scales and the Infant Psychological Development Scale. *Developmental Psychology*, 1973, **8**, 317-326.

Klein, R. P. Detecting interaction between continuous variables: Multiple regression vs. analysis of variance. Unpublished manuscript, Social & Behavioral Sciences Branch, National Institute of Child Health & Human Development, National Institutes of Health, Bethesda, Md., 1974.

Kohen-Raz, R. Scalogram analysis of some developmental sequences of infant behavior as measured by the Bayley Infant Scale of Mental Development. *Genetic Psychology Monographs*, 1967, **76**, 3-21.

Konner, M. J. Infancy among the Kalahari Desert San. In P. H. Leiderman & S. Tulkin (Eds.), *Cultural and social influences in infancy and early childhood*. Stanford: Stanford University Press, 1975.

Korner, A. F. Sex differences in newborns with special reference to differences in the organization of oral behavior. *Journal of Child Psychology and Psychiatry*, 1973, **14**, 19-29.

Korner, A. F., & Thoman, E. B. Visual alertness in neonates as evoked by maternal care. *Journal of Experimental Child Psychology*, 1970, **10**, 67-78.

Korner, A. F., & Thoman, E. B. The relative efficacy of contact and vestibular-proprioceptive stimulation in soothing neonates. *Child Development*, 1972, **43**, 443–453.

Kulka, A., Fry, C., & Goldstein, F. Kinesthetic needs in infancy. *American Journal of Orthopsychiatry*, 1960, **3**, 562–571.

Lambert, W. W. Interpersonal behavior. In P. H. Mussen (Ed.), *Handbook of research methods in child development*. New York: Wiley, 1960.

Leiderman, P. H., & Leiderman, G. F. Familial influences on infant development in an East African agricultural community. In P. H. Leiderman & S. Tulkin (Eds.), *Cultural and social influences in infancy and early childhood*. Stanford: Stanford University Press, 1975.

Lenneberg, E. H. *Biological foundations of language*. New York: Wiley, 1967.

Levine, S. A. A further study of infantile handling and adult avoidance learning. *Journal of Personality*, 1956, **25**, 70–80.

Levine, S. A. The effects of infantile experience on adult behavior. In A. Bachrach (Ed.), *Experimental foundations of clinical psychology*, New York: Basic Books, 1962.

Levy, D. *Maternal overprotection*. New York: Columbia University Press, 1943.

Lewis, M. State as an infant-environment interaction: An analysis of mother-infant interaction as a function of sex. *Merrill-Palmer Quarterly*, 1972, **18**, 95–121.

Lewis, M. Infant intelligence tests: Their use and misuse. *Human Development*, 1973, **16**, 108–118.

Lewis, M., & Goldberg, S. Perceptual-cognitive development in infancy: A generalized expectancy model as a function of the mother-infant relationship. *Merrill-Palmer Quarterly*, 1969, **15**, 81–100.

Lewis, M. (with the collaboration of Goldberg, S., & Campbell, H.). A developmental study of information processing within the first three years of life: Response decrement to a redundant signal. *Monographs of the Society for Research in Child Development*, 1969, **34**(9, Serial No. 133).

Lewis, M., & McGurk, H. Evaluation of infant intelligence. *Science*, 1972, **178**, 1174.

Liddicoat, R., & Koza, C. Language development in African infants. *Psychologica Africana*, 1963, **10**, 108–116.

Lusk, D., & Lewis, M. Mother-infant interaction and infant development among the Wolof of Senegal. *Human Development*, 1972, **15**, 58–69.

McCall, R. B., Hogarty, P. S., & Hurlburt, N. Transitions in infant sensori-motor development and the prediction of childhood IQ. *American Psychologist*, 1972, **27**, 728–748.

McCall, R. B., & Kagan, J. Attention in the infant: Effects of complexity, contour, perimeter and familiarity. *Child Development*, 1967, **38**, 939–952.

McCall, R. B., & Melson, W. H. Complexity, contour, and area as determinants of attention in infants. *Developmental Psychology*, 1970, **3**, 343–349.

McNeill, D. The development of language. In P. H. Mussen (Ed.), *Carmichael's manual of child psychology*, Vol. 1. (3rd ed.) New York: Wiley, 1970.

Mason, W. A. Early social deprivation in the nonhuman primate: Implications for human behavior. In D. C. Glass (Ed.), *Environmental influences*. New York: Rockefeller University Press, 1968.

Miller, G. A., Galanter, E. H., & Pribram, K. H. *Plans and the structure of behavior*. New York: Holt, Rinehart & Winston, 1960.

Moore, T. Language and intelligence: A longitudinal study of the first eight years. *Human Development*, 1967, **10**, 88–106.

Moss, H. A. Methodological issues in studying mother-infant interaction. *American Journal of Orthopsychiatry*, 1965, **35**, 482–486.

Moss, H. A. Sex, age and state as determinants of mother-infant interaction. *Merrill-Palmer Quarterly*, 1967, **13**, 19–36.

Moss, H. A., & Robson, K. S. The relation between the amount of time infants spend at various states and the development of visual behavior. *Child Development*, 1970, **41**, 509–517.

Moss, H. A., Robson, K. S., & Pedersen, F. A. Determinants of maternal stimulation of infants and consequences of treatment for later reactions to strangers. *Developmental Psychology,* 1969, 1, 239–246.

Murphy, L. B. *Widening world of childhood.* New York: Basic Books, 1962.

Murphy, L. B. Assessment of infants and young children. In L. L. Dittman (Ed.), *Early child care: The new perspectives.* New York: Atherton Press, 1968.

Murphy, L. B. Infants' play and cognitive development. In M. W. Piers (Ed.), *Play and development.* New York: Norton, 1972.

Orlansky, H. Infant care and personality. *Psychological Bulletin,* 1949, 46, 1–48.

Pavenstedt, E. A comparison of the child-rearing environments of upper-lower and very low-lower class families. *American Journal of Orthopsychiatry,* 1965, 35, 89–98.

Piaget, J. *The origins of intelligence in the child.* New York: International Universities Press, 1953. (First published, 1936.)

Pinneau, S. R. The infantile disorders of hospitalism and anaclitic depression. *Pyschological Bulletin,* 1955, 52, 429–462.

Prescott, J. W. Early social deprivation. In D. Lindsley & A. Riesen (Eds.), *Perspectives on human deprivation: Biological, psychological and sociological.* National Institute of Child Health and Human Development, National Institutes of Health, Washington, D.C.: U.S. Government Printing Office, 1968.

Prescott, J. W. Early somatosensory deprivation as an ontogenetic process in the abnormal development of the brain and behavior. In I. E. Goldsmith & J. Moor-Jankowski (Eds.), *Medical primatology 1970.* Basel: Karger, 1971.

Provence, S. The first year of life: The infant, In L. L. Dittman (Ed.), *Early child care: The new perspectives.* New York: Atherton Press, 1968.

Provence, S., & Lipton, R. *Infants in institutions.* New York: International Universities Press, 1962.

Repucci, N. D. Parental education, sex differences, and performance on cognitive tasks among two-year-old children. *Developmental Psychology,* 1971, 4, 248–253.

Rheingold, H. L. The measurement of maternal care. *Child Development*, 1960, **31**, 565–575.

Rheingold, H. L. The effect of environmental stimulation upon social and exploratory behavior in the human infant. In B. M. Foss (Ed.), *Determinants of infant behavior*. New York: Wiley, 1961.

Rheingold, H. L., Gewirtz, J. L., & Ross, H. Social conditioning of vocalizations in the infant. *Journal of Comparative and Physiological Psychology*, 1959, **52**, 68–73.

Rheingold, H. L., & Samuels, H. R. Maintaining the positive behavior of infants by increased stimulation. *Developmental Psychology*, 1969, **1**, 520–526.

Ribble, M. A. *Rights of infants*. New York: Columbia University Press, 1943.

Riesen, A. H. Sensory deprivation. In E. Stellar & J. Stellar (Eds.), *Progress in physiological psychology*, Vol. 1. New York: Academic Press, 1966.

Robson, K. S. The role of eye-to-eye contact in maternal-infant attachment. *Journal of Child Psychology and Psychiatry*, 1967, **8**, 13–25.

Robson, K. S., & Moss, H. A. Patterns and determinants of maternal attachment. *The Journal of Pediatrics*, 1970, **77**, 976–985.

Robson, K. S., Pedersen, F. A., & Moss, H. A. Developmental observations of diadic gazing in relation to the fear of strangers and social approach behavior. *Child Development*, 1969, **40**, 619–627.

Rosenzweig, M., Krech, D., Bennett, E., & Diamond, M. Modifying brain chemistry and anatomy by enrichment or impoverishment of experience. In G. Newton & S. Levine (Eds.), *Early experience and behavior*. Springfield, Ill.: Charles C Thomas, 1968.

Rotter, J. B. *Social learning and clinical psychology*. New York: Prentice-Hall, 1954.

Rovee, C. K., & Rovee, D. T. Conjugate reinforcement of infant exploratory behavior. *Journal of Experimental Child Psychology*, 1969, **8**, 33–39.

Rubenstein, J. Maternal attentiveness and subsequent exploratory behavior. *Child Development,* 1967, **38,** 1089–1100.

Sayegh, Y., & Dennis, W. The effect of supplementary experiences upon the behavioral development of infants in institutions. *Child Development,* 1965, **36,** 81–90.

Schaefer, E. S., & Bayley, N. Maternal behavior, child behavior, and their intercorrelations from infancy through adolescence. *Monographs of the Society for Research in Child Development,* 1963, **28**(3, Serial No. 87).

Schaffer, H. R., & Emerson, P. E. Patterns of response to physical contact in early human development. *Journal of Child Psychology and Psychiatry,* 1964, **5,** 1–13.

Schaffer, H. R., & Emerson, P. E. The development of social attachments in infancy. *Monographs of the Society for Research in Child Development,* 1964, 29(3, Serial No. 94).

Schwartz, A., Rosenberg, D., & Brackbill, Y. An analysis of the components of social reinforcement of infant vocalization. Paper presented at the biennial meeting of the Society for Research in Child Development, Santa Monica, Calif., March 1969.

Sears, R. R. Survey of objective studies of psychoanalytic concepts. *Social Science Research Council Bulletin,* 1943, **51,** 156.

Siqueland, E. R. The development of instrumental exploratory behavior during the first year of human life. Paper presented at the meeting of the Society for Research in Child Development, Santa Monica, Calif., March 1969.

Skinner, B. F. *Science and human behavior.* New York: Macmillan, 1953.

Spearman, C. *The abilities of man.* New York: Macmillan, 1927.

Spitz, R. A. Hospitalism: An inquiry into the genesis of psychiatric conditions in early childhood. *Psychoanalytic study of the child,* 1945, **1,** 53–74.

Spitz, R. A. *No and yes: On the genesis of human communication.* New York: International Universities Press, 1957.

Spitz, R. A., & Wolf, K. The smiling response. *Genetic Psychology Monographs,* 1946, **34,** 57–125.

Staats, A. W., & Staats, C. K. *Complex human behavior.* New York: Holt, Rinehart & Winston, 1963.

Thoman, E. B., & Korner, A. F. Effects of vestibular stimulation on the behavior and development of infant rats. *Developmental Psychology,* 1971, 5, 92–98.

Thomas, A., Birch, H., Chess, S., Hertzig, M., & Korn, S. *Behavioral individuality in early childhood.* New York: New York University Press, 1963.

Thompson, W. R., & Grusec, J. E. Studies of early experience. In P. H. Mussen (Ed.), *Carmichael's manual of child psychology,* Vol. 1. (3rd ed.). New York: Wiley, 1970.

Todd, G., & Palmer, B. Social reinforcement of infant babbling. *Child Development,* 1968, 39, 591–596.

Tulkin, S. R., & Kagan, J. Mother-child interaction in the first year of life. *Child Development,* 1972, 43, 31–41.

Tulkin, S. R., & Konner, M. J. Alternative conceptions of intellectual functioning. *Human Development,* 1973, 16, 33–52.

Uzgiris, I. C. Patterns of cognitive development in infancy. *Merrill-Palmer Quarterly,* 1973, 19, 181–204.

Uzgiris, I. C., & Hunt, J. McV. Attentional preference and experience: II. An exploratory longitudinal study of the effect of visual familiarity and responsiveness. *Journal of Genetic Psychology,* 1970, 117, 109–121.

Uzgiris, I. C., & Hunt, J. McV. *Toward ordinal scales of psychological development in infancy.* Urbana: University of Illinois Press, 1974.

Wachs, T. D. Utilization of a Piagetian approach in the investigation of early experience effects: A research strategy and some illustrative data. Paper presented at the annual meeting of the American Psychological Association, Montreal, Sept. 1973.

Walters, R. H., & Parke, R. D. The role of distance receptors in the development of social responsiveness. In L. P. Lipsitt & C. C. Spiker (Eds.), *Advances in child development and behavior,* Vol. 2. New York: Academic Press, 1965.

Warren, N. African infant precocity. *Psychological Bulletin,* 1972, 78, 353–367.

Washburn, R. W. A study of the smiling and laughing of infants in the first year of life. *Genetic Psychology Monograph,* 1929, **6,** 397–537.

Watson, J. S. The development and generalization of "contingency awareness" in early infancy: Some hypotheses. *Merrill-Palmer Quarterly,* 1966, **12,** 123–135.

Watson, J. S. Smiling, cooing and "the game." *Merrill-Palmer Quarterly,* 1972, **4,** 323–339.

Watson, J. S., & Ramey, C. Reactions to response-contingent stimulation in early infancy. *Merrill-Palmer Quarterly,* 1972, **18,** 219–227.

Wechsler, D. Cognitive, conative and non-intellective intelligence. *American Psychologist,* 1950, **5,** 78–83.

Weisberg, P. Social and nonsocial conditioning of infant vocalizations. *Child Development,* 1963, **34,** 377–388.

Werner, E. Sex differences in correlations between children's IQ's and measures of parental ability and environmental ratings. *Developmental Psychology,* 1969, **1,** 280–285.

White, B. L. An experimental approach to the effects of experiences on early human development. In J. P. Hill (Ed.), *Minnesota symposia on child psychology,* Vol. 1. Minneapolis: University of Minnesota Press, 1967.

White, B. L., & Castle, P. W. Visual exploratory behavior following postnatal handling of human infants. *Perceptual and Motor Skills,* 1964, **18,** 497–502.

White, R. W. Motivation reconsidered: The concept of competence. *Psychological Review,* 1959, **66,** 297–333.

Willerman, L., Broman, S., & Fiedler, M. Infant development, preschool IQ, and social class. *Child Development,* 1970, **41,** 69–77.

Wolff, P. H. Observations on the early development of smiling. In B. M. Foss (Ed.), *Determinants of infant behavior II.* New York: Wiley, 1963.

Wolff, P. H. The natural history of crying and other vocalizations in infancy. In B. M. Foss (Ed.), *Determinants of infant behavior IV.* New York: Barnes & Noble, 1969.

World Health Organization. *Deprivation of maternal care.* Public Health Paper No. 14, Geneva, 1962.

Wortis, H., Bardach, J., Cutler, R., Rue, R., & Freedman, A. Child-rearing practices in a low socioeconomic group. *Pediatrics,* 1963, **32,** 298–307.

Yarrow, L. J. Maternal deprivation: Toward an empirical and conceptual re-evaluation. *Psychological Bulletin,* 1961, **58,** 459–490.

Yarrow, L. J. Research in dimensions of early maternal care. *Merrill-Palmer Quarterly,* 1963, 9, 101–114.

Yarrow, L. J. Separation from parents during early childhood. In M. L. Hoffman and L. W. Hoffman (Eds.), *Review of Child Development Research,* Vol. 1. New York: Russell Sage Foundation, 1964.

Yarrow, L. J. Enrichment and deprivation: Towards a conceptual and empirical differentiation of the early environment. In F. J. Monks, W. W. Hartup and J. de Wit (Eds.), *Determinants of Behavioral Development,* New York: Academic Press, 1972.

Yarrow, L. J., & Goodwin, M. S. Some conceptual issues in the study of mother-infant interaction. *American Journal of Orthopsychiatry,* 1965, **35,** 473–481.

Yarrow, M. R., Campbell, J. D., & Burton, R. V. *Child rearing.* San Francisco: Jossey-Bass, Inc., 1968.

AUTHOR INDEX

Numbers in italics refer to the pages on which the complete references are cited.

Ainsworth, M., 16, 33, 75, 85, 86, 87, *229, 230*

Ambrose, A., 75, 76, *229*

Ames, E., 43, 98, *230*

Anderson, A., 51, *229*

Bardach, J., 33, *243*

Bayley, N., 15, 59, 64, 83, 115, 116, *229, 230, 231, 234, 240*

Beckwith, L., 31, *230*

Bell, S., 33, 85, 86, 87, *229, 230*

Bennett, E., 3, 99, *239*

Bergman, T., 78, *230*

Berlyne, D., 42, 43, 60, *230*

Birch, H., 81, *241*

Bishop, B. M., 16, *230*

Bloom, K., 84, *230*

Bowlby, J., 30, 75, 76, 88, 95, *230*

Brackbill, Y., 59, 79, 83, *230, 240*

Brennan, W., 43, 98, *230*

Brody, S., 75, 87, 95, *230*

Broman, S., 64, *242*

Bronson, W. C., 51, *230*

Brossard, L. M., 30, 41, 74, 75, 79, 95, *231*

Burton, R. V., 15, *243*

Butler, B. V., 64, 116, *233*

Caldwell, B. M., 4, *231*
Cameron, J., 59, 83, *231*
Campbell, J. D., 15, *243*
Casler, L., 69, 74, 77, 95, *231*
Castle, P. W., 76, *242*
Chess, S., 81, *241*
Chomsky, N. A., 58, 59, *231*
Clarke-Stewart, K. A., 16, 46, 48, 112, *231*
Corman, H. H., 52, *231*
Cutler, R., 33, *243*

Décarie, T. G., 30, 41, 74, 75, 79, 95, *231*
Dember, W. N., 50, *231*
Dennis, W., 96, *240*
Deutsch, C. P., 12, *231*
Diamond, M., 3, 99, *239*

Emerson, P. E., 85, *240*
Erickson, M., 84, *230*
Escalona, S. K., 16, 52, 81, 87, *231, 232*
Etzel, B. C., 86, *232*

Fantz, R. L., 30, 42, 43, 99, *232*
Fiedler, M., 64, *242*
Fiske, D., 60, *232*
Foster, M., 96, *232*
Fraiberg, S., 78, *232*
Frank, L. K., 29, 72, 73, *232*
Freedman, A., 33, *243*
Freedman, D. G., 78, *232*
Friedman, D. A., 78, *232*
Friedman, S., 96, *232*
Fries, M., 3, *232*
Fry, C., 72, *236*

Galanter, E. H., 18, *237*
Geber, M., 75, *232*

Gewirtz, H. B., 16, *233*
Gewirtz, J. L., 16, 33, 59, 83, 86, *232, 233, 239*
Goffeney, G., 64, 116, *233*
Goldberg, S., 75, *233, 236*
Goldfarb, W., 3, *233*
Goldstein, F., 72, *236*
Goodwin, M. S., 87, 90, *243*
Gray, S. W., *233*
Greenberg, D. J., 42, 99, *233*
Grusec, J. E., 4, *241*
Guilford, J. P., 51, *233*

Haith, M., 78, *230*
Harlow, H. F., 29, 72, 73, *233, 234*
Harlow, M. K., 29, 72, *234*
Haugan, G. M., 74, 83, 84, *234*
Hebb, D. O., 43, *234*
Heider, G. M., 16, 81, *232*
Helson, H., 5, 18, 101, *234*
Henderson, N. B., 64, 116, *233*
Hertzig, M., 81, *241*
Hindley, C., 116, *234*
Hogarty, P. S., 51, 116, *237*
Hollingshead, A. B., 11, *234*
Honzik, M., 116, *234*
Hunt, J., 52, *234*
Hunt, J. McV., 5, 18, 42, 43, 50, 60, 94, 95, 96, 160, *233, 234, 241*
Hurlburt, N., 51, 116, *237*

Jones, S. J., 31, 83, *234*

Kagan, J., 16, 46, 48, 64, 115, *234, 235, 237, 241*
Kaila, E., 78, *235*
Kessen, W., *235*
Kilbride, J. E., 75, *235*
Kilbride, P. L., 75, 235
King, W., 115, *235*
Klaus, R. A., *233*

Klein, R. P., *235*
Kohen-Raz, R., 52, 64, *235*
Konner, M. J., 75, *235*, *241*
Korn, S., 81, *241*
Korner, A. F., 30, 64, 74, 76, *235*,
    236, *241*
Koza, C., 75, *237*
Krech, D., 3, 99, *239*
Kulka, A., 72, *236*

Lambert, W. W., 17, *236*
Leiderman, G. F., 75, *236*
Leiderman, P. H., 75, *236*
Lenneberg, E. H., 31, *236*
Levine, S. A., 3, 95, *236*
Levy, D., 3, *236*
Lewis, M., 6, 33, 42, 46, 48, 51, 64,
    85, 160, *235*, *236*, *237*
Liddicoat, R., 75, *237*
Lipton, R., 3, 31, 33, 57, 59, 75
    100, *238*
Livson, N., 59, 83, *231*
Lusk, D., *237*

McCall, R., 43, *237*
McGurk, H., 48, *237*
McIntire, R. W., 74, 83, 84, *234*
McNeill, D., 58, 59, *237*
Maddi, S., 60, *232*
Mann, L., 78, *230*
Marshall, M. H., *235*
Mason, W. A., 29, 76, *237*
Melson, W. H., 43, *237*
Messick, S., 51, *229*
Miller, G. A., 18, *237*
Moore, R., 43, 98, *230*
Moore, T., 59, 83, 116, *237*
Moss, H. A., 16, 19, 31, 46, 78, 83,
    85, *234*, *237*, *238*, *239*
Murphy, L. B., 51, 81, 90, *238*

Nevis, S., 43, 99, *232*

Orlansky, H., 3, *238*

Palmer, B., 59, 83, *241*
Parke, R. D., 29, 80, *241*
Pavenstedt, E., *238*
Pedersen, F. A., 78, *238*, *239*
Piaget, J., 5, 94, 95, *238*
Pinneau, S. R., 3, *238*
Prescott, J. W., 29, *238*
Pribram, K. H., 18, *237*
Provence, S., 3, 31, 33, 57, 59, 75,
    100, *238*

Ramey, C., 42, 69, 98, *242*
Repucci, N. D., 116, *238*
Rheingold, H. L., 16, 30, 33, 41,
    59, 83, *239*
Ribble, M. A., 3, *239*
Riesen, A. H., 99, *239*
Robbin, M. C., 75, *235*
Robson, K. S., 31, 78, *237*, *238*,
    239
Rosenberg, D., 59, 83, *240*
Rosenweig, M., 3, 99, *239*
Ross, H., 33, 59, 83, *239*
Rotter, J. B., 6, *239*
Rovee, C. K., 96, 97, *239*
Rovee, D. T., 96, 97, *239*
Rubenstein, J., 16, 25, 65, 159, *240*
Rue, R., 33, *243*

Salapatek, P. H., *235*
Samuels, H. R., 41, *239*
Sayegh, Y., 96, *240*
Schaefer, E. S., 116, *230*, *240*
Shaffer, H. R., 85, *240*
Schwartz, A., 59, 83, *240*
Sears, R. R., 3, *240*
Seegmiller, B., 115, *235*
Siqueland, E. R., 97, *240*
Skinner, B. F., 5, *240*
Spearman, C., 51, *240*

Spitz, R. A., 3, 73, 75, 78, *240*
Staats, A. W., 82, *241*
Staats, C. K., 82, *241*
Stayton, D., 87, *229*

Thoman, E. B., 30, 74, 76, *235,*
   236, 241
Thomas, A., 81, *241*
Thompson, W. R., 4, *241*
Todd, G., 59, 83, *241*
Tulkin, S. R., 16, *241*

Uzgiris, I. C., 42, 52, 96, *233, 241*

Vietze, P., 96, *232*

Wachs, T. D., *241*

Walters, R. H., 29, 80, *241*
Warren, N., 75, *241*
Washburn, R. W., 78, *242*
Watson, J. S., 6, 42, 43, 69, 98,
   160, *242*
Wechsler, D., 50, *242*
Weisberg, P., 83, *242*
Werner, E., 116, *242*
White, B. L., 30, 41, 76, 96, *242*
White, R. W., 18, 51, 56, 160, *242*
Willerman, L., 64, *242*
Wolf, K., 75, 78, *240*
Wolff, P. H., 78, 79, 87, *242*
Wortis, H., 33, *243*

Yarrow, L. J., 3, 4, 16, 33, 59, 69,
   87, 88, 90, *243*
Yarrow, M. R., 15, *243*

SUBJECT INDEX

Adaptation level theory, 5, 101
Affect
  accompanying presentation of
    play materials, 37–38, 90–91
  expression of positive affect, 19–
    20, 35–37, 37–39, 87–89, 164,
    213–214
  intercorrelations with other envi-
    ronmental variables, 32, 36-37,
    178, 179
  play, 36–37, 38–40, 88–90, 204–
    205
  relations with infant develop-
    ment, 87–90, 184
  smiling, 36–38, 88–90, 203–204
Auditory stimulation

  intercorrelation with other
    environmental variables, 31–
    32, 178, 179
  measures of, 31, 202–203
  relations with infant development,
    79–81, 182

Bayley Scales of Infant Development
  clusters derived from, 24–25, 52–
    59
  fine motor, 53–55
  goal directedness, 54–57
  gross motor, 53–55
  object permanence, 55, 58
  secondary circular reactions,
    55, 57

Bayley Scales of Infant Development,
    clusters derived from (*continued*)
    social responsiveness, 54–55
    visually directed reaching and
        grasping, 54, 56–57
    vocalization and language, 55, 59
    intercorrelations of clusters, 60–
        63, 180, 181
    Mental Developmental Index, 24,
        61–63, 64–66
    Psychomotor Developmental
        Index, 24, 61–63, 64–66
    sex differences, 64–66
Bidirectional influences, 80–81,
    101, 165–166, 168–170

Caregivers
    primary, 10–11, 192
    substitute, 10–11, 118, 171–172
Case descriptions, 117–153
Cognitive-motivational functions
    environmental correlates of, 73–
        74, 77, 85–86, 88–90, 93–94,
        96–98, 101–102, 106–111
    goal directedness, 54, 57
    intercorrelations of measures,
        60–63, 66–67, 180, 181
    problem solving, 25, 58, 225–227
    secondary circular reactions, 55, 57
    theoretical significance, 159–160
    visually directed reaching and
        grasping, 54, 56–57
Complexity of inanimate envi-
    ronment
    intercorrelations with other envi-
        ronmental variables, 32, 44,
        178, 179
    measure of, 19, 43–44, 220–223
    relations with infant development
        97–99, 159, 182
Contingency
    infant's awareness of, 85, 160
    intercorrelations with other
        environmental variables,
        32, 34, 178, 179
    measures of
        response to distress, 33–34,
            85–87, 202, 205–206, 214
        response to positive vocaliza-
            tion, 33–34, 82–85, 202
    relations to infant development,
        81–87, 183
    theoretical importance of, 31–33,
        164–165
Cross-cultural studies, 75
Crying, 86–87
    (*See also* Contingency; Maternal
        responsiveness; Mother-infant
        interaction)

Differentiation of the early envi-
    ronment, 3, 4–5, 27–28, 102,
    155–157, 160–161, 163–166,
    173–175
Direction of effects, 80–81, 101,
    165–166, 168–170

Exploratory behavior
    environmental correlates of, 89–
        90, 92–93, 97, 100–102, 107,
        182–187
    intercorrelations with other in-
        fant measures, 61, 63, 180,
        181
    interobserver reliability, 26
    measures of, 25–26, 59–60, 196
    (*See also* Preference for novelty)
Expression of positive affect
    intercorrelations with other envi-
        ronmental variables, 36–38
    measure of, 19–20, 35–37, 213–
        214
    relations with infant development,
        87–89, 184

Fine motor development
  environmental correlates of, 73–
    74, 82, 85–86, 93–94, 96–98,
    105–108, 159, 182–187
  intercorrelations with other in-
    fant measures, 60–63, 180–
    181
  measure of, 53–55

Goal directedness
  environmental correlates of, 73–
    74, 77, 92, 85–86, 88–89, 92,
    94, 105, 107, 109–110,
    182–187
  intercorrelation with other in-
    fant measures, 60–63, 180–181
  measure of, 54, 57
Gross motor development
  environmental correlates of, 73,
    82, 85–86, 96–98, 105–108,
    159, 182–187
  intercorrelations with other in-
    fant measures, 60–63, 180–
    181
  measure of, 53–55

Inanimate environment
  intercorrelations with other envi-
    ronmental variables, 32, 44,
    178–179
  measures of, 19, 23–24, 40–46,
    209–211, 215–223
  relations with infant develop-
    ment, 95–102, 187
  sex differences, 47
  (See also Complexity of inani-
    mate objects; Responsiveness
    of inanimate objects; Variety
    of inanimate objects)
Intelligence in infancy, 50–52
  (See also Bayley Scales of Infant
    Development)
Intervention programs, 7–8, 170–173

Intrinsic motivation, 5, 160

Kinesthetic-vestibular stimulation
  intercorrelations with other envi-
    ronmental variables, 31–32,
    178–179
  measure of, 30, 72, 203
  relations with infant develop-
    ment, 73–77, 105–108, 109–
    111, 182
  theoretical importance of, 29–30,
    72, 157–159, 161

Language stimulation, 31–34, 79–
    81, 202
Language and vocalization
  environmental correlates of, 73,
    77, 79, 82–85, 91–94, 106,
    109–110, 182–187
  intercorrelations with other in-
    fant measures, 61–62, 180–
    181
  measures of, 55, 58–59, 197–198
Level of social stimulation
  intercorrelations with other envi-
    ronmental variables, 32, 40,
    178–179
  measure of, 38–40
  relations with infant develop-
    ment, 91–95, 186
  sex differences, 46–48

Maternal responsiveness
  relations with infant develop-
    ment, 81–87, 183
  response to infant's distress, 33–
    34, 85–87, 202, 205–206, 214
  response to infant's positive vocal-
    izations, 33–34, 82–85, 202
Mediation of play objects by care-
    giver
  intercorrelation with other envi-
    ronmental variables, 32, 37–
    38, 178–179

Mediation of play objects by caregiver (*continued*)
  measure of, 37–38, 206–208
  relations with infant development, 90–91, 185
Mental Developmental Index, 24, 61–63, 64–66
Methodological issues
  combinations of environmental variables, 103–104, 109
  isolation of variables, 173–175
  time-sampling vs. narrative records, 15–17
  toward better methods, 163–166
Methodology
  coding of contingencies, 17
  data collection, 13–15, 20
  inter-observer reliability, 20–24, 25–26
  measures of infant functioning, 24–26, 52–60
  ratings of mother-infant interaction, 19–20
  sample, 10–13
  time-sample categories, 21–24
Modalities of social stimulation
  auditory, 31, 79–81, 202
  distance receptor stimulation, 30–31, 77–81, 201, 202
  intercorrelations among modalities, 31–32, 178–179
  kinesthetic-vestibular, 29–30, 74–77, 158–159, 203
  relations with infant development, 71–81, 182
  tactile, 29–31, 72–74, 201, 202–203
  visual, 30–31, 201
Mother-infant interaction
  auditory stimulation, 31, 79–81
  contingent response to infant distress, 33–34, 85–87
  contingent response to infant

  vocalization, 33–34, 82–85
  expression of positive affect, 19–20, 35, 37, 36–38, 87–89
  intercorrelations among measures, 31–32, 34–38, 40, 44, 48, 178–179
  kinesthetic-vestibular, 29–30, 74–77, 158–159
  mediation of play materials, 37–38, 90–91
  modalities of stimulation, 28–31, 71–81
  observational categories, 21–24, 194–211
  observational methods, 15–24
  play, 36–37, 38–40, 88–90
  relations with infant development, 71–114, 182–187
  smiling, 36–38, 88–90
  tactile stimulation, 29–30, 72–74
  variety of social stimulation, 38–40, 46–48
  visual stimulation, 30–31, 77–79
Motor development (gross and fine)
  environmental correlates of, 73–74, 82, 85–86, 93–94, 96–98, 105–108, 159, 182–187
  intercorrelations with other infant measures, 60–63, 180–181
  measures of, 24, 53–55
  (*See also* Bayley Scales of Infant Development)
Multiple regression analyses, 104–105
Multivariate analyses, 103–112, 161–162
Mutual visual regard
  intercorrelations with other environmental measures, 31–32, 178–179
  measures of, 31, 201
  relations with infant development, 79, 80–81, 84, 182

Object permanence
  environmental correlates of, 73–
    74, 77, 82, 85, 89–90, 93–94,
    97, 101, 105, 158–159, 182–
    187
  intercorrelations with other in-
    fant measures, 60–63, 180–
    181
  measures of, 25, 55, 58
Observational methods
  categories, 21–24, 189–211
  duration of observation, 20
  reliability, 20–24
  time sampling vs. narrative rec-
    ords, 15–18
  (See also Methodological issues;
    Methodology)
Optimal levels
  arousal level, 76, 105
  levels of stimulation, 94–95,
    111–112, 167–168

Person permanence, 89–90, 94
Play
  component of level and variety,
    38–40
  intercorrelations with other envi-
    ronmental variables, 32, 36,
    178–179
  measure of, 36–37, 204
  relations with infant develop-
    ment, 88–90, 184
Preference for novel stimuli
  environmental correlates of, 82,
    89, 97, 100–102, 107–108,
    182–187
  intercorrelations with other in-
    fant measures, 61, 63, 180–
    181
  inter-observer reliability, 26
  measures of, 25–26, 59–60
  (See also Exploratory behavior)

Problem solving
  environmental correlates of, 74,
    97, 101, 107–108, 182–187
  intercorrelations with other in-
    fant measures, 60–63, 180–
    181
  measure of, 25, 58, 225–227
Psychodynamic theory, 2–4, 35
  critique of studies, 3–4
  research on early development,
    2–3
  (See also Affect)
Psychomotor Developmental Index,
    24, 61–63, 64–66

Reaching and grasping
  environmental correlates of, 82,
    85, 93–94, 97, 99, 107, 109–
    110, 182–187
  intercorrelations with other in-
    fant measures, 60–63, 180–
    181
  measure of, 25, 54–55, 56–57
Reliability
  Bayley Scales, 24
  exploratory behavior and prefer-
    ence for novelty, 26
  problem solving, 25
  sex differences in reliability, 115
  split-half reliability of Bayley
    clusters, 53–55
  time-sample interaction catego-
    ries, 20–24
  (See also Methodology)
Responsiveness of inanimate objects
  correlations with infant develop-
    ment, 96–98, 187
  intercorrelations with other envi-
    ronmental variables, 32, 44,
    178–179
  measure of, 19, 42–43, 215–220
  sex differences, 47

Response to infant distress, 33–34, 85–87, 183, 205–206, 214
Response to infant positive vocalization, 33–34, 82–85, 183, 202

Sample characteristics, 10–13
Secondary circular reactions
    environmental correlates of, 73, 82, 85–86, 88–89, 93–94, 97–99, 107–109, 182–187
    intercorrelations with other infant measures, 60–63, 180–181
    measure of, 25, 55
Sex differences
    in the impact of the early environment, 69–70, 112–116, 162–163, 182–187
    infant characteristics, 64–66
    intercorrelations among infant measures, 180, 181
    in patterns of stimulation, 46–58, 162–163, 178–179
    statistical issues, 112–115
Smiling
    component of social mediation, 37–38
    intercorrelations with other environmental measures, 32, 36, 178
    measure of, 36–38, 203–204
    relations with infant development, 88–90, 184
Social class, 170–172
    Hollingshead Index, 11
    socioeconomic level, 11–13
Social responsiveness
    environmental correlates of, 73–74, 77–78, 80, 88–89, 93–94, 106, 109, 182–187
    intercorrelations with other infant measures, 60–63, 180–181
    measure of, 24, 54–56
Specifity of environmental effects, 102
Stimulation

contingent upon infant signal, 31–34, 81–87, 202, 205–206, 214
    correlations with infant development, 71–95, 95–102, 182–187
    inanimate, 40–46, 209–211, 215–223
    individual differences in sensitivity to, 6–7, 49
    intercorrelations among variables of, 31–32, 34, 36–38, 40, 44, 178–179
    issues of deprivation and enrichment, 3–4, 29–30, 69–70, 96, 99, 167–168
    modalities of, 28–31, 71–81, 201–203
    models of, 166–168
    optimal levels of, 167–168
    seeking, 5, 165–166
    time-sampling categories, 7, 21–24, 189–211
    (See also Mother-infant interaction)

Tactile stimulation
    intercorrelations with other environmental variables, 31–32, 178–179
    measure of, 30, 72, 201–203
    relations with infant development, 72–74, 182
    theoretical importance of, 29–30
Theories of environmental influences, 5–6, 18, 28–31, 33, 35, 37–43

Variety of inanimate objects
    correlations with infant development, 97, 100–102, 187
    interaction with, 109–111
    intercorrelations with other environmental variables, 32, 44, 178–179

measure of, 19, 24, 42, 211
multiple regression analyses,
     105–107
sex differences, 47
Variety of social stimulation
     correlations with infant func-
          tions, 91–95
     intercorrelations with other envi-
          ronmental variables, 32, 40,
          102, 178–179

measure of, 38–40
sex differences, 46–48
Verbal stimulation (*see* Auditory
     stimulation)
Visual stimulation, 30–31, 77–81,
     84, 201
     (*See also* Mutual visual regard)
Visually-directed reaching and
     grasping (*see* Reaching and
     grasping)